DEVELOPING PROGRAMS IN ADULT EDUCATION

Edgar J. Boone
NORTH CAROLINA STATE UNIVERSITY

Prentice-Hall, Inc. Englewood Cliffs, N. J. 07632

Library of Congress Cataloging in Publication Data

Boone, Edgar John, (date)
   Developing programs in adult education.
   Includes bibliographies and index.
   1. Adult education—Curricula—Planning.
I. Title.
LC5219.B55 1985   374   84-18019
ISBN 0-13-204694-6

Dedicated to my parents, John and Daisy Holmes Boone; my wife, Ethel Bower Boone; and our sons, John Bower and David Warner Boone, who have been and continue to be my major sources of inspiration, devotion, and commitment to lifelong learning.

Editorial/production supervision and
   interior design: Diana Drew and Mark Stevens
Cover design: Joseph Curcio
Manufacturing buyer: John B. Hall

Printed in the United States of America

10 9 8 7 6 5 4 3 2 1

ISBN 0-13-204694-6   01

Prentice-Hall International, Inc., *London*
Prentice-Hall of Australia Pty. Limited, *Sydney*
Editora Prentice-Hall do Brasil, Ltda., *Rio de Janeiro*
Prentice-Hall Canada Inc., *Toronto*
Prentice-Hall Hispanoamericana, S.A., *Mexico*
Prentice-Hall of India Private Limited, *New Delhi*
Prentice-Hall of Japan, Inc., *Tokyo*
Prentice-Hall of Southeast Asia Pte. Ltd., *Singapore*
Whitehall Books Limited, *Wellington, New Zealand*

Contents

Foreword

The leadership of the adult education movement in this country has historically come from its practitioners. Accordingly, the literature of the field has been concerned predominantly with principles of good practice. (This tendency is characteristic of any new field of social practice; the construction of theoretical frameworks usually comes later.)

This is not to say that there were no theoreticians in the early days of adult education; Eduard C. Lindeman, Edward L. Thorndike, and Lyman Bryson in the twenties and thirties and Cyril O. Houle from the forties on come to mind. But, except for Houle, they had little interest in the programming aspect of adult education. The literature on programming, including my own works, has tended to focus on principles and practices derived from an analysis of accumulated experience. Attempts were made to put the principles and practices into conceptual models (such as my "andragogical" model and Houle's fundamental system of educational design), but none of them presented a comprehensive theory of the entire programming process with assumptions and concepts stated explicitly and systematically.

In the last decade or so the number of scholars in our field concerned with theory has grown exponentially. It would take the rest of the space allotted to this Foreword just to list the names of those currently contributing to our literature. High on my list would be that of Edgar J. Boone, who for over two decades has been evolving his theory of programming in adult education. He has, in fact, become so absorbingly identified with this undertaking that his course on this subject at North Carolina State University has been dubbed by his students "Booneology."

Boone's conceptual model possesses certain characteristics that cause it to stand apart from other models in my mind. It identifies the concepts around which the processes and subprocesses of planning, designing, implementing, evaluating, and accounting for educational programs are organized, and it makes explicit the assumptions or philosophical tenets on which these concepts are based. It is, in short, a thinking person's approach. It defines the purpose of adult educational programs as being to produce changes in the behavior of individuals, learning groups, and systems, strongly emphasizing adult education's responsibility to bring about changes in society. It is highly systems-oriented and interdisciplinary in its analysis of the programming process. It places a high value on collaboration among all parts of a system in carrying out the process. But the book also identifies the tasks flowing from each concept and provides practical examples of how these tasks can be implemented. For example, it contains one of the clearest and most down-to-earth portrayals of the social-mapping technique that I have seen.

The target audience toward which the book is addressed, as I sense it, comprises the "professionals" in our field—the professors of adult education, their graduate students, and the program directors in organizations and institutions that provide education for adult learners. But the text should also provide stimulating ideas and helpful guidelines for the sophisticated "amateurs" among us. And it has the decided advantage of being neutral so far as the institutional settings to which it is applicable are concerned.

The book's principal significance lies in the contribution it makes toward refining the theoretical framework for thinking about and practicing adult educational programming. But its greatest contribution may be in furthering research into the programming process. The last chapter is one of the richest sources of ideas about needed research in our field that has yet appeared. The author's outlook is encapsulated in this passage from page 229: "The existence of a coherent model in no sense relieves the student of the responsibility for the critical and reflective thinking required to develop a personal philosophy of adult education. Rather, the model should be used as a guide for thinking, as a means to help sort out the important issues and questions, and not as a source of ready-made answers."

This book will be a standard reference in our field for many years, and I predict it will soon be referred to as a "classic."

Malcolm S. Knowles
Professor Emeritus
North Carolina State University

Preface

The diversity that characterizes adult education is one of the field's major strengths. However, this diversity can be disconcerting to the professional adult educator, who continuously develops and delivers educational programs, in diverse areas, for both new and old clientele. It can be bewildering to the graduate student who is studying programming in adult education from the perspective of another discipline or from experience in a single program area. In daily practice, adult education serves a vast array of adult audiences through an almost equally broad variety of programs and institutions.

The theory of adult education derives from several fields: content area disciplines, educational psychology, organizational theory, sociology, economics, and educational research and evaluation, to name a few. This breadth of sources from which to draw is the sign of a robust and growing field, but it can be an awesome challenge. Successful programming in adult education depends upon the recognition of multiple sources of theory, principles, and practices. Its concepts give potential and practicing adult educators a simple, flexible base that is adaptable to the complexities of programming for adult audiences and organizations.

Lengthy debate has continued through the years about whether or not adult education, in fact, constitutes an identifiable discipline. This adult educator's rebuttal is that a relatively small number of basic concepts underlie the programming process in adult education and its subprocesses of planning, design and implementation, and evaluation and accountability. Understanding these subprocesses and their basic concepts allows the adult educator to choose an appropriate model for the situation in which he or she works. In other words, the model or form that adult education takes will differ in programs designed to serve either the literacy needs of rural, agrarian adults or to maintain the skills of highly trained professionals. But the basic programming process is the same in both instances. The adult educator's first responsibility, as change agent and programmer, is to analyze the sociocultural context of the desired change, identify educational needs in the particular instance, and act in congruence with the supporting adult education organization.

This book represents knowledge gained over twenty years of research, teaching, and actual application of my interpretation of programming in adult education, which I call "the conceptual programming model." It is intended to meet the longstanding programming needs of students and practitioners in adult education or related fields, as well as the needs of those who plan and manage educational enterprises for adult learners. This is not a detailed handbook. It is a comprehensive, yet practical, conceptual framework for planning, designing and implementing, and evaluating and accounting for planned adult education programs.

The sequence of topics discussed begins with a description of the programming process in adult education. Programming, as defined in Chapter 1, includes the individual and collective efforts of the adult education organization, its adult educators, and its client systems in planning, designing and implementing, and evaluating and accounting for planned educational programs. It includes all of the planned and collaborative activities of adult educators, learners, and their spokesmen in designing and effecting educational strategies that should culminate in behavioral change in the targeted client subsystem and subsequent alterations of the system itself. Several basic assumptions are advanced that help to define programming in adult education, the planned program, and the role of the adult educator as change agent and programmer.

Examined in Chapter 2 are differing models of the adult education programming process and the variety of settings in which these models are applicable. Nine programming models are reviewed: those of Beal, Blount, and Johnson (1966); Boone, Dolan, and Shearon (1971); Boyle (1981); Freire (1970); Houle (1972); Kidd (1973); Knowles (1970); Lippitt, Watson, and Westley (1958); and Tyler (1971). Similarities and differences in the nine models are noted, with particular emphasis on context, scope, philosophy, perspective, applicability, and main theme.

A theoretical approach to the programming process in adult education is presented in Chapter 3. The nature, structure, and function of programming are examined. The objectives and philosophical tenets of programming are explicated. The evolution of the scientific approach to programming is discussed, with special emphasis on theory construction and model building. Chapter 3 concludes with a presentation of the conceptual programming model and its three major subprocesses: planning, design and implementation, and evaluation and accountability.

A comprehensive approach to the planning subprocess is detailed in

Chapter 4. In the conceptual programming model, planning is viewed as a deliberate, rational, continuing process of precise educational activities by adult educators, operating from an organizational base, in their roles as change agents and programmers. The first step in any educational program planning is an analysis of the organization and its renewal process, in which the organization continuously examines its functions, structure, and processes and the needs of its publics, so that it does not depart from its stated mission. The second step is linkage—that is, studying, analyzing, and mapping its publics, identifying its target publics and their leaders, and interfacing with those leaders and their followers in collaborative identification, assessment, and analysis of expressed educational needs within those publics.

In Chapter 5, we show how the design and implementation subprocess has as its primary focus the actual design, development, and implementation of a planned program as a purposeful educational response to needs confirmed in the planning subprocess. The design/implementation subprocess has three distinct but interrelated components: (1) translating analyzed expressed needs into hierarchies of needs and objectives, (2) creating sequenced increments or plans of action for executing the planned program within designated periods of time, and (3) formulating and executing educational strategies for implementing plans of action and, ultimately, the planned program.

The evaluation and accountability subprocess of the conceptual programming model is explored in Chapter 6. As a continuous, coordinated process involving the total system and individual subsystems, evaluation consists of making judgments about program outcomes based on established criteria and known, observable evidence. The evaluation dimension, as treated in the conceptual programming model, operates as a continuous macro feedback loop from input to output and back to input. Accountability is the process through which adult educators report the outcomes of program evaluation, primarily to the learners and their leaders, the adult education organization, funding sources, the profession, and, where appropriate, the governance body. Program outcomes are used, as warranted, to revise, refine, and renew the adult education organization and its programming process.

In Chapter 7, we summarize and discuss the generality of the conceptual programming model, identify research questions about the conceptual programming model that need to be subjected to further inquiry, and test and discuss the implications that the conceptual model has for practicing adult educators and for the professional preparation of students who aspire to careers in adult education. Finally, adult educators are challenged to examine, test, accept, reject, modify, and extend the conceptual programming model or to develop a new approach to programming in adult education.

In my own professional experience, this conceptual framework for programming has brought a sense of consistency to my behavior as an adult educator and to the practices I follow in planning, designing and implementing, and evaluating and accounting for programs to meet adult educational needs. It not only has profoundly affected my philosophy and approach to the preparation of professionals in adult education; it has given me security in knowing what to do, and why to do it.

Sincere acknowledgment and appreciation are extended to Adele Porter Covington, friend, colleague, and entrepreneur, who has shared many writing chores over the years, for editing the entire manuscript and considerably improving its quality and readability. Sincere appreciation is extended to Drs. Estelle E. White, Patrick A. Cabe, Stanley P. Littlefield, R. David Mustian, and Richard T. Liles for their counsel and contributions regarding the preparation and content of the manuscript. Thanks are also extended to Drs. Randall Barnett, Jasper Lee, Lin Compton, William Flowers, Malcolm Knowles, John Peters, Lee Hoffman, Ronald W. Shearon, Manfred Thullen and Joan W. Wright for their helpful critiques and suggestions concerning the book.

A note of gratitude goes to North Carolina State University, the North Carolina Agricultural Extension Service, and the North Carolina Community College System. These organizations have provided me with rich and challenging professional experiences.

Last, but certainly not least, a special note of appreciation is extended to the more than 2000 graduate students in adult education at North Carolina State University, the University of Wisconsin, the University of Puerto Rico, and at Louisiana State University, who have participated in a graduate course I teach entitled "The Programming Process in Adult Education." Over the years, the course has come to be affectionately referred to, by graduate students and colleagues alike, as "Booneology."

E.J.B.

Chapter One

Introduction

During the past century, adult education has evolved as a distinct field of professional practice and as a new type of educational system. As a field of professional practice, its purpose is to effect planned change in the behavior of individual adult learners, learner groups, and relevant systems. As an educational system, adult education provides a conceptual framework within which a myriad of related organizations, programming processes, delivery systems, and evaluation techniques can be classified, analyzed, and studied. From these two perspectives of adult education, concepts, constructs, and theories have evolved through observation, experience, and research. The resulting body of knowledge serves in the further development and refinement of the field and facilitates its practice by adult educators.

The stage of development of adult education at this time in its relatively brief history is praiseworthy. Although adult education can be classified as robust and growing, its continued growth and evolution will depend, to a large measure, on its theorists and practitioners generating more refined inquiry into its operation in various contexts, that is, on further refinement in theory formulation and further development in principles of practice. Adult educators' relentless search for ordered, systematic thinking will continue. The question is, Where do we look for inspiration?

The focus of this work is on developing and illustrating the application of a conceptual model of the programming process in adult education. The model draws from many concepts, constructs, and theories that have been generated by adult educators and other scholars in closely allied disciplines. The author's objective is to present a conceptual model that can be used to guide the adult educator or others in planning, designing, implementing, evaluating, and accounting for adult education programs.

Programming, as defined here, includes the individual and collaborative efforts of the adult education organization, the adult educators, and the learners in planning, designing, implementing, evaluating, and accounting for educational programs. The process encompasses *all* of the planned, coordinated, and collaborative activities of adult educators, lay leaders, learners, learner groups, and systems (such as neighborhoods, communities, and special-interest groups) in designing and effecting educational strategies that should culminate in behavioral change in individual learners and within learner groups and systems. Feedback from the experience may be used in subsequent alteration or renewal of the adult education organization itself.

Programming includes

Developing a thorough understanding of and commitment to the mission, philosophy, functions, structure, processes, and culture of the organization with which the adult educator is affiliated and commitment to its continual renewal as a dynamic, change-focused system.

Studying, analyzing, and mapping publics within the organization's environment.

Identifying target publics.

Identifying and interfacing with leaders of those publics.

Identifying, assessing, and analyzing needs specific to the target public through collaboration with leaders, learner groups, and individual learners.

Translating and incorporating expressed needs into a planned program.

Designing and implementing plans of action to carry out the planned program.

Evaluating the impact of the planned program and plans of action in effecting behavioral change in the learners.

Using evaluation findings and feedback for program revisions, organizational renewal, and for accounting to the learners and their leaders, the adult education organization, funding sources, the profession, and, where applicable, the governance group.

The foregoing conceptualization of programming is consistent with Schroeder's (1980) definition of adult education as "a developmental process used to link various agent and client systems for the purpose of establishing directions and procedures for adult learning programs" (p. 42). In his view, the adult educator's concern is with assessing needs, setting objectives, selecting and organizing learner experiences, choosing and implementing teaching strategies, and evaluating outcomes—in a word, programming.

The concept of programming set forth here suggests that adult educators must broaden their perspective from concern with stages of program development and instructional design to include those features of participating systems that affect the nature of programming and the change process. For example, the mission and philosophy of the adult education organization, the sociocultural characteristics of learner groups or systems and their environment, and the unique personal characteristics and style of the adult educator are important considerations in programming. The adult educator operates in systems. All efforts are directed toward change in systems. The adult education organization is a system; the adult learner group is a system; the process employed in developing and implementing an educational program is a system; and the program itself is a system.

Adult education programming generally involves administrators, teachers and counselors, and policy makers. These categories of programmers range from county extension agents to directors of continuing education in community colleges and universities, to training directors in industry, to persons involved in planning and delivering educational programs in a variety of community agencies. For the most part, these programmers operate from adult education organizations. All, in the same way, interact with other organizations, learner groups, and individual learners as they involve themselves in programming activities. They have in common four major responsibilities: (1) to identify, assess, and analyze educational needs specific to the target publics; (2) to plan and design educational programs to fit those expressed needs; (3) to implement the planned programs; and (4) to evaluate and account for the outcomes of such programs.

The concept of programming in adult education, as set forth here, is based on certain assumptions. Thus, to expand this concept, a statement of assumptions about programming, the planned program, and the adult educator, in the roles of change agent and programmer, is in order.

ASSUMPTIONS ABOUT PROGRAMMING

Several basic assumptions within the context of programming help to define and describe the process. These assumptions undergird and permeate the total programming process, beginning with planning and extending through evaluating and accounting for program outcomes.

First of all, programming is directed toward change in behavior of the individual adult learner, of learner groups, and of systems. All of these audiences are systems, and it is toward these systems that adult educators' efforts are directed.

In the case of the individual adult learner and adult learner groups, reference is to *change* in their knowledge, skills, and attitudes. In the case of systems (family, neighborhood, community, special-interest group, and others), reference is in terms of change directed toward the aggregate of people who comprise the system and the system itself. Individual members of a system have goals and objectives that generally are congruent with those of the system itself. Thus, to effect change in a system, adult educators must focus on individual members' beliefs, attitudes, and objectives, as well as those of the system. Successful attainment of planned change in a system involves collaboration among the adult education organization, leaders of the system, and members of the system. The outcome of such collaboration may be the alteration of attributes of the system and its subsystems through the development of a new system or alteration of the old one. An example of a planned change in a system may be the development and adoption of a countywide water system in a rural county. The need is for a water system, and the educational program is to convince county residents of the need, obtain their commitment to act, define the objectives to be achieved, develop educational strategies to achieve the objectives, and invoke the action steps needed to achieve the objectives. The outcomes are the development of a countywide water system and change in patterns of cooperation and relationships between groups (subsystems) of people in the county.

A second assumption is that programming is a decision-making process. Identifying adult learners, learner groups, and their leaders and interfacing with them in collaborative identification, assessment, and analysis of their needs, translating those analyzed needs into program objectives, planning the educational program, invoking action strategies to implement the program, selecting and implementing learning activities, and determining methods for evaluating and procedures for accounting for program outcomes are all accomplished in a systematic, decision-making, and value mode. Conscious choices and decisions are made throughout the programming process. Such choices and decisions are made collaboratively by representatives of all systems involved in the programming process.

The third assumption is that programming is a collaborative effort involving both the adult education organization and its learners and their leaders in identifying, assessing, and analyzing the educational needs of those learners. Continual interaction and collaboration between the two systems may lead to their functioning, albeit temporarily, as a unified system.

The fourth assumption is that programming in adult education is a system; that is, its parts (relevant concepts and processes) are interrelated, ordered, and linked to form a collective whole. Encompassed within programming are three major subprocesses: (1) planning, (2) design and implementation, and (3) evaluation and accountability. Subsumed under each of these subprocesses are a number of relevant assumptions and concepts. As a holistic system, programming provides a framework to guide the efforts of adult educators in reviewing, synthesizing, and classifying research findings germane either to the total process or to one or more of its subprocesses.

The fifth assumption is that programming is the principal means by which the adult education organization obtains feedback. The use of such feedback often helps to keep the organization alert and sensitive to changes in its environment and forms the base for organizational renewal.

In addition to assumptions about the programming process are assumptions about the planned program itself.

ASSUMPTIONS ABOUT THE PLANNED PROGRAM

The first assumption about the planned adult education program is that it consists of several universal components that exist at different levels and over different time spans. These components include a description of the needs of individual adult learners and learner groups, a statement of program objectives, and a description of educational strategies to achieve the stated objectives and to fulfill the stated needs. Moreover, this planned program reflects the nature and capabilities of the adult education organization, the nature of the learners and learner groups, the content area(s) involved, the support structure(s) to be used in program design and implementation, and a description of evaluation and accountability strategies.

The second assumption is that a planned program should exist in two time dimensions: a long-range program and short-range plans of action. The long-range program logically encompasses two or more shorter-range plans of action, with the latter effectively comprising the former. The overall needs of the learners, the general goals of the planned program, the methods to be employed in program design and implementation, and the evaluations to be made over the long run will be reflected in the year-by-year, phase-by-phase plans of action. Accountability, of course, is the final step in the long-range program.

A third assumption is that a planned program exists in a hierarchical order. That is, the planned program generally includes long-range and broad-based educational needs and the general strategies for dealing with them. At the lower levels of the hierarchy are sequential plans of action designed to implement the broad-based program. These plans of action encompass specific objectives as reflected in course offerings, workshops, conferences, or individually oriented activities, with their own special content and delivery modes.

Given the stated assumptions about programming and the planned program, what assumptions are pertinent to the adult educator?

ASSUMPTIONS ABOUT THE ADULT EDUCATOR

The primary assumption about the adult educator concerns the role itself. First and foremost, the adult educator's role must be perceived as including that of both change agent and programmer. As a change agent, the adult educator plans and directs the change process as it relates to the individual learner, learner groups, or the system. The change agent functions as a helper and facilitator in involving and helping potential learners to become aware of their needs, formulating educational goals or objectives to meet those needs, devising and implementing means for achieving those objectives, and subsequently fulfilling their needs. The change agent assists learners in evaluating their successes or failures in needs attainment and helps them replan, when necessary. The change agent functions as an educator. Knowles (1980) reinforces this assumption through his assertion that the adult educator must focus on involving the actual and potential learners in assessing needs, setting goals, selecting change strategies, implementing educational plans, and evaluating program outcomes. He stresses that adult education programs must be developed with the full knowledge and consent of the learners.

The second assumption relates to the adult educator as a programmer. In most instances, the adult educator cannot single-handedly institute a planned program. As a programmer, the adult educator functions within the context of an adult education organization, in which interactions with colleagues can significantly affect programming decisions. Planned programs are structured within the context of the organization's external system, whether it be a neighborhood, a community, a county, a state, or a combination of such systems. Ideally, the programmer would choose to incorporate into the process the inputs of the learner group. In this way, institution of the planned program represents the combined efforts of at least the adult education organization and the learners.

The third assumption is that the programmer's personal characteristics and style influence the programming process. These characteristics include personal values and goals, mastery of certain concepts and principles of programming, and skill in programming procedures. The programmer's values and goals usually are reflected in a personal philosophy of adult education, which serves as an important component of a guiding framework within which the programmer operates. This personal philosophy often is the final criterion upon which professional decisions are based.

The fourth assumption is that the programmer needs a conceptual base from which to operate in the change process. Concepts forming this base act as the background of understandings that guide decisions or intelligent choices to be made by the programmer. These concepts combine to form a conceptual framework or a *cognitive map* that undergirds the programmer's decisions and choice of activities. Lippitt, Watson, and Westley (1958) speak to this assumption when they emphasize that the adult education programmer must possess a strong conceptual base from which to view a programmatic situation, as well as special diagnostic skills in planning and directing the change process. Further, they imply that the programmer must understand and agree with the organization's mission and philosophy.

The fifth assumption is that the programmer makes decisions or choices at every stage and step in the programming process. As a decision maker, the programmer must have an adequate factual and conceptual base from which to make choices among available options. The soundness of decisions taken will strongly influence the quality of the planned program and its outcomes.

The sixth and final assumption is that the programmer must be skillful in planning, designing, implementing, evaluating, and accounting for program outcomes. Specific skills include, among others, the ability to communicate effectively, to assess needs, to write objectives, to select general educational strategies, to market programs, and to develop evaluation devices. These skills are influenced and shaped by the programmer's cognitive map. For example, needs assessment instruments may be selected and refined on the basis of their psychometric properties, but their use particularly depends on the programmer's knowledge of the capabilities of the adult education organization, the sociocultural characteristics of the learners, and the goals of the planned program. This assumption has considerable support in the literature. Lippitt, Watson, and Westley (1958), for example, assert that every adult educator, as change agent and programmer, should have "specific skills of interpretation and fact finding" (p. 276), and should have training in both change concepts and diagnostic skills. The diagnostic skills referred to are those techniques needed for posing pertinent questions, for establishing reliable patterns of observation, and for using valid methods in collecting, processing, and interpreting data. Such a conceptual orientation is viewed as essential to the change agent or programmer's "ability to formulate systematically the process of change" (p. 277).

The very context in which the adult educator as programmer functions is a challenging one. The interdependence of learner groups poses a series of complex problems originating from several systems: group, organization, and community. Precisely because of the great potential for things to go wrong, specialized training is needed according to the type of system(s) with which the adult educator, as change agent, is expected to interact. One must recognize that, in general, a system is open and dynamic, with the potential for various problems to arise from its subsystems or from the total system.

Knox (1980) also speaks to the complexity of the role of the programmer. He sees the role as involving skills in strategy, innovation, initiating and bringing about change, creative problem solving, active seeking out of alternatives and opportunities, reforming goals and priorities, negotiating, resolving conflicts, dynamic leadership, diplomacy, and a high degree of risk taking and entrepreneurship.

One may conclude from the six assumptions about the role of adult educators as either change agents or programmers that they are major strategists who thoroughly understand and are skillful in the use of certain psychological, sociological, and educational concepts in linking the organization to its publics. Such linkage is achieved through analyzing and mapping publics, identifying target publics of adult learners, identifying leaders of those publics, and interfacing with those leaders and the learners in collaborative needs identification, assessment, and analysis. Further, adult educators possess the conceptual and technical skills to translate analyzed needs into viable programs, plans, and change(s). These conceptual tools and technical skills are coupled with the ability to relate effectively to the mission, philosophy, functions, structure, and processes of the adult education organization and the beliefs, values, and goals of the learner group(s).

UNDERSTANDING THE ROLES
OF THE ADULT EDUCATOR IN PROGRAMMING

Effective functioning by the adult educator, as change agent and programmer, in implementing the programming process depends upon a thorough understanding of several key concepts. These concepts have their origin in the social and behavioral sciences. Collectively, they form a major part of the previously mentioned cognitive map of the adult educator.

As change agents and programmers, adult educators need a framework within which to make decisions and take actions on the programs they develop. A cognitive map represents the integration of concepts and their interrelationships into a framework that is useful in directing the mental processes involved in making decisions and choices. Laszlo (1972) refers to a cognitive system as constituted of mind-events, including perceptions, sensations, feelings, volitions, dispositions, thoughts, memories, and imagination; that is, anything present in the mind. Concepts within this system cohere as interdependent constituents, not as a mere collection of diverse aggregates of thoughts. Therefore, the term *cognitive map* is used here to refer to a conceptual framework composed of concepts and their interrelations that form the programmer's understanding of the component processes of programming.

Systems, culture, change, decision making, and needs are among the more important concepts in a change agent's or programmer's cognitive map. These concepts are explored fully in Chapter 4 (Planning), Chapter 5 (Design and Implementation), and Chapter 6 (Evaluation and Accountability). To emphasize their importance in programming, it seems appropriate to include here a brief introduction to each of these concepts. Also presented is a plan for establishing the relationship that ought to exist among these concepts as they interact to form the basis of a change agent's or programmer's cognitive map.

Systems

In general, a system is viewed as consisting of several parts that together form a unitary whole. Ackoff (1960) views a system as "any entity, conceptual or physical, which consists of interdependent parts" (p. 1). Maccoby (1976) cites as a case of systems thinking the ability to view the prospectus as a whole and to integrate several ideas into an overall plan. Peters and Kozoll (1980) cite Rice and Bishopric's viewpoint that a system also consists of "a patterned, functioning relationship among components" (p. 5). We emphasize that gaining a perspective on programming in adult education requires a degree of *systems thinking*.

Systems have universal characteristics and behavioral patterns. An understanding of these universalities can be applied to decisions at several points in the programming process, including

Analysis of the adult education organization as a system, including its subsystems and their interrelationships.

Analysis of a learner group, organization, or community that is the target of a change effort.

Development of a profile of any other organization(s) involved in a collaborative effort or to which the programmer may defer program plans.

Evaluation of the program or plan itself as a system, and programming as a systems approach to change.

Assessment of the total context within which change is to take place.

We are surrounded by countless thousands of systems, each of which varies in structure, ranging from the simplest to the most complex. The products of these systems are equally varied. The principal product or outcome of adult education programs, for example, is positive behavioral change among participants in programs offered by adult education organizations. Further, the collaborative efforts of adult educators and learner groups in the programming process, from planning to evaluation, also constitute a system. These and other applications of the systems concept in programming are explored.

Culture

Culture refers to the behavior or way of life of a definable grouping of people. *Culture* may be thought of as all the learned and expected ways of life shared by members of a society: artifacts, buildings, tools, and other physical things, as well as techniques, social institutions, attitudes, beliefs, motivations, and value systems known to the group. From this definition, one can see that culture includes the commonly accepted ways of thinking as well as the more tangible achievements of group life (Bertrand, 1967).

Concepts such as culture, subculture, cross-cultural change, cultural bias, and the culture of the disadvantaged are increasingly a part of an adult educator's cognitive map. Current efforts of adult educators to motivate and effect change in disadvantaged segments of society whose motivation and value systems differ from the norm have been and continue to be a perplexing but challenging task. In relating to these segments of society, the adult educator functions as a teacher, a communicator, and a change agent. It seems reasonable, therefore, that the adult educator must be aware of existing motivations and value systems of learner groups to understand how and why such differences exist and how programming and planned change are affected by these differences.

Study, analysis, and mapping of the organization's external environment facilitate understanding of the cultural differences in the lifestyles of potential learners and learner groups within that public. Thus, an adult educator's decisions with regard to specific programming strategies should be based on the particular cultural group at which the program may be directed.

Change

Change refers to alteration of the structure or behavior of systems, or both. Change may be planned or unplanned. *Planned change* refers to a purposeful decision to make improvements in a system, usually with the help of a change agent. Bennis et al. (1969) define planned change as "a conscious, deliberate, and collaborative effort to improve the operations of a human system, whether it be self-system, social system, or cultural system, through the utilization of scientific knowledge" (p. 4).

Beal and his co-workers (1966) refer to *social action* as undertaking change in collective behavior in an effort to resolve problems in a social system. Social action is relevant to the programmer role because this role is performed within and among social systems. One significant social system is the programmers' professional organization, a system that largely determines their mission, professional philosophy, operating procedures, contacts, and boundaries of influence. This organizational unit within the larger system, in turn, can itself be regarded as a social system, as can each and every organization, community, neighborhood, and family with which programmers relate. The entire effort of programmers is in some way tied to social systems, and any educational program being planned represents intended change(s) in the collective behavior of people in those systems.

The initial option for action identified by a programmer usually is perceived as it relates to one or more systems within that programmer's range of responsibility. For example, the director of noncredit programs in a university will interpret program ideas based on a personal concept of the community or segments of the community being served by the unit responsible for noncredit programs. Moreover, the university will be perceived as "delivering" the program to learner groups. It is equally possible that this programmer, in planning and implementing the noncredit program, will envision a cooperative relationship with one or more other organizations or systems.

The second and third options obviously would involve changes in the cooperating systems, and would define some type of social action. Such programming calls for a strategy unlike decision making involved in routine planning, wherein a system merely adds to or repeats existing programs without significantly changing its structure or behavior. The strategy involved in the more complex case would be akin to that described by the social action process. The social action process and the conceptual model depicting social action are developed more fully in Chapter 2 (Review of Major Writings).

Decision Making

Decision making almost always is referred to as a process. Griffiths (1964) defines a *process* as "a cycle of events in which a consistent quality or direction can be discerned" (p. 92). The process may be depicted as (1) the cycle of events by which criteria are established by an administrator against which the performance of others is applied or measured or (2) the cycle of events occurring in the mind of the individual while choosing among available options.

The first approach to depicting the decision-making process is typified in step-by-step or phase-by-phase decision models, sometimes called *systems approaches* to decision making. Although different writers apply different approaches to the concept, the themes are similar. Certain stages of decision making are universally employed by administrators who are interested in making the most effective and efficient decisions for their organizations. Variations in the basic theme deal largely with nomenclature and the range of personal and organizational factors affecting the decision-making process.

The second approach to depicting decision making involves the mental cycle individuals undergo in choosing their response to a stimulus to change. For example, when faced with the decision to adopt or reject an innovation, individuals usually move from first knowledge of the innovation, through a persuasion stage, then to a decision stage, and finally to a point where confirmation is sought for the decision made (Rogers, 1972). Although, as Rogers cautions, some decision makers may not always follow this exact sequence, all of these events are involved in the decision-making process. Moreover, decision makers are influenced by such factors as their own personality, values, background, and communication sources; the nature of the social system(s) involved; and the nature of the innovation, among other factors.

Whether decision making is depicted from the point of view of the person who makes decisions for others to follow, or from the perspective of personal or group decisions, the process involves a series of events, usually occurring in some order and influenced by personal and systemic factors. The approach here is to depict programming as involving decisions made by the programmer and significant others, and to build a framework for programming from the factors thought to influence the process itself. Thus, programming is a decision-making process; the decision makers are the programmer, members of the adult education and other organizations, leaders of the learner groups, and the learners themselves. Moreover, all decisions, and hence the decision-making process, are influenced importantly by personal and systemic factors.

Needs

Tyler (1971) defines a *need* as the difference between the present condition of the individual learner or learner group and a social norm that can be identified. The gap between where these learners are in relation to the social norm consitutes a need. For example, a social norm in consumer education may be that consumers will know basic management concepts and possess the skills needed to make informed and intelligent decisions in the marketplace. An analysis of consumers' knowledge about and skills in resource management may reveal that they lack knowledge and understanding of financial management concepts and practices and thus are ill-prepared to make informed and sound decisions in the marketplace.

Tyler identifies several sources of information that suggest educational needs of learners. The primary source of such information is the learners themselves. A study of learners will provide a perspective on their environment, their sociodemographic characteristics, their interests, and the relevance of program content to them. A second source of information is a study of the learners' contemporary life to determine their culture, lifestyle, bases for lifestyle, and vocabulary (concepts, skills, and values). Such knowledge aids in designing programs relevant to the learners' social context. The argument for the study of contemporary life is that the learners' recognition of the similarities between the situations encountered in life and that which is being learned will increase the likelihood of the learning being applied. A third source of information is suggestions from subject-matter specialists, a source of needs most commonly used and most often criticized. Often specialists may propose needs and objectives for individual learners or learner groups that may be too highly technical and specialized. Nonetheless, these specialists generally set the norms upon which needs may be based.

Adult educators must identify, assess, and analyze learners' expressed/felt needs in collaboration with the individual learner, learner groups, and their leaders. It is imperative that adult educators thoroughly understand the needs concept if they are to function effectively in this collaborative effort.

PROGRAMMING IN RETROSPECT

In this introduction to the programming process in adult education, all aspects of the process are treated as systems-related. The emphasis is on how the parts and elements of educational programs interact and relate to other parts and elements, not on how parts and elements of the program stand by themselves. Therefore, the discussion deals with the systems concept of programming as a process, the planned program itself, assumptions about the process, and concepts basic to programming. Concepts presented here are intended to be helpful in analyzing and understanding the major subprocesses of programming in adult education—that is, planning, design and implementation, and evaluation and accountability.

The conceptual programming model in adult education differs from existing models in several ways:

First, programming is viewed as a dynamic system that includes a number of interrelated and interdependent processes and concepts.

Second, programming is viewed as the principal means by which an adult education organization evaluates its relevancy and effectiveness as a change organization within its environment, and engages in renewal, as needed.

Third, emphasis is placed on the adult education organization being proactive as contrasted to reactive in its behavioral stance in the change arena.

Fourth, the programming concept emphasizes the important role the adult education organization plays in the total programming process.

Fifth, the conceptual model is predicated on the proposition that adult educators, functioning as change agents and programmers, collaborate with individual learners, learner groups, and their leaders in identifying, assessing, and analyzing expressed/felt educational needs.

Sixth, educational programs exist in at least two time dimensions and at least two levels of specificity: a long-range planned program and its component short-range plans of action.

Seventh, the conceptual model specifies an orderly set of processual tasks to be engaged in when applying a specific concept to a given situation.

The conceptual programming model and programming models advanced by leading experts in the adult education field are presented, analyzed, and compared in Chapter 2. To facilitate the presentation, it would seem desirable to offer definitions of terms pertinent to programming and used throughout this work.

GLOSSARY OF TERMS

Accountability: the capability and the responsibility to account for the commitment of resources in terms of program results or outcomes. This accounting involves both the stewardship of resources and the evaluation of achievements in relation to specified objectives.

Adult education: "a process whereby persons whose major social roles are characteristic of adult status undertake systematic and sustained learning activities for the
purpose of bringing about changes in knowledge, attitudes, values, or skills"
(Darkenwald and Merriam, 1982, p. 9).

Adult education organization: any agency, organization, or institution that has as one
of its primary responsibilities the education of adults.

Adult learner: a participant in any adult learning opportunity, whether special or regular,
to develop new skills or qualifications, or to improve existing skills and qualifications, or to acquire information.

Adult learner group: a group of adults in the population at whom learning opportunities are directed.

Behavioral change: an alteration in either the knowledge, attitudes, or skills or any
combination of these behaviors of an adult learner or learner group.

Change agent: a professional, practicing adult educator or lay leader who consciously
endeavors to relate to a learner, learner group, or system (client system) for the
purpose of creating awareness of a need; definition and acknowledgement of the
need; agreement on the need to change; definition of goals/objectives with regard
to the need; decisions on change strategies to be pursued; action on strategies;
and plans for evaluation. The change agent functions as an educator, a facilitator,
and an action strategist.

Change strategy: the overall design and packaging of learning activities and teaching
methods that adult educators develop and use to intervene with individual learners,
learner groups, and systems to motivate and effect change among them with regard
to a defined educational need(s) and objective(s).

Cognitive map: a set of interrelated concepts formed and organized by adult educators to guide their thinking and actions in programming.

Concept: an idea or mental image a person forms in his or her mind in order to understand and cope with something in his or her actual experience. A concept is composed of both meaning and feeling, which may or may not be expressed in words.

Conceptual model: a pattern of interrelated concepts used to guide the thoughts and
actions of an adult educator in implementing the programming process. A conceptual model for programming in adult education is a verbal or graphic structure that represents, within the parameters of its specified purpose, a conceptualization of programming in adult education.

Construct: the interrelations of concepts; the programming process in adult education
is both a conceptual model and a construct.

Culture: the behavior or lifestyle of a definable grouping of people; all the learned
and expected physical and mental aspects of life shared by members of a society.

Decision making: an orderly cycle of events in which a consistent quality or direction
can be discerned; orderly execution of the sequenced events leads to a decision
or action on available options.

Deductive change: refers to change that begins with a generalization which infers a
factual conclusion within the context of the major postulate.

Delivery system: an organizational and administrative mode for providing learning
opportunities.

Design and implementation: the second subprocess of the programming process in adult
education, which begins with the design of the planned program and extends
through its implementation. The three dimensions of the subprocess are (1) the
planned program, (2) the component plans of action, and (3) the action strategies.

Educational needs: the difference between the current situations of learners and a
societal norm or standard that can be identified; the gap between where learners
are in relation to an identifiable societal norm.

Evaluation: "the process of judging (or a judgment as to) the worth or value of a program. This judgment is formed by comparing evidence as to what the program 'is' with criteria as to what the program 'should be' " (Steele, 1970, p. 7).

Evaluation and accountability: the third subprocess of the programming process in adult education, which is concerned with making informed judgments about the effectiveness of the planned program and plans of action based on established criteria and observable evidence. The subprocess is based on three concepts: (1) determining and measuring program outputs, (2) assessing program inputs, and (3) using evaluation findings and feedback for program revisions, organizational renewal, and accounting to the learners and their leaders, the adult education organization, funding sources, the profession, and, where applicable, the governance body.

Feedback loop: the path through a feedback system from input to output and back to input.

Inductive change: refers to change that begins with a specific set of observations and moves to a generalization.

Interaction: the reciprocal contact or interstimulation and response between individuals and groups. Four characteristics of interaction are (1) a plurality of actors (two or more); (2) communication between the actors by means of symbols; (3) a duration or time dimension possessing a past, a present, or a future, which, in part, determines the character of the ongoing action; and (4) an objective, whether or not, from the standpoint of the actors, its specification coincides with that of an objective observer.

Interfacing: a process by which human beings confront common areas of concern, engage in meaningfully related dialogue, actively search for solutions to mutual problems, and purposefully cope with their solutions.

Lay leader: a person in a group or system whose characteristics and traits influence the thinking and actions of those who are members of the group or system; there may be both formal and informal leaders in the group or system.

Linkage: the blending of the adult education organization and its publics into a common function; the blending of two or more systems to achieve a common purpose. In the conceptual programming model, linkage is basic to the entire programming process and consists of four elements: (1) study, analysis, and mapping of the publics within which the organization functions; (2) identification of target publics; (3) identification of and interfacing with leaders of target publics; and (4) collaborative identification, assessment, and analysis of educational needs specific to the target publics.

Mapping: an element of the linkage process in which the adult educator, as change agent, engages for the purpose of identifying and delineating learner groups and systems to be served by the adult education organization. Criteria for mapping in an adult education organization are (1) maintaining a constant interchange with the societal context (acting on and reacting to it); (2) providing alternatives to meet the problems of mapping evolving out of new environmental forces; (3) having the ability to recognize those parts of the organization that are responsive to mapping; and (4) having an arrangement for preserving or propagating successful experiences.

Objectives: conditions sought, attainment of which is observable, measurable, and qualifiable; what a learner should be able to do when his or her behavior changes in the intended way.

Organizational renewal: the organization's adjustment or rearrangement of its resources, both human and material, to accommodate changes in its environment predicated on feedback obtained through continual interaction with its learners and their leaders and evaluation of outcomes of planned programs.

Planned change: the utilization of scientific knowledge in a conscious, deliberate, and collaborative effort to improve the operations of a human system, whether it be a self-system, social system, or cultural system.

Planned program: the master perspective (plan) for behavioral change toward which adult educators direct their efforts. The planned program consists of (1) a statement of broad-based educational needs, (2) a statement of objectives keyed to those needs, (3) specification of teaching strategies for achieving the objectives, and (4) specification of macro outcomes of the planned program.

Planning: the first subprocess of the programming process in adult education; a deliberate, rational, continuing sequence of activities through which the adult educator acquires a thorough understanding of and commitment to the organization's functions, structure, and processes, and becomes knowledgeable about and committed to a tested conceptual framework for programming, continuous organizational renewal, and linkage of the organization to its publics.

Plan of action: short-range, specific teaching strategies to guide the efforts of the adult educator in fulfilling learner needs and attaining the long-range objectives of the planned program; for each objective of the planned program, specific plans of action must be designed and implemented.

Proactive behavior: a stance taken by the adult education organization in projecting and predicting the future state of affairs of a situation or phenomenon; anticipating and planning for the future.

Process: a series of interrelated steps or actions leading to a specific end or goal.

Processual task: an orderly set of actions engaged in by an adult educator in applying a specific concept to a particular situation.

Programming process: a comprehensive, systematic, and proactive process, designed to facilitate desirable changes in the behavior of adult learners and the environment or system in which they live, and encompassing, in a purposeful manner, the total planned, collaborative efforts of the adult education organization, the adult educator in the roles of change agent and programmer, representatives of the learners, and the learners themselves.

Public: a group of people, within the operational boundaries of the organization, who (1) share common interests and identity, (2) manifest frequent or continuous interaction, and (3) are spatially distributed over a relatively small area or a larger territory.

Reactive behavior: the response to needs or crisis situations as they occur.

Social action: planned change in collective behavior in an effort to resolve problems in a social system; more specifically, planned, collaborative action that is consciously evoked by the alteration of attributes of systems and subsystems through the development of new systems and the alteration of old ones.

System: an entity, conceptual or physical, that consists of interrelated parts. Programming is directed toward change in the behavior of the individual learner, learner groups, and systems. All of these audiences are systems. Further, the adult education organization is a system; the process employed in developing and implementing the planned program is a system; and the planned program itself is a system.

Target public: an identified group or system, within its publics, toward which the adult education organization focuses its efforts in effecting behavioral change.

Theory: a set of interrelated constructs, definitions, and propositions that present a systematic view of phenomena by specifying relations among variables for the purpose of explaining and predicting phenomena.

The foregoing definitions, in some cases, represent the author's concept of the term defined; others are compilations of definitions from several sources as interpreted by the author; and others are quoted directly from their source. In all cases, the terms are defined as used in the conceptual model for programming in adult education. In view of the number of concepts, processes, elements, and dimensions encompassed in the programming process, and their interrelatedness, the author urges the reader to become thoroughly familiar with these definitions.

REFERENCES

ACKOFF, R. L., "Systems, Organizations, and Interdisciplinary Research," *General Systems,* 5 (1960), 1–8.

BEAL, G. M., R. C. BLOUNT, R. C. POWERS, and W. J. JOHNSON, *Social Action and Interaction in Program Planning.* Ames: Iowa State University Press, 1966.

BENNIS, W. G., K. D. BENNE, R. CHIN, and K. E. COREY, eds., *The Planning of Change.* 2nd ed. New York: Holt, Rinehart and Winston, 1969.

BERTRAND, A. L., *Basic Sociology: An Introduction to Theory and Method.* New York: Appleton-Century-Crofts, 1967.

DARKENWALD, G. G., and S. B. MERRIAN, *Adult Education: Foundations of Practice.* New York: Harper & Row, Publishers, 1982.

GRIFFITHS, D., "Administrative Theory and Change in Organizations," in *Innovation in Education,* ed. M. B. Miles. New York: Teachers College, Columbia University, 1964.

KNOWLES, M., "The Growth and Development of Adult Education," in *Building an Effective Adult Education Enterprise,* ed. J. M. Peters and Associates. San Francisco: Jossey-Bass, Publishers, 1980.

KNOX, A. B., "Preface," in *Developing, Administering, and Evaluating Adult Education,* ed. A. B. Knox and Associates. San Francisco: Jossey-Bass, Publishers, 1980.

LASZLO, E., ed., *The Relevance of General Systems Theory.* New York: George Braziller, 1972.

LIPPITT, R. L., J. WATSON, and B. WESTLEY, *The Dynamics of Planned Change.* New York: Harcourt, Brace & World, Inc., 1958.

MACCOBY, M., *The Gamesman.* New York: Simon and Schuster, 1976.

PETERS, J. M., and C. P. KOZOLL, "Organization in the Field," in *Building an Effective Adult Education Enterprise,* ed. J. M. Peters and Associates. San Francisco: Jossey-Bass, Publishers, 1980.

ROGERS, E. M., "Change Agents, Clients, and Change," in *Creating Social Change,* ed. G. Zaltman, P. Kotter, and R. Kaufman. New York: Holt, Rinehart and Winston, 1972.

SCHROEDER, W., "Typology of Adult Learning Systems," in *Building an Effective Adult Education Enterprise,* ed. J. M. Peters and Associates. San Francisco: Jossey-Bass, Publishers, 1980.

STEELE, S., "Program Evaluation—A Broader Definition," *Journal of Extension,* 8 (Summer 1970), 5–18.

TYLER, R. W., *Basic Principles of Curriculum and Instruction.* Chicago: University of Chicago Press, 1971.

Chapter Two

A Review
of
Major Writings

When facing the tasks of conceptualizing programming in adult education and then putting the related concepts into practice, we encounter two major obstacles. First, those adult educators considered to be programming experts have proferred differing models of the programming process; second, a consistent application of any model is made difficult because of the wide variety of contexts within which adult education is practiced.

These obstacles are addressed in an attempt to clarify the programming aspect of adult education, a task not previously undertaken in the literature. First, we will review nine major programming models that deal with processes relevant to programming in adult education (Beal et al., 1966; Boone, Dolan, and Shearon, 1971; Boyle, 1981; Freire, 1970; Houle, 1972; Kidd, 1973; Knowles, 1970; Lippitt, Watson, and Westley, 1958; Tyler, 1971). We will describe their similarities and differences and draw overall conclusions. This format provides both a review of the respective conceptual models for comprehension and analysis and a sense of which model (or models) appears to be most applicable to specific situations.

To facilitate understanding the nine different programming models, we have organized each model on the notion that programming in adult education encompasses three basic subprocesses: planning, design and implementation, and evaluation and accountability. Each of the nine models is incorporated in Table 2-1 by alphabetical order of the author's surname. As clearly shown in the table, the three subprocesses tend to overlap, and some of the models tend not to use all three of the suggested subprocesses. Nonetheless, this type of grid allows each of the nine programming models to be analyzed, understood, and compared with others. Table 2-1 will be referred to at appropriate points when reviewing each of the nine models and when describing similarities and differences in the models.

BEAL, BLOUNT, POWERS, AND JOHNSON (1966)

Because Beal and his co-workers are concerned with social action within the context of rural extension work, they present a detailed analysis of the stages involved in that process. The most distinctive feature of this model is that each of the odd-numbered stages (from 3 to 31) is evaluative, because the authors see evaluation as ongoing and, therefore, integral to each stage in the social action or programming process. Thus, each even-numbered stage (from 2 to 32) has preceding evaluative activities.

Having analyzed and reflected on the conceptualization and progression of the Beal et al. model, one can see that it is sociological and social system-oriented, advocates a process of social action that is analytic and systematic in activities, and seeks a carefully built consensus for action.

The model progresses from analysis of social systems to convergence of

TABLE 2-1   Selected programming models

Author	Planning	Design & Implementation	Evaluation & Accountability
Beal, Blount, Powers, & Johnson (1966)	**Step 1:** Analysis of existing social systems. **Step 2:** Convergence of interest. **Step 4:** Study prior social situation. **Step 6:** Delineate relevant social systems. **Step 8:** Contact with "initiating sets." **Step 10:** Legitimation with key leaders. **Step 12:** Contact with "diffusion sets." **Step 14:** Need definition by more general, relevant social systems. **Step 16:** Commitment to action. **Step 18:** Formulation of goals. **Step 20:** Decision on means of action.	(Even) **Step 22:** Plan of action. **Step 24:** Mobilization of resources. **Steps 26-28:** Action steps.	(Odd) **Steps 3-31:** Ongoing evaluation. 　Objectives met? 　What next? **Step 33:** Total program evaluation. **Step 34:** Continuation.
Boone, Dolan, Shearon (1971)	**The institution & its renewal process:** Understanding & commitment to the functions of the institution: 　Philosophy 　Objectives. Understanding of and commitment to the institution's organizational structure: 　Roles 　Relationships. Knowledgeable about & skilled in management: 　Staffing 　Staff development 　Supervision 　Accountability. Understanding of & commitment to a tested conceptual framework for programming. Understanding of & commitment to continuous institutional renewal. **Linking the institution to its publics through need analysis & leader involvement:** 　Study, analysis, & mapping of county and/or area. 　Identification & analysis of subsystems within county and/or area. 　Identification of target subsystems.	**Long-range program:** 　Specification of macro needs. 　Delineation of macro objectives. 　Designation of strategies for attaining objectives. **Plans of work:** 　Delineating, ordering, & sequencing micro needs. 　Specifying instructional-level objectives. 　Selecting & organizing learner activities. 　Formulating plans for evaluation. **Activating plans of work:** 　Mobilizing & utilizing resources. 　Monitoring the teaching-learning process. 　Reinforcing learners. 　Revising & redirecting activities based on feedback.	**Program evaluation & accountability:** 　Determining program outputs. 　Assessing program inputs. 　Utilizing evaluative findings for program revisions, institutional renewal, & accountability to publics, funding sources, & to the profession.

TABLE 2-1 (continued)

Author	Planning	Design & Implementation	Evaluation & Accountability
Boone et al. (cont'd.)	Identifying & interfacing with leaders of target subsystems.		
	Formation of leadership systems representative of target subsystems.		
	Needs identification & analysis specific to target subsystems.		
	Relating needs of target subsystem to the larger system & identifying macro needs common to two or more subsystems.		
Boyle (1981)	Establish a philosophical basis for programming.	Select & organize learning experiences.	Determine the effectiveness, results, & impact.
	Analyze problems & needs or concerns of people & communities.	Identify instructional design with appropriate methods, techniques, & devices.	Communicate program value to appropriate decision-makers.
	Involve potential clientele.	Utilize effective promotional priorities.	
	Determine intellectual & social development levels.	Obtain resources necessary to support the program.	
	Select sources to investigate & analyze in determining program objectives.		
	Recognize organizational & individual constraints.		
	Criteria for establishing program priorities.		
	Degree of rigidity/flexibility of planned programs.		
	Legitimation & support of formal & informal power situations.		
Freire (1970)	**Steps:**		
	Research an area *completely*.		
	Meet with significant groups to discuss aims.		
	Call for volunteers to gather necessary data about area life.		
	Team of "experts" & area residents analyze totality *as if a code* & determine interactions.	———————————— Also evaluative.	
	Observe *moments in area life* & compile data.		
	Team evaluates & recognizes data.	———————————— Also evaluative.	
	Locate nuclei of contradictions.		
	Select contradictions to develop (visual/oral) "*codes.*"		
	Start "decoding" dialogues in area.		

TABLE 2-1   (continued)

Authors	Planning	Design & Implementation	Evaluation & Accountability
Freire (cont'd.	Team studies results of dialogues for "themes." Break themes into "thematic" components. Codify thematics. Prepare didactic materials out of codification.	————————————— Materials presented to area residents.	Also evaluative.
Houle (1972)	**Identifying possible educational activities:** Via dissatisfaction, accident, media, extra money/old interest, group interaction, reaching "thresholds." **Deciding to proceed:** Via being asked, choosing among alternatives. **Identifying & refining objectives:** "Intended result of educational activity." Elements: professional goals, rational ends, teacher/learner needs & resources. Attributes: rational, practical, be at end of desired action, pluralistic, need balanced judgment, hierarchical, discriminative, change during learning process. Refinement = milieu x nature of learners x content x design x aspiration x motivation. Objective statement: Should conform to reality. Is abstract notation. Defines desired learner accomplishments. Results from cooperative development. Should be clear. Includes necessary supports. Study people's level of awareness (real consciousness) of contradictions. **Suitable format designed:** Resources + leaders + methods + schedule + sequence + social reinforcement + individualization + roles/relationships set + evaluation criteria set + design clear to all.	**Format fitted into larger life patterns:** Help learners enter & exit. Necessary shifts in learner lifestyle. Financial support. Public relations. **Plan put into effect:** Via prior planning.	**Results measured & appraised:** Standard evaluation procedure. Back to first stage.

TABLE 2-1 (continued)

Author	Planning	Design & Implementation	Evaluation & Accountability
Kidd (1973)	**Identifying learners' needs:** Via exploration, investigation, current interests as starting point. **Curriculum development:** Field of study. Tyler's "screens": Educational philosophy. Understanding learning. Set objectives (via Mager & Tyler). Develop learning experience (with Houle's steps).	**Learning situation (= engagement):** Need exploration. Specific forms/devices. Group reinforcements. Subject-matter exploration.	**Evaluation:** Change, growth, objectives. Standard methodology.
Knowles (1970)	**Climate-setting:** Organizational purpose promotes educative environment, democratic philosophy, growth, & change modeling. Through policy statements & committee structures. **Organizational structure:** Via program committees. **Need diagnosis:** Of individuals. Of organizations. Of community. **Objective-definition:** As guidelines & bench marks. Organize needs into priority system (as educational & operational needs). Screen needs through institutional philosophy, feasibility, individual interests. Surviving needs are program objectives.	**Comprehensive program operation:** Recruiting/training. Management of facilitators & procedures. Educational counseling. Budget/finance. **Learning experience design:** Aim is *unity*. Via art principles: line, space/shape, tone, color, texture. Choice of many learning formats.	**Evaluation/rediagnosis:** A question of values: quantification/behavioral change vs. involvement/self-development. When? Who? Purpose: improvement of program & its operation Process: consider educational/operational objectives, development questions, collect data, analyze, modify.
Lippitt, Watson, & Westley (1958)	**Development of a need for change:** Problem awareness. Change agent engaged. **Establishment of a change relationship:** Problem understanding. Trust developed. Degree of effort necessary. Organization of responsibility. Trial periods? **Working toward change:** Clarification/diagnosis: information, analysis, client reaction. Alternative routes/goals.		**Terminal relationship:** Dependency? Skills/flexibility gained? Conflicts? Substitute change agent? Substitute process?

TABLE 2-1   (continued)

Author	Planning	Design & Implementation	Evaluation & Accountability
Lippitt, et al. (cont'd.)	Goals/intentions set: information exchanged, motivation explored, possible anxiety. Intentions become efforts: change agent support necessary, possible struggles; client needs feedback. **Generalization/stabilization of change** Peer/community support. Organizational/structural changes.	Goals/intentions set: information exchanged, motivation explored, possible anxiety. Intentions become efforts: change agent support necessary, possible struggles; client needs feedback. **Generalization/stabilization of change** Peer/community support. Organizational/structural changes.	
Tyler (1971)	**Educational purposes:** Three sources: Learners themselves. Contemporary life. Subject specialists. Screens: Institutional philosophy. Psychology of learning. Stating objectives: "Desired changes in students." Behavior & content. Grid approach.	**Selecting learning experiences:** General principles: Opportunity to practice desired behavior. Satisfaction from behavior. Reactions desired are possible. Many experiences fulfill one objective. One experience can have many outcomes. **Organizing learning experiences:** Horizontal & vertical. Criteria: continuity, sequence, integration. Elements: values, concepts, skills. Principles: Chronology Greater breadth of application Breadth & activity Description-then-analysis Specifics-then-principles Unified world view.	**Evaluation:** Do experiences produce results? Strengths & weaknesses. Basic notions: Degree of change. Evaluate early, late, & afterward. Any valid evidence OK. Procedure: Objective. Evidence necessary. Behavior demonstration situations. Instrument. How to express behavior. Objective rating.

interest on a problem; to more specific analysis; to contact with "initiating sets" (those persons who will get ideas moving); to legitimation via key leaders; to "diffusion sets" (persons who will "spread the word"); to more specific needs (definition); to action (commitment); and then to the more standard steps of goal setting, means of action, plans of action, and resource mobilization and action stages. As in the other models, these "planning" steps imply action stages flowing naturally from what is planned; for example, if a community cleanup is planned, all necessary actions will be initiated.

Finally, all the evaluative activities in this model revolve around the question of whether or not objectives are met. To point up the fact that the process is ongoing, "continuation" is specified as the step in this model that leads back to Stage 1.

BOONE, DOLAN, AND SHEARON (1971)

The Boone-Dolan-Shearon "conceptual schema" of programming in the co-operative extension service is an expansion and refinement of the Beal group's model and Tyler's conceptualization of programming (see Table 2-1). As one reads through the "processual tasks" (actions undertaken in the *process* of extension educational work) under each heading, the major effort is to specify the systems, educational needs, learning objectives, learning experiences, and plans for evaluation. Compared to the Beal et al. model, this model brings in a more *educational* framework for defining and organizing the learning activities essential to extension work.

The Boone-Dolan-Shearon model operates under a set of four basic assumptions/values considered vital to understanding the thrust of the processual tasks described. First, the adult educator, as change agent and programmer, must understand and be committed to the philosophy, objectives, roles, and relationships of the organization. Second, the educator requires understanding of and skills in staffing, staff development, supervision, and evaluation and accountability. Third, the educator must have a commitment to a tested conceptual framework for programming that (1) links the organization and its publics through needs analysis and leader involvement and (2) tailors program design and implementation to the publics' needs. Fourth, the educator needs an understanding of and commitment to organizational renewal.

The Boone-Dolan-Shearon programming model ranges from identification and mapping of the main systems and subsystems; to leadership identification and interfacing/development; to macro needs/objectives delineation; to strategy design; to defining micro needs, micro objectives, learning activities, and evaluation plans; to activating plans of action; and then to program evaluation and accountability (Table 2-1).

BOYLE (1981)

In *Planning Better Programs*, Boyle (1981) discusses programming as a comprehensive synthesis of theory, analysis, and practice. The perspective and scope of Boyle's views of programming have several distinctive features. First, he carefully links programming to the concept of continuing education/lifelong learning; that is, programming is seen as the opportunity structure for the continuing demand for lifelong learning. The terms *programming* and *program develop-*

ment are used synonymously in an attempt to reduce the perplexing nature of thoughts, ideas, and practices that Boyle feels the concept of programming can communicate. Rather than offer an actual model for programming, Boyle presents the 15 relevant concepts upon which he believes the program development process rests. The first nine of these concepts refer more to the planning stage, the next four to design and implementation, and the final two to evaluation (see Table 2-1). To encourage the reader to appreciate the dynamics of the process, Boyle suggests that these concepts and action phases may vary according to the program situation. To this end, he carefully classifies program types as developmental, institutional, and informational.

Boyle's approach to programming does not lend itself to any one theoretical model. Thus, he makes six assumptions about the role of planned change that he believes become the focus or basis for the development of a continuing education program. These assumptions are (1) planned change is a necessary prerequisite to effective economic and social progress for people and communities; (2) the most desirable change is predetermined and democratically achieved; (3) continuing education programs, if properly planned and implemented, can make a significant contribution to planned change; (4) educational changes in knowledge, skills, and attitudes of people are necessary to achieve economic, environmental, and social change; (5) it is possible to select, organize, and administer a continuing education program that will contribute to the social and economic progress of people and communities; and (6) people and communities need the guidance and leadership of an adult educator to help them solve their problems and achieve more desirable ways of living and making a living.

These assumptions undergird a variety of theoretical approaches and concepts that Boyle synthesizes and elaborates upon in differing contexts. For example, his approach to change involves a framework of institutional model building, premised upon the notion that change is introduced by formal organizations. On the other hand, his approach to needs is derived from Lewinian field theory and the notion of dynamic tensions; that is, imbalance in the organism indicates a need to be satisfied; satisfaction of this need causes a reduction in tension and equilibrium is restored to the organism. His approach to design and implementation is heavily indebted to Tyler (1971), while his approach to evaluation is based on Steele's (1970) definition of evaluation as "the process of judging (or a judgment as to) the worth or value of a program. This judgment is formed by comparing evidence as to what the program 'is' with criteria as to what the program 'should be' " (p. 8).

FREIRE (1970)

Freire (*Pedagogy of the Oppressed*) must be regarded as providing us with a programming context, a methodology, and a set of values quite different from the other eight authors reviewed. Before analyzing Freire's approach to programming in adult education, one should be aware that Freire developed his "pedagogy" out of his literacy work with poor, oppressed peasants in northeastern Brazil. Thus, his values are concerned with "freedom from oppression" and a humanizing and humanistic liberation. His methodology is both dialectic and dialogic; that is, it is aimed at resolving the contradictions inherent in the perspectives of the oppressed poor and utilizes a reflexive pattern of analysis and active dialogue (*praxis* is Freire's term), as indicated in the planning steps in Table 2-1. Freire's aim is a "problem-posing pedagogy" in which learners begin to question, analyze, and act upon their world, the end result being liberation from oppression.

The core of activity depicted in Table 2-1 is to study an area and its people and then to present back to them the "themes" distilled from both that analysis and feedback gathered from them in the process of data collection. The basic process is to perceive existential "contradictions"; to codify or present them in oral and visual form, or both; to have the people decode those contradictions; to develop themes for the decoding; and thence to prepare didactic materials.

So, unlike our other authors, Freire presents an *inductive* model, as compared to Tyler's *deductive* model, for example, that evolves from a praxis of thought and action set in the context of an ongoing dialogue with a target group. As indicated in Table 2-1, evaluation is continuous, as in the Beal et al. model; it is built into the process as a constant review of both information and perceptions about that information.

Finally, the original content of Freire's programming efforts was literacy work, geared to the most powerful words in the themes of those Brazilian peasants. Thus, one might assume that the content of an applied Freirean pedagogy depends on the focus of the adult education organization, the instructors involved, and the themes identified by the target groups. In community development, for example, the theme might be, "How can we get fire protection?" or, with older adults, it might be, "How can we stay independent as long as possible?"

Freire can be difficult to understand, due to both the uniqueness of his dialectic methodology and terminology and the profoundly political context of his values. But he does provide another programming model of great potential worth for the field of adult education.

HOULE (1972)

One distinctive feature of Houle's model is the attention and detail he gives to the planning phase of programming. Perhaps even more important, in *The Design of Education* Houle poses seven powerful assumptions for the design of education:

1. Any learning episode occurs in a specific situation and is profoundly influenced by that fact.
2. The analysis or planning of educational activities must be based on the realities of human experience and upon their constant change.
3. Education is a practical art.
4. Education is a cooperative rather than an operative art.
5. The planning or analysis of an educational activity usually is undertaken in terms of some period the mind abstracts from complicated reality for analytic purposes.
6. The planning or analysis of an educational activity may be undertaken by an educator, a learner, an independent analyst, or some combination of the three.
7. Any design of education can be understood best as a complex of interacting elements, not as a sequence of events.

Just as other writers construct their program designs on certain values, Houle builds upon his assumptions. Although Houle's model is adequately summarized in Table 2-1, it is worthwhile to note how his beliefs influence his programming concept. What comes through clearly in *The Design of Education* is the practical focus Houle has in this model. The first two stages look at programming through the learner's eyes. Designing learning formats requires a complete set of administrative actions. Designation of the fifth stage as "format fitted into larger life patterns," is quite revealing in that it specifically recognizes the fit between learning activities and the broader scope of the learner's life. Finally, for increased understanding, it is worth nothing that Houle's programming perspective (like that of Knowles) is one of a continuing education administrator. That fact marks his concern for detail and for the learner, who has many choices to make with regard to a variety of educational opportunities.

KIDD (1973)

Kidd is perhaps the most eclectic of the authors whose programming models are described herein and illustrated in Table 2-1. Specifically, in *How Adults Learn,* his section on curriculum development basically follows Tyler's (1971) recommendations about using "screens" to refine educational objectives and about setting learning objectives (with passing reference to the value of Mager's [1962] work in defining objectives). Then Kidd refers his readers to Houle's (1972) work on developing learning experiences, which we have just discussed.

However, in his mathematical approach to programming, Kidd is distinctive in being learner-centered, precise, and analytic in curriculum development. In his first programming stage, identifying learners' needs, he advocates starting with learners' current interests and letting them explore their own needs, as well as investigating such needs through standard needs assessment methods. In addition, in Kidd's third stage, the learning situation itself, we note that his stated aim is the *engagement* of the learner, primarily through exploration of both learner needs and the subject matter itself. Because the learning experiences can take various forms and use many methods, Kidd urges that group reinforcement be built into all group learning situations.

With regard to evaluation, Kidd cites AEA/USA recommendations in targeting the vital question in the final stage of programming: How much change and growth has there been?'' Kidd then proposes a standard evaluation methodology to help answer that question.

KNOWLES (1970)

In *The Modern Practice of Adult Education,* Knowles structures his programming model (summarized in Table 2-1) on his androgogical philosophy, a philosophy that assumes adults move toward self-direction, use their experience as a learning resource, are ready to learn in accordance with sociodevelopmental tasks, and desire immediate application of learning. These assumptions imply self-diagnosis of learning needs, participation in planning and learning experiences, and self-evaluation.

Although these values underlie Knowles's concept of programming, they are tempered, as Knowles gives a concrete and detailed description from a continuing education program perspective. So, ideal values are combined with down-to-earth pragmatism in this model. For example, Stage 1, climate-setting, is achieved through the institutional mechanism of organizational purposes, policy statements, and committee structures; and Stage 2, participative planning, occurs through program committees.

At Stage 3, needs diagnosis, and Stage 4, objectives definition, Knowles shifts to more traditional program actions. Needs diagnosis is achieved by a variety of means (e.g., interviews, surveys) at the individual, organizational, and community levels. Potential objectives then are divided into educational and operational categories and screened through the "filters" of institutional philosophy, feasibility, and individual interests. The surviving needs become program objectives.

Unity is Knowles's aim for Stage 5, learning experience design, and he expresses organizing principles here from a unique perspective, that of art. So, one is advised to choose among many possible learning formats via the principles of line, space/shape, tone, color, and texture.

Following these five stages is comprehensive program operation, or managing what has been planned. Finally, Knowles poses a choice of focuses for evaluation: for those valuing desired behavioral change, quantitative techniques are appropriate; for those valuing self-development, participant evaluation in programming is more appropriate.

LIPPITT, WATSON, AND WESTLEY (1958)

In *Dynamics of Planned Change,* Lippitt, Watson, and Westley (1958) are somewhat less structured in their model of "planned change" than is Tyler (1971), for example, as can be observed in Table 2-1. Since their purpose is to define a more general *process* of change than is the case in the other models reviewed here, they tend to be much less specific.

One may gain a sense of the process Lippitt and his co-workers elaborate upon by reflecting on the five main stages in their model. Change is the objective and the process, so the client and change agent go from awareness of the need for change, establishing the "change relationship," to working toward change, to stabilization of that change, and finally to the change agent establishing a terminal relationship with the client system. Within these major stages, the subheadings denote the actions between the client and change agent (as between learner and teacher). Information is continually exchanged, terms are developed and tested, new behaviors are tested, established emotional needs are explored, and support is sought from other sources.

The "terminal relationship" stage, under which several questions are listed (see Table 2-1), may need some explanation. These questions note the evaluative concerns common at the end of a change effort and imply the learning goals of such efforts (independence, skills, and adaptability gained; conflict successfully dealt with). As in other programs, one asks, Was this the way we should have done this? So, we normally question the need to shift the change agent, or the change process, or both.

TYLER (1971)

The programming process in Tyler's *Basic Principles of Curriculum and Instruction* is organized around four main questions:

1. What educational purposes (objectives) should the organization seek to attain?
2. How can learning experiences be selected that are likely to be useful in attaining these objectives?
3. How can the selected learning experiences be organized for effective instruction?
4. How can the effectiveness of these learning experiences be evaluated?

Although Tyler does not propose formal stages of educational programming (see Table 2-1), he does present a legitimate process of curriculum/program development that is adaptable to formal adult education endeavors.

To answer his first organizing question, "What educational purposes (objectives) should the organization seek to attain?" Tyler suggests three sources to define educational purposes: (1) the learners themselves—learning gaps growing out of comparisons with standards of learning, community needs, and individual interests and needs, met and unmet, (2) contemporary life, and (3) subject-matter specialists. The educational philosophy of the organization serves as a screen for other elements here, refining what is to be undertaken in light of the social values held by the organization. Knowledge of the psychology of learning helps set bounds on what can be learned, within the given time and the current environment of the organization.

Stating educational objectives is Tyler's next step in defining educational purposes. The statement focuses on behavioral changes desired in learners, and the content of those objectives specifies the domain of that desired behavior. Tyler suggests a grid demonstrating that content can be defined on one axis, and an ascending range of behavior can be set on the other axis, thus specifying *which behavior* is sought within *what content* and giving a total picture of the program objectives.

Once these tasks have been performed, Tyler's second question, "How can learning experiences be selected that are likely to be useful in attaining these objectives?" is addressed. Tyler defines *learning experiences* as the interaction of learner behavior and the learning environment, and poses five general principles of selection: (1) that the opportunity to practice the desired behavior is provided; (2) that satisfaction is gained from behavior produced; (3) that the desired reactions are possible; (4) that many experiences can fulfill any objective; and (5) that one experience can lead to multiple outcomes.

Having answered the second organizing question, Tyler answers the third question by defining the concepts applicable to organizing learning experiences for effective instruction, organization being both horizontal (in daily blocks) and vertical (cause sequences over time). His criteria for organization are (1) continuity, (2) sequence, and (3) integration. The learning elements within these criteria are values, skills, and concepts. In addition, Tyler posits several principles of organization within the frameworks previously set up: chronology; increasing application, breadth, and range of activity; description followed by analysis of content; specific information followed by intellectual principles; and a unified world view.

The outline in Table 2-1 gives a quick summary of Tyler's approach to evaluation. His primary focus is on desired results, with a secondary concern for the curriculum's strengths and weaknesses. Tyler looks for behavioral change and for valid evidence with regard to standards, and he recommends sequential evaluations. The procedure he recommends for answering the fourth organizing question, "How can the effectiveness of these learning experiences be evaluated?" is reflected in the list of questions that need to be answered in the process of evaluating any group of learners.

SIMILARITIES AND DIFFERENCES
IN THE PROGRAMMING MODELS

While perusing this literature review, undoubtedly the reader has made mental notes about the similarities and differences in the models and authors presented (perhaps in answer to the practical question, Which of these can I use in my job or in my studies?). What follows here is a quick overview of the major similarities and differences in the programming models reviewed. Since a full treatment of these aspects could quite easily become a full-length book, Table 2-2 is provided both as a schematic for comparison and as a tool for further reflection and analysis. In Table 2-2, the aspects of each model are categorized by its context, its scope, its underlying philosophy, its perspective on programming, its primary situational applicability, and its main theme.

TABLE 2-2 Similarities and differences of the programming models

Author	Context	Scope	Philosophy	Perspective	Applicability	Main "Theme"
Beal, Blount, Powers, & Johnson (1966)	Extension work.	Program.	Traditional democratic & applied sociological theory.	Sociological, programmatic, analytic, & applied traditional extension model.	Community/ county programs, traditional social action/ community development settings, educational program/development.	Social action. Utility of social systems approach & social action. Implied notion of the process.
Boone, Dolan, & Shearon (1971)	Adult education, extension work, community development.	Program & group learning experiences.	Democratic/ educational applied sociological & psychological theory, synthesizing.	Sociological, curriculum development, programmatic, analytic, & conceptual approach.	Educational program/institutional development, community/ county extension programs, social action programs.	Social system analysis, leader involvement, needs analysis, formal systematic curriculum development "processual tasks" for change agents, "felt needs."
Boyle (1981)	Continuing education programming.	Program: developmental, institutional, informational.	Eclectic/ pragmatic curriculum development.	Lifelong learning.	Formal & informal extension community.	Change as an assumption in programming; institutional model building; Lewinian concept of needs; evaluation to determine program effectiveness.
Friere (1970)	Education for liberation.	National-community programs/ projects.	· Dialectical, humanistic, Christian, processual, participative, inductive.	Situations of liberation from oppression, political, class societies; radical social change, theoretical.	Nonformal education, literacy work, community/rural development, radical social change, situations of oppression & injustice.	"Problem-position pedagogy"— liberation & humanization vs. oppression & dehumanization, contradictions, codification of life situations.

TABLE 2-2 (continued)

Author	Context	Scope	Philosophy	Perspective	Applicability	Main "Theme"
Houle (1972)	Continuing adult education & other adult education programs.	Program.	"Existential"/ phenomenological.	Administrative, decision-making.	Continuing education & other program situations.	Seven assumptions. Practical tasks. Integration with existential realities.
Kidd (1973)	Range of adult education programs/ learning situations.	Program & smaller focuses.	Humanistic— pragmatic.	Learner-centered, applied educational design, synthesization of existing knowledge— processual.	Range of adult education programming/learning situations.	"The learning transaction"/ engagement of learners/how to synthesize relevant concepts & activities.
Knowles (1970)	Continuing adult education & other adult education situations.	Program.	Humanistic, andragogical, pragmatic, democratic.	Andragogical adult education model— applied educational program design— learner-centered.	Continuing education & other group/ organizational adult education programs.	Andragogy— practical, programmatic activities, democracy, humanism, need analysis, the "craft" of program design.
Lippitt, Watson, & Westley (1958)	Organizational development. Community development. T-groups.	Ongoing "development" project/ program. Group educational projects.	Applied group psychological theory (esp. Kurt Lewin). Process. Philosophies— humanistic psychology.	Process of change— development focus. Applied theory.	Organizational development consultant tasks. Community organization learning facilitation.	Human relationship of change agent & clients. Collaboration—facilitation as an important skill.
Tyler (1971)	Elementary, secondary, higher.	Educational curriculum/ program.	Logico-deductive rationalist tradition.	Formal curriculum development, rationalism, formalism.	Formal adult education curriculum development.	Four basic questions.

The most basic similarity in our models (one which is self-evident, yet worth repeating) is that all of them have basic programs/processes of educational development in which the following elements are present: (1) problem/need definition; (2) setting of objectives, goals, and means; (3) some formal and informal learning activity; and (4) either an explicit or an implicit evaluation. So, what we have seen is an intellectual order of stages and steps in presentation, combined with an interaction of these stages and steps in practice.

Other threads bind these models together. All are adaptable to most, if not all, adult education contexts (although some are obviously more adaptable than others). All of the programming processes are based on either explicit or implicit educational and social philosophies (although there are differences among these philosophies, which we will explore). Also, all of our authors express concern, in varying degrees, for the needs and interests of learners.

Perhaps the most consistent similarity within the nine models is the pattern of emphasis. Most of the activities are concentrated on planning, a reflection of concern for careful design, whether for intellectual reasons or for thorough interaction with learners, or both. Boyle, in particular, devotes full chapters to philosophical concerns, the role of the programmer, and the rationale for involving the learner in programming.

Also notable is the nearly total agreement among the authors. Most are specific about defining goals and objectives (exception: Freire); most explicitly advocate engagement of and participation by learners in the process (exception: Tyler); most see learners' needs and interests forming the *primary* base for program development (exception: Tyler); and the majority of the authors offer a fairly standard treatment of evaluation (exceptions: Freire; Knowles; and Lippitt, Watson, and Westley).

Even though we have viewed this range of programming models within a common framework, and definite similarities have been noted, there is an amazing diversity of approaches within the models, reflecting both the broad scope of the adult education field and the many contingent uses for the models. The differences in approach to programming seem to be more of degree than of substance, and the degrees of difference appear to lie primarily in two areas: the values or philosophy of the author(s) and the purpose(s) for which each model was developed.

We can see these differences in approach more clearly by checking the first four columns in Table 2-2 (context, scope, philosophy, and perspective). In addition, we can generalize about the authors' philosophies and purposes. Beal and his associates are extension-oriented rural sociologists, with values appropriate to that context. Boone, Dolan, and Shearon write primarily for an extension audience, significantly integrating more formal educational methodology with an applied value base and perspective. Boyle draws heavily upon cooperative extension experience, but extends his approach to cover all continuing education programs. Freire melds humanism into an inductive educational methodology, the purpose of which is to liberate the oppressed through appropriate educational content.

The degrees of difference in these models are seen more concretely with regard to basic programming tasks. The differences are most pronounced in the approaches to planning, needs identification, defining objectives, and program implementation (and can be traced by working from model to model in Table 2-1).

Needs identification concepts and practices range from completely individual identification, to a combination of analysis and individual identification, to an educator's analysis of needs. Both the Houle and the Lippitt-Watson-Westley models are predicated upon the individual (or group of individuals) identifying a need and then seeking the assistance of either a change agent or an educational organization. The Beal et al. model and the Boone-Dolan-Shearon model both combine interaction with individuals/groups with social analysis (although they seem to emphasize analysis), while Kidd and

Knowles stress individual identification (with analysis secondary). Boyle seems to share Knowles's specific concept of an educational need, and develops his approach to needs assessment via a Lewinian field theory framework. Tyler, then, stands alone in his intellectual approach to needs identification via three sources of educational purposes.

The approaches to defining objectives are even more diverse in the nine models. There is only one definite pairing of authors in this area: Tyler uses a grid of behavior and content to define objectives; Kidd also recommends that procedure. To a much lesser degree the Beal and Lippitt groups concur in that "goal formulation" occurs in their models. Yet, in the former, goal formulation is simply one step; in the latter, goal formulation is the result of ongoing dialogue and refinement. Boyle suggests that setting priorities is a multigroup process that uses personal, organization, clientele, community, political, and resource screens to turn needs into program priorities and then into objectives. The remainder of the authors see objectives formulated as they go through "filters." Houle poses a set of interactive elements, and Freire never explicitly puts objective defining into his model.

A very loose unity within diversity about program implementation is apparent in the models: it flows mainly from prior planning actions. This is seen most specifically in the Beal et al., Freire, and Houle models, and is implicit in the other models. The Boone-Dolan-Shearon model poses four basic "processual" tasks to implement the more elaborate needs identification/defining objectives task; the Kidd model stresses means of engaging learners in the program developed, using Houle's and Tyler's frameworks; the Knowles model presents basic, practical, administrative suggestions; the Lippitt-Watson-Westley model shows change efforts coming out of the planning relationship; and the Tyler model uses criteria, elements, and principles to organize learning experiences out of the "behavior and content" objective-defining task.

THE PROGRAMMING MODELS IN RETROSPECT

Looking back on this brief review of the literature on programming in adult education, we can affirm that the phrase "unity within diversity" rings true. For all the differences in the models presented, there is great similarity in their applicability, the range and diversity of which are detailed in Table 2-1. One can both categorize them for more intellectual and academic purposes *and* pick and choose among them according to which model(s) or aspects of the model(s) best fit one's specific needs "in the field." Such is the state of the art in programming in adult education.

Countless more generalizations might be made about the nine programming models presented and discussed in this chapter. However, the similarities and differences noted give us a more general conceptualization of the programming process. This more general conceptualization is derived from observation, inquiry, and research, as noted in Chapter 3. The discussion in Chapter 3 also provides a scientific approach to depicting and examining the programming process that should have utility for all adult educators affiliated with an organization and who have programming responsibilities.

REFERENCES

BEAL, G. M., R. C. BLOUNT, R. C. POWERS, and W. J. JOHNSON, *Social Action and Interaction in Program Planning.* Ames: Iowa State University Press, 1966.

BOONE, E. J., R. J. DOLAN, and R. W. SHEARON, *Programming in the Cooperative Extension Service: A Conceptual Schema.* Misc. Ext. Publ. #72. Raleigh: North Carolina Agricultural Extension Service, 1971.

BOYLE, P. G., *Planning Better Programs.* New York: McGraw-Hill Book Company, 1981.

FREIRE, P., *Pedagogy of the Oppressed.* New York: Herder and Herder, 1970.

HOULE, C., *The Design of Education.* San Francisco: Jossey-Bass, Publishers, 1972.

KIDD, R. J., *How Adults Learn.* New York: Association Press, 1973.

KNOWLES, M. S., *The Modern Practice of Adult Education: Andragogy versus Pedagogy.* New York: Association Press, 1970.

LIPPITT, R. L., J. WATSON, and B. WESTLEY, *The Dynamics of Planned Change.* New York: Harcourt, Brace & World, Inc., 1958.

MAGER, R. F., *Preparing Instructional Objectives.* Palo Alto, Calif.: Fearn Publishers, 1962.

STEELE, S., "Program Evaluation—A Broader Definition," *Journal of Extension,* 8 (Summer 1970), 5–18.

TYLER, R. W., *Basic Principles of Curriculum and Instruction.* Chicago: University of Chicago Press, 1971.

Chapter Three

A *Theoretical Approach to Programming*

In Chapter 2 we established that numerous and varied approaches exist for describing how programs are generated in adult education. Close examination of the models reveals a plethora of ideas about programming. Yet, in these models, little or no attention is given to the role of the organization in influencing the programming behavior of the adult educator. To this writer's knowledge, no explanation has been offered concerning the role that programming should play in the continuous evaluation and renewal of the adult education organization's functions, structure, and processes. The authors of the programming models explicated in Chapter 2 offer almost no elaboration or explanation of the process through which the adult education organization consciously attempts to establish linkage with learner groups for the purposes of identifying, analyzing, and assessing their needs and designing and implementing programs to alleviate those needs.

Further, the models described in Chapter 2 show a lack of consensus among the authors as to a prevailing conceptual framework for programming in adult education. Agreement with this generalization is indicated by Knox (1980) and Buskey and Sork (1982). Knox notes that the adult education practitioner is apt to discuss or use "distinctive methodologies that reflect procedures typical in the type of agency and the specific agency in which he works" (p.xiii). After analyzing numerous models for "planning" programs reported in books, monographs, articles, and other writings, Buskey and Sork conclude that each model tends to represent the author's recommendations for how one should go about the planning process. Only in rare instances are similarities or differences acknowledged between the model presented and those proposed by others. These writers' criticisms, and those of others in the behavioral and social sciences, are taken into account in this effort to formulate a conceptual model for programming in adult education.

Our approach incorporates a unified and comprehensive concept of programming within a framework of three essential interrelated subprocesses: (1) planning, (2) design and implementation, and (3) evaluation and accountability. This framework also provides for relevant concepts subsumed under each of the three subprocesses considered essential in the adult education programming process.

The discussion in this chapter deals with a programming construct that has generalizable aspects for programming efforts undertaken by adult educators. To present the construct requires a description of its nature, structure, and functions. The discussion expounds on an approach to the development of a conceptual model in the theory-building process.

THE NATURE, STRUCTURE, AND FUNCTION OF PROGRAMMING

Programming in adult education is a broad-based process that has as its primary objective planned behavioral change in the adult learner, learner groups, and systems. It involves the collaborative, planned efforts of adult educators, leaders (formal and informal) of learner groups and systems, as well as individual learners, in planning, designing and implementing, and evaluating and accounting for programs to alter the behavior of individual human subjects and, indirectly, the system(s) of which they are a part. Programming is a dynamic, continuous process that may be viewed as a never-ending, circular system. That is, its component subprocesses are interrelated and, in reality, inseparable.

Programming is a *proactive* process in that it is always futuristic in its thrust. It is a system that links the adult education organization with learner groups and systems in a collaborative effort to identify group members' educational needs, to assess and analyze those needs, to design and implement programs to meet those needs, and to gather and report evidence of the extent to which the program met those needs.

In a summative way, programming in adult education might be defined as

A comprehensive, systematic, and proactive process encompassing the total planned, collaborative efforts of the adult education organization, the adult educator in the roles of change agent and programmer, representatives of the learners, and the learners themselves in a purposive manner and designed to facilitate desirable changes in the behavior of learners and the environment or system in which they live.

Programming in adult education organizations can be equated with the manufacturing process in an industrial complex. The manufacturing process embodies all the functions, tasks, and events that contribute to producing, processing, and marketing a product: determination of consumers' preferences, indentification of potential markets, development of product specifications, marshaling and assembling of resources, and production. In a like manner, programming in the adult education organization embodies all of the processes, functions, and tasks of the adult education professional staff and learners in planning, designing and implementing, and evaluating and accounting for a planned educational program intended to produce behavioral change in adult learners.

Objectives of Programming

The objectives of programming in adult education are to provide

A logical and rational framework for directing and giving meaning to the efforts of adult educators in effecting educational programs designed to alter learner behavior.

A means of linking the adult education organization to its publics through analyzing, mapping, and defining its publics, identifying its target publics and their leaders, and interfacing with leaders and learners of those target publics in collaboratively identifying, assessing, and analyzing their educational needs, and designing and implementing programs to meet those needs.

An arena for adult educators to demonstrate the visionary leadership and pro-active behavior vital to creating a long-term and positive effect on the lifestyles of their systems of adult learners.

An opportunity for adult education organizations to nurture those conditions that, ideally, may be brought about through education.

These four objectives conceivably might be expanded to include others. The major point to be emphasized is that programming provides a rational, continuous, systematic approach through which the adult education organization can focus its efforts in responding to the educational needs of its publics and its ongoing organizational renewal.

Philosophical Tenets of Programming

Several basic tenets give credence to programming in adult education. Each of the seven philosophical tenets offered here is discussed briefly to provide the reader with a perspective of the rationale for the system and process through which adult education programs are planned, designed and implemented, and evaluated and accounted for.

1. First and foremost, adult educators must acquire and become committed to a unified framework of basic beliefs about adult education to guide their efforts in their roles as change agent and programmer.

Obviously, the foremost task of the adult education organization is education. The adult educator's concern is to alter or change, through education, the behavioral patterns of learners to the extent that they become better equipped to cope with and adapt to the almost daily changes that occur within their environments.

The adult education organization operates in a planning society and has as one of its primary functions the nurturing of a climate that encourages and facilitates collaborative planning, by users and providers, of educational programs to meet both the current and long-term needs of people. Adult educators are responsible for having available at all times adequate, factual information to use in assessing the current situation of their learners. Only when adult educators and their learners are armed with facts about the current state of affairs and forecasts for the future can informed decisions be made about educational needs.

Reasonable, accurate assumptions about the future are preconditions for understanding the potential consequences of any action. Without such understanding, planning is impossible. Most people are interested in improving both their current and future situations and, if provided with complete, appropriate, factual information, will act rationally to attain specified goals and objectives. Further, their leaders, who are involved in making decisions that affect their future welfare, respond more favorably to programs that embody those decisions in which they have participated than to "expert-designed" programs super-imposed on them by persons external to the local setting.

> **2.** Adult educators must be committed to the premise that programming is concerned with making a start toward conditions that ideally might be.

Because most of the conditions cited by Toffler (1970) are byproducts of the triumphs and tragedies of modern technology, we might think the corrections for these conditions would come through improved technology. Not entirely so, says Robb (1970): "Technology is neither good nor evil. The problem of technology is man himself. [And, as adult educators,] we have to believe in . . . [the ability] of human beings to learn and profit from past experience" (p.4).

The goal of programming always has been to nurture conditions that ideally might be brought about through education. Through the years, programming has been considered an administrative function, democratically determined and educationally sound, that responds to changing conditions and provides for decentralized responsibility.

Programming begins with a consciousness of the current state of affairs of people, their resources, and how those resources are being used within a designated social, political, or geographic context. From that point, programming moves on to defining conditions that might be more ideal. The definition of the "ideal state" has its roots in normative standards that have both a knowledge and a value base. We might look at a few examples.

Consider the problem of accelerated change. Should we encourage people to adapt to an accelerated rate of change? Or, should we teach them ways to resist the accelerated rate of change? Should we continue to promote the satisfactions of "lives based on having," as in the past? Or, considering the current depletion of the world's resources, should we devote more attention to helping people build "lives based on doing or being"?

Consider the problem of land-use planning. Should we encourage leaders and elected officials to commit time, resources, and money to planning for the use of land, knowing full well that the value of such efforts may not be realized for another two or three decades?

Consider the problem of housing. Should leaders and the people be prodded to become concerned about the future condition of housing in a community where housing might be quite adequate for the present time?

Consider the price-cost squeeze being experienced by consumers in both urban and rural areas. Should adult educators mount a program designed to provide consumers with all possible information about production, processing, and retail costs? Further, should adult educators mount a money-management program designed to help consumers realize as much as possible from dollars spent?

These few examples suggest that we need to clarify for ourselves the philosophical stance that adult educators should take as they cope with various alternatives in trying to fulfill their leadership role in a transient society. They further suggest that adult educators must acquire and exhibit, at all times, "visionary leadership." To exhibit this type of proactive behavior, adult educators must work continually at renewing and replenishing their information base about societal conditions.

Although the situation described here may appear paradoxical, adult educators, nonetheless, must display the capacity to respond promptly in crisis situations. At the same time, they must think about and plan for programs whose results will be of a long-term or futuristic nature.

3. To function effectively as planners and implementers, adult educators must regard themselves as planners and must continually engage in acquiring and expanding their cognitive maps.

This means that adult educators, as planners and implementers, need the broad picture of the philosophy, the purposes, the concepts, the processes, and the techniques of programming. Moreover, they need a working understanding of the concepts, theories, and principles found useful in the social and behavioral sciences to explain the situations with which they deal and to guide their decisions through the planning process. Particularly, planners need to acquire sensitivity and commitment to the changing needs of the learners to be served. Further, they need to know how to effect linkage with their publics through mapping and identifying target publics and their leaders, and how to interface with those leaders and their followers (the learners).

4. Planners need to understand the sociocultural context within which they are endeavoring to plan and implement educational programs.

Sociocultural context is the framework in which adult education functions. Adult educators work in a partially ordered society; that is, some events are causally connected to adult education, and some are not. The latter are beyond our control but may affect our results. We are a planning society, not a completely planned society. We function in this society, not as independent adult education organizations, but in relation to others in the community. Leaders can never plan without considering the rest of society. So it behooves adult educators to be familiar with the linkages in the social structure and with the reference groups or leaders that are important to the publics they seek to serve.

Adult educators must be familiar with and understand the relationships and communication channels that are important to participants in adult education programs, as well as the aims and roles the learners expect of the leaders to whom they turn for guidance and sanction. Adult educators must be knowledgeable about the nature of other organizations that are functioning within the community, their roles and structure, the policies under which they function, and the educational offerings they provide.

An understanding of sociocultural context and especially the concept of linkage is most valuable, as the foreshortened relationship span in many communities requires the adult educator to build bonds both quickly and effectively among strangers and long-time residents alike. A thorough analysis of the sociocultural context of the publics and the desired linkage can be useful preparation for mapping publics, for identifying target publics and their leaders, and for initiating informal and meaningful dialogue with those leaders, through which to identify the educational needs and concerns of target publics.

5. Adult educators, as change agents and programmers, need to be thoroughly knowledgeable about the concept of collaboration between the provider and the user in decision making.

The concept of collaborative provider-user decision making refers to the joining of the provider's experience with the user's or learner's experience when participating in planning. Every increase in technical knowledge and mechanical invention increases dependence on the providers. The indispensability of the provider is accepted; what is needed is a clearer understanding of the relation of the provider to the user and the part each plays in decision making.

Back in the 1930s, Mary P. Follett (1940) called attention to the many difficulties encountered in trying to connect providers' findings with the will of the people. She observed that providers, secure in the belief that they were "right," did not hesitate in their presentation of "facts" to stampede the general public into acceptance of their opinions. In justice to the providers, she added, the public showed little inclination to resist crowd tactics that rushed them into decisions without education on the matters under consideration.

An understanding of the concept of collaborative decision making comes when the user knows that the provider is not one who has access to the secrets of the All-Wise. Rather, the provider has a particular kind of experience that the user should add to his or her own kind of experience, and vice versa, for both have an important role to play. The adult educator's task of guiding this delicate balance in programming is difficult but essential to sound educational programs that people will both respond to and support.

6. Adult educators must face the major challenge of translating expressed needs of learners into a meaningful program design and in developing effective strategies for its implementation.

Concepts from the fields of economics and educational phychology are valuable tools in accomplishing the tasks of translating needs and developing program designs. First, there must be clear, feasible objectives, understood equally by adult educators, leaders of learner groups, members of learner groups, and individual learners. Deciding on these objectives is no easy task. Since, by definition, education means a change in human behavior, the objectives must be regarded in terms of intended behavioral change among the learners. Only when adult educators are able to describe what behavioral change they wish to effect are they ready to design an educational program.

Program objectives should be considered from several aspects. Is the learning possible in the time allotted, or will mastery require more time than allocated for the program? Is the behavior possible of attainment, given the age or mental and emotional capacities of the learners? Will the cost fall within the limits of available resources? These are some of the questions revolving around feasibility in selecting objectives.

In a planned program, we must identify a whole progression of learning behaviors that range from simple awareness, through many levels of knowledge and skill development, into valuing and commitment. The same progression of learning behaviors may apply to many content areas, depending on what experts identify as necessary to betterment of the conditions under which people live and work. The notion of a progression of behaviors to be learned is based on the educational concept that the complex forms of learning, such as problem solving, require mastery of the simpler forms, such as ability to discriminate or knowledge of principles.

Educational phychology provides two other important concepts. One is the notion of *teachable moment,* that is, the time when people are ready to learn (Havighurst, 1952). Many of us have experienced a violation of that notion when trying to promote ideas whose time for acceptance had not yet arrived. The second concept is that of *opportunity to practice.* This concept is basic to the whole notion of learning experience. A *learning experience* is an opportunity for the learner to practice the desired behavior. It other words, it is not what the "teacher" does that constitutes a learning experience; it is what the learner does.

In these times of transient interests and concerns, adult educators must be certain that the economist's concept of *demand* is considered in determining educational priorities. Can adult education serve all the educational needs for all people? Do not our goals always exceed our means and resources? If the adult education organization's fixed amount of time is to be used where it will generate maximum results, adult educators will have to consider how strong the demands are and the point at which diminishing returns will make their efforts less than effective.

In the complexity of organizational structures operating in most communities, adult educators must think carefully about still another economic principle, that of *comparative advantage.* Considering its unique talents or other resources, where can the adult education organization, compared to other educational organizations, make a better contribution to effecting behavioral change? This and many other principles are quite adequately defined and described within the behavioral science bodies of knowledge. And many adult educators have become acquainted with them. Planners wishing to professionalize their performance in programming would do well to explore such principles.

Suffice it to say, for each objective in the planned program, the design must provide at least one learning experience that is tailored to the situation.

7. The adult educator must evaluate and report how well the planned program effected the desired behavioral change among the participants.

Much has been said and written about accounting for results obtained through educational programs. We are apt to hear and read a great deal more as the next critical years unfold!

Programming in adult education is not complete until plans have been devised and carried out to utilize tested and valid methods for collecting and analyzing evidence of behavioral change. The more complex the program, the more involved is the accounting. Yet, program outcomes or outputs must be weighed in relation to program inputs, and validity and reliability of evidence must be tested before adult educators can use their findings in directing the next program efforts. Only then has the full cycle of the programming process been completed.

In summary, the foregoing philosophical tenets constitute this adult educator's philosophy of programming in adult education. From this brief discussion, the reader must certainly have concluded, and rightly so, that programming is a complex process. Progress is evolutionary, unfolding, and gradual. Its product is uniquely designed for a given situation. Programming is a judgmental process, based on values held worthwhile by both programmers and users. It can be, to all involved, an enlightening and consciousness-enlarging experience.

One may assume that adult educators have the knowledge and skills needed to make program decisions about "what" to do, "how" to do it, and "why" it should be done. But how is the adult educator to recognize the "right" answers to programming questions in a particular situation? For answers that will make the most valuable contribution to program decision making, the adult educator must turn to an organized body of scientific knowledge about the programming process. Such knowledge can be made available through scientific inquiry. Thus, the discussion that follows focuses on programming as an area of inquiry, followed by the transition from inquiry to theory building.

PROGRAMMING: AN AREA OF INQUIRY

Inquiry, in a broad sense, is not new to adult educators; it has been a continuing part of their learning process. A structured process of investigation is referred to as inquiry. *Inquiry* may be defined as a search for knowledge based on a systematic, investigative, problem-solving procedure organized to seek answers to clearly stated questions. From the scientific point of view, what concepts, theories, and principles should be encompassed in the programming process? To generate substantive answers to this question requires the researcher to use an adaptation of the *scientific approach* discussed later in this section.

Throughout the history of adult education, numerous approaches to inquiry have been used to gather information about programming, such as observation, personal experience, and trial and error, among others. However, these informal approaches to inquiry fail to provide information necessary to answer complex questions relevant to the programming process. Results of the trial-and-error approach, for example, generate only those concepts useful for practical purposes and in establishing a common-sense approach to programming inquiry. However, common-sense answers to programming questions lack validity for making general and reliable decisions about programming. When common sense alone is employed to answer questions, prediction becomes less accurate; but prediction remains the major function of science. Thus, the common-sense approach lacks the needed "structure." To overcome the pitfalls of the common-sense approach to inquiry, procedures were developed to assist researchers in structuring their ideas systematically in search of explanations to inquiry questions. The resulting systematic inquiry procedure strategies are referred to as deductive reasoning, inductive reasoning, problem solving, and the scientific approach. A brief discussion of these strategies is in order.

The oldest inquiry strategy is *deductive reasoning.* Deductive reasoning has its genesis in the syllogism model of thinking, wherein the viability of a conclusion rests on the truthfulness of a postulate. Deductive reasoning refers to reasoning that begins with a generalization that infers a factual conclusion within the context of the major postulate. *Generalization* is the process of inferring beyond the sample studied to a larger population, using information acquired from the sample. If the basic generalization or major postulate is false, the conclusion will be in error. For example:

Major postulate   = All adults with gray hair are over 60 years of age.
Minor postulate   = This adult has gray hair.
Conclusion   = This adult is over 60 years of age.

Since the major postulate stated here is not true, the conclusion is in error (the adult described in the minor postulate could have been 40 years of age instead of over 60). Since deductive reasoning cannot establish truth and add to what is already known, it does not serve as a substantial strategy of inquiry in programming. Yet, in spite of its limitations, deductive reasoning does provide a means for linking theory and observations. It enables one to deduce, from existing theory, phenomena that should be observed. Deductions from theory can provide hypotheses, which are vital to scientific inquiry.

Inductive reasoning begins with a specific set of observations and moves to a generalization. Early inquirers undoubtedly gathered information from many sources to form common-sense answers about educational programming, but many years passed after the introduction of deductive reasoning before the more formal system of inductive reasoning was employed in the inquiry process. Observations by early inquirers revealed that, over time, certain causes seemed to be related to observed effects. For example: educational programs are more effective when based on the needs of their participants. Such deductive reasoning still is used to form hypotheses.

In inductive reasoning, inquiry is structured into two stages: (1) collection of information (data) through many specific observations and (2) moving from the specific to making a generalization. Limitations encountered in and surrounding data collection give little credence to the generalization(s) developed. Hence, in its purest form, inductive reasoning amounts to a way of gathering data that lacks direction (structure). Unless one knows what to look for in the data collected, generalization(s) may be hard to make.

Because deficiencies were recognized in both deductive and inductive strategies, researchers were obliged to seek ways to build subjectivity into inquiry and still not prejudice the results. It is an accepted phenomenon that those who seek answers must have some direction; that is, to be productive in any inquiry, one must be searching for something. However, total subjectivity is difficult when dealing with the human element.

The next stage in the evolution of educational inquiry led researchers to combine deductive and inductive strategies to inquire into what is commonly referred to as *problem solving*. This phenomenon relies on inductive reasoning to generate a hypothesis and deductive reasoning to test that hypothesis. Problem solving is used in seeking answers to many questions. Replacement of the major postulate used in deductive reasoning by a research hypothesis structures the inquiry in answering questions and provides checks and balances for inquiry strategy. Through combining hypotheses that are considerably supported, researchers can develop *theory* and eventually establish *principles* and, ultimately, *laws*. Hence, the output of problem solving is knowledge: new information about the relationships between or among the variables studied.

The search for answers to programming questions requires that some kind of structure be employed to direct adult educators' investigation into inquiry questions. The need for structure in inquiry gave rise to what is called the *scientific approach* to answering questions and thus to problem solving. At the outset, the scientific approach was intended to be more efficient than those strategies previously discussed.

The scientific approach to seeking answers to questions serves as a *model,* that is, a representation of a particular situation, for use in structuring an attack on new questions and old questions that still need satisfactory answers or solutions. By combining inductive and deductive reasoning in inquiry, the scientific approach to problem solving is generated. The key part or dimension of this approach is the *hypothesis*. A hypothesis is generated from gathered information and is formulated to serve as the basis for deductively testing the tenability of a position taken by the investigator; it is derived through the actual thought processes of the inquirer about the problem under investigation, and is a generalization that amounts to conjecture about the solutions to the problem under study. Kerlinger (1964) defines a *hypothesis* as "a conjectural statement of the relation between two or more variables" (p. 20). He also sets up two criteria for "good" hypotheses: (1) hypotheses are statements about the relation between variables and (2) hypotheses carry clear implications for testing the stated relations; that is, a hypothesis must contain two or more variables that are measurable, and it must specify how the variables are related.

Through the scientific approach to inquiry, problem solving can be structured for both direct and indirect testing. *Problem solving* should be considered as a way of structuring an attack on a question that utilizes inductive reasoning to generate one or more hypotheses. Deductive reasoning, then, is used in testing by providing support for or evidence against the hypothesis. The use of a hypothesis is a principal difference between the scientific approach and inductive reasoning. In the scientific approach, one predicts what will be found, if the hypothesis is true, and then systematically observes to confirm or reject the hypothesis. In inductive reasoning, one makes observations first and then organizes the information gained. Hence, hypotheses serve to bridge the gap between generalizations obtained inductively and the deductive approach to testing that generalization. The most widely used model today in organizing procedures for problem solving is the scientific approach to inquiry, wherein the investigator moves inductively from observations to hypotheses and then deductively from hypotheses to the logical implications of the hypotheses. Basically, such an approach deduces the consequences that would follow if the hypothesized relationship were true.

The scientific approach, as depicted in Figure 3-1, consists of a series of major steps that should be followed. These steps may vary somewhat from re-

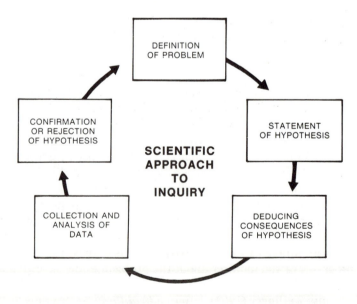

FIGURE 3-1   Schema depicting the scientific approach to inquiry

searcher to researcher. The principal idea is that it is a *systematic* approach to inquiry whose parts are interdependent.

The scientific approach includes five steps:

1. Defining a problem or a question that is in need of a solution or an answer.
2. Stating hypotheses formulated to serve as tentative explanations of the problem; this step requires a prior review of the literature related to the problem.
3. Deducing consequences of the hypothesis; if the hypothesis were true, what would be observed?
4. Collecting and analyzing data, through observation, experimentation, and testing.
5. Confirming or rejecting the hypotheses on the basis of whether or not evidence was produced to support the hypothesized relationship(s) between variables.

In the scientific approach, no claim is made to prove a hypothesis. Rather, the researcher merely concludes that the finding or evidence from testing the implied relationship does or does not support the hypothesis.

The evolution of inquiry from the common-sense approach to the scientific approach is depicted as an inverted hierarchy in Figure 3-2. The illustration

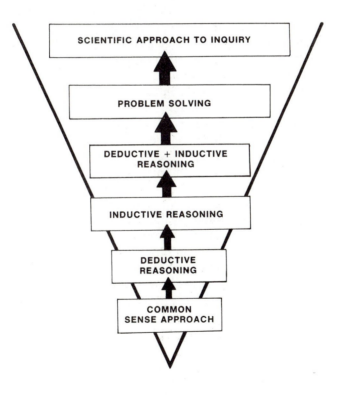

FIGURE 3-2 A hierarchy depicting the evolution of the scientific approach to inquiry

shows that the scientific approach to programming inquiry developed gradually over time and remains dynamic, because it proved to be a successful approach to understanding complex phenomena in the natural world. Note that the top of the inverted hierarchy is left open to provide space for future growth and development in research techniques, beyond the scientific approach—whatever and whenever that might be.

The researcher recognizes that, in any inquiry, some underlying assumptions will be taken for granted. Many of these assumptions must be accepted as true, whether or not they are clearly supported. So it is with the researcher who uses the scientific approach to inquiry. Two basic assumptions undergird the scientific approach.

The first assumption is that science is based on the belief that all natural phenomena have identifiable, sequential, antecedent factors, that is, are lawful or ordered. This assumption often is referred to as *universal determinism* It was not until human beings looked beyond supernatural explanations and began to depend on observations of nature itself to provide answers that modern science began to develop. When researchers predict that, under specified conditions, certain events will occur, the assumption of lawfulness serves as the underlying rationale for such predictions. For example: (1) behavioral scientists assume that human behavior is predictable; and (2) chemists expect that, when a mixture of manganese dioxide and potassium chlorate is heated, oxygen will be released. Also undergirding this assumption is the belief that events in nature are orderly and regular, and that this order and regularity can be discerned, to a degree, through the scientific approach to inquiry.

The second assumption in the scientific approach is that, in time, truth can be derived only from direct observation. This reliance on empirical observation differentiates science from nonscience.

Each of the inquiry techniques discussed in this section must be viewed as important in its own right, as each approach helps to solve problems of a specific type. It is not our purpose here to make judgments about the relative value of the different techniques, nor are any intended.

The basic goal of science is theory building, which provides explanations, predictions, and controls. Hence, the discussion that follows focuses on moving from inquiry to theory building in programming by way of the structured inquiry research approach. The discussion turns toward the potential of programming theory building as one organizing framework for future inquiry into understanding the programming process in adult education.

FROM INQUIRY TO THEORY BUILDING
IN EDUCATIONAL PROGRAMMING

Adult educators, in their daily course of carrying out the programming process, are faced with the task of making decisions about how to plan, design and implement, and evaluate and account for planned programs. Although there are a number of sources of knowledge, such as experience, authority, and tradition, the most valuable contribution to decision making in programming is the organized body of scientific knowledge about the programming process. Based on a recognized need for a perspective or an organizing framework for further study of the programming process, we will turn to theorizing as a means of bringing some structure to existing assumptions and propositions about adult education programming. Drawing on a multidisciplinary knowledge base, we will attempt to demonstrate that there is substance in the area of programming in adult education worthy of our efforts toward theory building. To do this, we will review briefly the process of theory building, then generate a conceptual framework or construct to guide the programming process, and finally describe briefly our conceptualization of the interrelationships of concepts and constructs (subprocesses) encompassed within the conceptual programming model.

Theory Defined

The basic aim of science is theory, that is, to find general explanations of natural events. Kerlinger (1964) defines *theory* as "a set of interrelated constructs . . . , definitions, and propositions that presents a systematic view of phenomena by specifying relations among variables, with the purpose of explaining and predicting the phenomena" (p. 11). He goes further to explain:

> This definition says three things. One, a theory is a set of propositions consisting of defined and interrelated constructs. Two, a theory sets out the interrelations among a set of variables (constructs) and, in so doing, presents a systematic view of the phenomena described by the variables. Finally, a theory explains phenomena. It does so by specifying what variables are related to what variables and how they are related, thus enabling the researcher to predict from certain variables to certain other variables. (P. 11)

Purposes of Theory

In the development of a science, several purposes are served by theory. Theory summarizes and puts in order existing knowledge in a particular area, such as programming in adult education. Theory summarizes, in a consistent way, the results of many separate investigations and provides meaning to previously isolated empirical findings. Theory provides an explanation for observed events and relationships. It shows what variables are related and how they are related. For example, a theory of programming would explain the relationship between the concepts of planning, design and implementation, and evaluation and accountability. The development of new knowledge is stimulated by theory, as it provides new insights for further research. Historical research findings show that revolutionary and significant advances come from new theories (Ary, Jacobs, and Razavieh, 1979).

Finally, theory summarizes facts and states a general uniformity beyond immediate observations. It also becomes a predictor of facts; that is, it enables extrapolation from the known to the unknown. Thus, the scientist uses facts both as building blocks from theory and as a way of verifying the theory. Theory stimulates and guides scientific inquiry and analyzes and explains its findings. On the other hand, scientific inquiry serves to test existing theories and to provide a basis for the development of new ones. This two-way relationship is continuous (Goode and Hatt, 1952).

THE BASIC LANGUAGE OF THE SCIENTIFIC APPROACH

The programming process requires a specific language for describing and summarizing observations in its domain. The scientific approach, discussed briefly in the preceding section, has a basic terminology. Researchers may use words taken from everyday language, yet ascribe to them new and specific meanings not commonly found in everyday usage. In this section, the reader is introduced to some key terms used in the scientific approach at both the descriptive and the theoretical levels.

Concepts—A Means of Communication

Thinking involves the use of language, which is a system of communication composed of symbols and a set of rules permitting various combinations of those symbols (Nachmias and Nachmias, 1976). Among the most significant communication symbols in the language of research are concepts, which serve as the foundation for all human communication and thought. Thus, a concept must be communicable, must arouse feeling, and must be so constructed that all of its components are known. Kerlinger (1964) defines a *concept* as

> . . . a word that expresses an abstraction formed by generalization from particulars. . . . [For example,] "weight" is a concept: it expresses numerous observations of things that are more or less "heavy" or "light." "Mass," "energy," and "force" are concepts used by physical scientists. They are, of course, much more abstract than concepts like "weight," "height," and "length." (P. 31)

Tinsley and Sitton (1967) refer to a concept as "an idea which a person forms in his mind in order to understand and cope with something in his experience" (p. 86). With this definition Tinsley and Sitton imply that (1) the formation of concepts is an individual matter, (2) the formation of concepts involves mental learning, (3) concepts are formed for a specific purpose, and (4) the formation of concepts is based on experience.

Selltiz et al. (1959) cited McClelland's definition of concepts as "a shorthand representation of a variety of facts" and his conclusion that the purpose for forming concepts is "to simplify thinking by subsuming a number of events under one general heading" (p. 41). Thus, the functions that concepts perform appear to be (1) to provide a system for organizing information to be used in identifying relationships, (2) to serve as sources of thinking, and (3) to serve as predeterminers of behavior.

Concepts are the chief ingredient in the building of theory. Merton (1957) contends that the interrelation of concepts to form a particular framework or conceptual schema marks the emergence of a theory. Kerlinger (1964) asserts, however, that an intermediate entity exists between the mere formation of concepts and the development of a theoretical or conceptual framework. He refers to this intermediate entity as a *construct*.

Constructs and Conceptual Model Building

Whereas concepts are formed by the interrelation of information, experiences, and feelings, constructs are formulated by the interrelation of concepts. Kerlinger (1964) insists that it is the conglomeration of constructs, not concepts, that enters into theoretical schemes or cognitive maps.

A *cognitive map* is a set of interrelated concepts, organized and developed into interrelated constructs for the purpose of providing a framework for thinking about a particular phenomenon. Constructs, then, provide a linkage system between unstructured but related abstract ideas and a schematic way of thinking. In the discussion regarding the conceptualizations of a variety of writers in the field of adult education, Houle (1972) suggests that these conceptualizations can be viewed as a system or set of interrelated ideas, principles, or practices that form a collective entity. Houle views a system, in this sense, as a conceptualization described or made operational in the form of a diagram, flow chart, conceptual model, or other structure, to facilitate identification of its components and ensure proper sequencing of those components.

A conceptual model, as defined by Theodorson and Theodorson (1969) is a "pattern of interrelated concepts (constructs) not expressed in mathematical form and not primarily concerned with quantification" (p. 261). The Theodorsons advocate that the utility of a model is determined by its potential to serve as a guide to action: "Models are tentative and limited [due primarily to the open-endedness of the concepts which constitute them], yet they are building blocks of theory, interpretation, empirical discoveries, prediction, and, in general, . . . progress" (p. 261).

Conceptual models are symbolic representations of reality and usually include only those factors pertinent to an operational understanding of a particular system. For Van Dalen (1966), such models are "simplified or familiar structures which are used to gain insights into phenomena that scientists want to explain" (p. 65). They propose that a model might be defined as a set of constructs specified in such a way that their formal connections are evident. A conceptual model for programming in adult education is a verbal or graphic structure that represents, within the parameters of its specified purpose, a conceptualization of programming in adult education.

Getzels (1968) lists several criteria for developing and constructing a conceptual model: (1) the model must provide a set of integrated concepts and relations capable not only of answering questions already asked, but posing questions that still need to be asked; (2) the concepts and relations must be operational in that they give direction to understanding and simultaneously provide blueprints for investigation; and (3) the model must be capable of handling as many of the commonplace or familiar issues as possible, within a single set of concepts and relations.

With these criteria met, the programming process in adult education, presented herein, might be said to represent a conceptual model. The question of whether or not it also represents a theory is at least partially answered by Inkeles (1964): "It is not always possible to distinguish between a scientific model and a scientific theory" (p. 28). Inkeles further contends that models are capable of generating any number of theories; yet, a single theory may be so powerful as to constitute a general model. Inkeles extends his argument with the following comparison:

> A theory we take to be a heuristic device for organizing what we know, or think we know, at any particular time about some more or less explicitly posed question or issue. A theory would, therefore, be more limited and precise than a model. A theory can ordinarily be proved wrong. In the case of a model, it can usually only be judged incomplete, misleading, or unproductive. (P. 28)

Operational Definitions

Operational definitions are the third important element in the basic language of the scientific approach. Before a hypothesis can be tested, the concepts or variables contained therein must be defined. Kerlinger (1979) best explained operational definitions when he wrote that such definitions

> . . . assign meaning to a construct or variable by specifying the activities or "operations" necessary to measure it or to manipulate it. An operational definition, alternatively, specifies the activities of the researcher in measuring a variable or in manipulating it. It is like a manual of instruction to the researcher: it says, in effect, "Do such-and-such in so-and-so manner." (P. 41)

For example, if one wishes to measure "intelligence" (anxiety, achievement, etc.), one first must define intelligence as "scores on X intelligence test, or intelligence is what X intelligence test measures. This definition tells us what to do to measure intelligence. It tells the researcher to use X intelligence test" (p. 41).

Further, suppose we wish to define the variable "leadership." One may define it operationally by listing behaviors that are presumably leadership behaviors and then having observers rate an individual's leadership behavior on a five-point scale.

Kerlinger (1979) maintains that there are two types of operational definitions, *measured* and *experimental*. Measured operational definitions describe how to measure (and observe) a variable. The two examples just discussed were measured operational definitions. They indicate to the researcher how to measure and observe a variable, that is, intelligence with X intelligence test scores and leadership with rating of observed behaviors.

Experimental operational definitions tell the researcher how a variable is to be manipulated. For example, a well-documented finding in educational research is that reward enhances learning. The theory undergirding the research is called *reinforcement theory.* If learners are told they have done well when doing something correctly, they will tend to remember and repeat the results when the same or similar conditions occur again. In a study of this type, reinforcement must be operationally defined by giving the details of how subjects are to be reinforced. Two groups of approximately equal characteristics are required. The first, or experimental group, receives treatment. The second, or control group, receives no treatment. In experimental situations, operational definitions specify what is done to manipulate the independent variable(s).

According to Kerlinger (1979), an operational definition "bridges the gap between concepts or constructs and actual observations, behaviors, and activities" (p. 42). A modified illustration of Kerlinger's gap idea is diagrammed here, which shows the two levels at which the researcher operates: (I) constructs and hypotheses and (II) observation/manipulation/measurement. As illustrated, the

gap between the two levels is bridged by operational definitions, which may be either measured or experimental. At level I, the variables to be measured must be identified and defined prior to hypothesizing. The researcher also works at this level when testing hypotheses. However, before moving from level I to level II, the gap between the two levels must be bridged with at least one operational definition. In addition to allowing the researcher to move from level I to level II, operational definitions allow movement back and forth between the two levels.

THEORY VERIFICATION

Because models may generate an indefinite number of theories, empirical verification of all the theories generated may be difficult, it not impossible. However, the foundational theories upon which a model is constructed are somewhat more amenable to judgment and validation (Inkeles, 1964).

Theories may be verified or justified within two distinct parameters: *concrete* and *abstract*. The former involves definite proof or disproof; the latter involves some form of judgment (Cunningham, 1958). Put in other terms, Foster (1979) wrote that concrete verification of a theory involves some uncontestable form of proof, whereas judgment (an abstract entity) must be exercised in determining just what constitutes this proof. (It must be added that "incontestable" proof may be hard to come by.)

Theories structured about abstract concepts, as are those undergirding the conceptual programming model presented herein, can be verified only as related to some human experience (Foster, 1979). Pollock (1975) supports this perspective in his comment that, if individuals' experience or background accommodates belief in a theory, they will perceive the theory as valid. Pollock adds that, despite the obvious weakness of this type of verification, most abstract verifications actually are based upon beliefs. In fact, Ingle (1976) maintains that much of the lack of agreement or understanding about the nature of things is due to insufficient information or misinformation.

It should be emphasized here that theory verification, on the basis of beliefs, can transpire only if the beliefs themselves are verified (Pollock, 1975). What, then, justifies a belief? Pollock (1975) submits the following as an answer:

> . . . to justify a belief one must appeal to a further justified belief. This means that one of two things can be the case. Either there are some [epistemologically basic] beliefs that we can be justified in holding without being able to justify them on the basis of any other belief, or else for each justified belief there is an infinite regress of (potential) justification [the nebula theory]. On this theory there is no rock bottom of justification. Justification just meanders in and out through our network or beliefs, stopping nowhere. (P. 26)

Although Pollock maintains that the nebula theory is a misrepresentation, he does support the notion of epistemologically basic beliefs; that is, beliefs in each tier are justified on the basis of beliefs in the tiers below. In this case, "justification proceeds in terms of reasons. When one belief justifies another, the former is said to be the reason for the latter" (p. 33).

Cunningham (1958) asserts that conformity of thought itself constitutes a form of theory verification. Ingle (1976) indirectly concurs by stating that an observation or judgment is not usually regarded as valid until there is general agreement that it is true.

Verification and *confirmation* are two concepts used to explicate justification in believing a theory on the combined basis of inductive and deductive inferences. Pollock perceives confirmation as a combination of straightforward inductions from instances and deductive conclusions drawn from the inductive conclusions, thus implying that theory verification or confirmation is based on individual observations. Such theory verification is based on the observed "consequences" of a theory, rather than having observed the theory in action. Such will be the case when theories are constructed about abstract, unobservable concepts. This view of theory verification is called the *hypothetico-deductive* method of confirmation (Pollock, 1974).

Preceding but analogous to Cunningham's (1958) abstract theory verification concept is Guttman's (1950) notion of *internal validity*. Guttman postulates that internal validity entails verifying whether or not the theory expresses a "logical" relationship. Cunningham (1958) explains that, inferentially, if the theory is logical, it is more amenable to judgment. Likewise, if conformity of judgment exists across a broad cross section of theorist in the field, the theory is to some degree verified.

Following up on Inkeles' (1964) suggestion (noted earlier) that the foundational theories upon which a model is constructed are amenable to judgment and validation, we turn to Guttman's (1950) earlier internal validity approach to theory verification, which supports constructing an index or "schema for routine description." This procedure, of breaking up the conceptual model into its foundational elements, assists in the development of a comprehensive conceptualization of the model. At the same time, the procedure tends to separate the large number of theories embodied in the conceptual model. Zetterberg (1965) reminds us that internal validity of the theory can be increased without empirical studies; rather, "the progress toward validity lies in a continuous adjustment of theorizing to the techniques of research, and in a continuous adjustment of techniques of research to theorizing" (p. 115).

A dual conceptual framework was used in generating the conceptual model for programming in adult education. The first conceptual framework is appropriate to conceptual model construction and verification, while the second focuses primarily on programming for adult education. The interrelation of these two conceptual frameworks provided the basis for the research that culminated in formulating the author's conceptual model for programming in adult education.

The preceding explication of model construction and theory verification lays the foundation for shifting our attention to examining the assumptions, concepts, constructs, and propositions upon which the conceptual model for programming in adult education is predicated.

A CONCEPTUAL MODEL FOR PROGRAMMING IN ADULT EDUCATION

Concepts and constructs are needed to provide a guide for thinking about programming in adult education and to support its practice. The first step in constructing a theory about such programming is to identify the undergirding concepts that describe and explain the programming process.

Drawing upon a wealth of concepts, theories, and principles derived from organizational, social, and behavioral sciences and cast into a heuristic programming construct or conceptual model, the author's conceptualization of the programming process is illustrated in Table 3-1. This conceptual model is useful for describing and explaining the planning, design and implementation, and evaluation and accountability subprocesses of educational programming. These subprocesses and their respective components are set forth for heuristic purposes in Table 3-1, are briefly described in the next section of this chapter, and are fully developed in Chapters 4, 5, and 6, respectively.

The schema summarizing the relationships that should exist among the various stages of theory development in programming is presented in Figure 3-3. The schema begins with identification of program objectives, tentative propositions, definitions, philosophical tenets, and a content analysis of relevant literature. Thus, Stage I provides a language for communication and the descriptive categories needed for progression of the inquiry process. In addition, there is a need to collect concepts that describe, inspire, and serve as sources for thinking and organizing. Stage II in the schema suggests that such concepts are drawn from organizational, social, and behavioral science theories and used in combination to generate new, relevant concepts, constructs, propositions, and assumptions. Theory results from a combination of constructs, their refinement, the generation of testable hypotheses, and empirical verification (Stages III, IV, and V, respectively). As Peters and Kozoll (1980) observe, "It is assumed that the nature of the resulting theory would be just as fluid as the stages of development that comprise its formulation" (pp. 122, 124). Only under such circumstances and at Stage V can verification studies be designed and implemented to accept, reject, modify, extend, or develop a new theory or theories, as illustrated by the broken line in Figure 3-3.

In the past, and often still today, the study of programming in adult education has focused more on Stages I and II than Stages III, IV, and V. The descriptive and case approaches to inquiry have been overworked at the expense of theory building and theory verification studies.

Assuming we have executed the tasks subsumed under Stages I and II in the programming theory development process, we turn to Stages III, IV, and V in constructing a theory for programming in adult education. The concepts that form the heuristic programming construct and the concepts encompassed within each of its three subprocesses, planning, design and implementation, and evaluation and accountability, are outlined in Figure 3-4. Starting with planned change, the macro concepts of programming proceed through the three subprocesses of programming. Subsumed under each of these three subprocesses are the related micro concepts and constructs.

We turn now to an analysis of the macro concepts that form the heuristic programming construct and then to the micro concepts encompassed within each of its three subprocesses. Detailed descriptions of the author's conceptualiza-

TABLE 3-1 A conceptual programming model

PLANNING		DESIGN & IMPLEMENTATION		EVALUATION & ACCOUNTABILITY
THE ORGANIZATION & ITS RENEWAL PROCESS	LINKING THE ORGANIZATION TO ITS PUBLICS	DESIGNING THE PLANNED PROGRAM	IMPLEMENTING THE PLANNED PROGRAM	
UNDERSTANDING OF & COMMITMENT TO THE FUNCTIONS OF THE ORGANIZATION: MISSION PHILOSOPHY OBJECTIVES.	STUDY, ANALYSIS, & MAPPING OF THE ORGANIZATION'S PUBLICS.	TRANSLATING EXPRESSED NEEDS INTO MACRO NEEDS.	DEVELOPING PLANS OF ACTION: TRANSLATING NEEDS INTO TEACHING OBJECTIVES.	DETERMINING & MEASURING PROGRAM OUTPUTS.
	IDENTIFYING TARGET PUBLICS.	TRANSLATING MACRO NEEDS INTO MACRO OBJECTIVES.	SPECIFYING LEARNING EXPERIENCES FOR EACH TEACHING OBJECTIVE.	ASSESSING PROGRAM INPUTS.
UNDERSTANDING & COMMITMENT TO THE ORGANIZATION'S STRUCTURE: ROLES RELATIONSHIPS.	IDENTIFYING & INTERFACING WITH LEADERS OF TARGET PUBLICS.	SPECIFYING GENERAL EDUCATIONAL STRATEGIES & LEARNING ACTIVITIES.	DEVELOPING PLANS FOR EVALUATING LEARNER OUTCOMES & ASSESSING LEARNING EXPERIENCES.	USING EVALUATION FINDINGS FOR PROGRAM REVISIONS, ORGANIZATIONAL RENEWAL, & FOR ACCOUNTING TO PUBLICS, PARENT ORGANIZATION, FUNDING SOURCES, THE PROFESSION, AND, WHERE APPROPRIATE, THE GOVERNANCE BODY.
KNOWLEDGEABLE ABOUT & SKILLED IN ORGANIZATION'S PROCESSES: SUPERVISION STAFF DEVELOPMENT EVALUATION & ACCOUNTABILITY.	COLLABORATIVE IDENTIFICATION, ASSESSMENT, & ANALYSIS OF NEEDS SPECIFIC TO TARGET PUBLICS.	SPECIFYING MACRO OUT-COMES OF THE PLANNED PROGRAM.	DEVELOPING & IMPLEMENTING STRATEGIES & TECHNIQUES FOR MARKETING THE PLANS OF ACTION.	
UNDERSTANDING OF & COMMITMENT TO A TESTED CONCEPTUAL FRAMEWORK FOR PROGRAMMING.			DEVELOPING & FOLLOWING THROUGH ON PLANS TO RECRUIT & TRAIN LEADER-LEARNER RESOURCES.	
UNDERSTANDING & COMMITMENT TO CONTINUOUS ORGANIZATIONAL RENEWAL.			MONITORING & REINFORCING THE TEACHER-LEARNER TRANSACTION.	

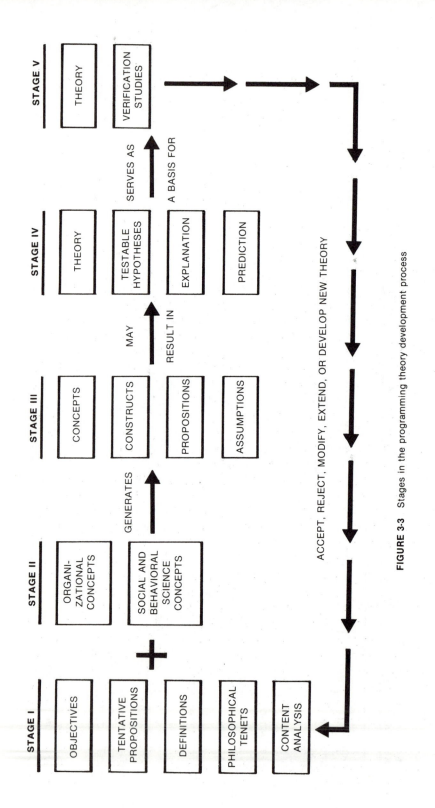

FIGURE 3-3 Stages in the programming theory development process

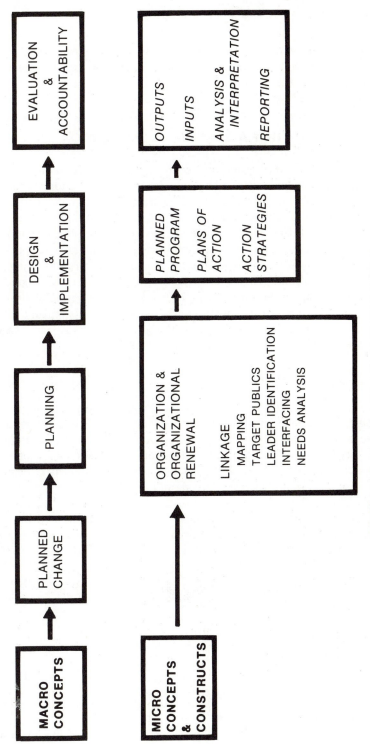

FIGURE 3-4 Concepts formulating the programming construct

tion of the interrelationships of concepts and constructs encompassed within the conceptual model (see Table 3-1 and Figure 3-4) are presented later in Chapters 4, 5, and 6.

ANALYSIS OF THE PROGRAMMING CONSTRUCT

An analysis of the programming construct, introduced in the preceding section, is needed to provide the reader with a more complete understanding of the phenomenon. As indicated in Figure 3-4, the programming construct is comprised of a number of connecting and interrelated concepts that are ordered under three major subprocesses: planning, design and implementation, and evaluation and accountability. The three subprocesses and the concepts subsumed under each provide a holistic systems approach to programming and planned change. This total programming process also may serve as a guide for reviewing, synthesizing, and classifying research findings germane either to the total process or to one of its constituent parts. The discussion that follows focuses on a brief analysis of the conceptual and theoretical aspects of the three subprocesses of programming in adult education.

Planning

The first subprocess in the conceptual programming model is planning. *Planning* is a deliberate, rational, continuing sequence of activities through which the adult educator acquires a thorough understanding of and commitment to the organization's functions, structure, and processes and becomes knowledgeable about and committed to a tested conceptual framework for programming, continuous organizational renewal, and linkage of the organization to its publics. This definition involves two distinct dimensions: (1) the organization and its renewal process and (2) linkage of the organization to its target publics through study, analysis, and mapping of the publics within which it functions; identifying target publics and their leaders; and interfacing with these leaders, individual learners, and learner groups in collaborative needs identification, assessment, and analysis. As a part of the conceptual programming model, planning is guided by certain assumptions:

Planning is a futuristic activity.

The planning behavior of the adult education organization is proactive rather than reactive.

Planning enhances efficiency in the adult education organization.

Planning is sequential or stepwise; it begins with the organization and its renewal process, continues through the sequential steps of the linkage process, and ends with analysis of identified educational needs.

Planning is collaborative; it involves representatives of all who are affected by it.

The planning subprocess in the conceptual programming model is depicted in Table 3-2.

TABLE 3-2   The planning subprocess

PLANNING	
The organization & its renewal process	**Linking the organization to its publics**
Understanding of & commitment to the organization's functions: Mission Philosophy Objectives.	Study, analysis, and mapping of the organization's publics.
	Identifying target publics.
Understanding of & commitment to the organization's structure: Roles Relationships.	Identifying & interfacing with leaders of target publics.
Knowledgeable about & skilled in the organization's processes: Supervision Staff development Evaluation & accountability.	Collaborative identification, assessment, and analysis of needs specific to a target public.
Understanding of & commitment to a tested conceptual framework for programming.	
Understanding of & commitment to continuous organizational renewal.	

Planning leads in sequential steps to the actual identification, assessment, and analysis of the needs of the target publics that the organization purports to serve. A major assumption undergirding planning is that the organization significantly influences the planning behavior of the adult educator as change agent and programmer. A second assumption is that the organization must interface effectively with leaders of its target publics and their followers (learners) to make an accurate identification, assessment, and analysis of their educational needs. Gordon Lippitt (1969) defines *interfacing* as "primarily a process by which human beings confront common areas of concern, engage in meaningfully related dialogue, actively search for solutions to mutual problems, and cope with these solutions purposefully" (p. 2). The interfacing function further implies a temporary merger of the organization and its target publics into a single, modified system within which effective interfacing is achieved between the adult educator, learners in the target publics, and their leaders.

The educational organization exists to facilitate positive behavioral change in its clientele and their sociocultural environment in concert with available resources. The organization projected in the planning subprocess is not static. Rather, it continually adjusts to serve the needs of relevant publics in a changing socioeconomic environment. The dynamics of the organization's mission, philosophy, functions, structure, and processes can greatly affect the planning behavior of the adult educator in the role of change agent.

The extent to which positive program outcomes or outputs are attained through planning efforts and, ultimately, the total programming effort of the adult education organization are contingent upon several organizational concepts. First among these is the degree to which a systematic framework is established and defined within which adult educators, as change agents and programmers, are expected to function. Adult educators must be knowledgeable about and committed to the mission and philosophy of the organization or system that provides a general framework for the planning behavior of its members and to the organizational objectives that guide and help regulate their planning behavior in achieving these objectives.

Second, adult educators must be knowledgeable about and skillful in management processes that are operational within their organization. The supervisory, staff development, and evaluation/accountability management processes and practices of their organization can either facilitate or hamper their planning efforts.

The third organizational concept that can affect the adult educator's planning behavior is the extent to which the organization maintains a tested conceptual approach to generating and effecting change programs with target publics. Such a tested conceptual framework should include concepts, theories, and principles derived from the behavioral and social sciences about planned change, linkage with publics, leader involvement, needs assessment, program design and implementation, and program evaluation and accountability. This tested conceptual framework becomes a major part of the cognitive map of the adult educator in linking with publics and interfacing with leaders and learners of those publics in identifying needs.

The fourth organizational concept of import to planning is the adult educator's acquisition of a keen sensitivity and commitment to objective, systematic analysis that will facilitate organizational responsiveness to the constantly changing needs of target publics. Further, in a society where needs of publics and patterns of thinking, feeling, and acting are in constant and rapid transition, the organization must renew itself by constantly adjusting its functions, structure, and processes to accommodate the changing sociocultural environment of its publics. Conceptually, the mission, philosophy, functions, structure, and processes of the organization should be the first consideration in delineating planning as a major subprocess of the conceptual programming model. Organizational renewal is a means by which objectives are readied for a concerted effort to meet the varied and frequently changing educational needs of its target publics. Adult educators' behavior in approaching their roles as change agents and programmers will be affected by the depth of their understanding of and commitment to the four organizational concepts discussed in this section.

Armed with an understanding of and commitment to their adult education organization and a clear concept of their roles as change agents and programmers, adult educators must now approach the difficult task of linkage, that is, studying, analyzing, and mapping the publics within which the organization functions; identifying its target publics and leaders of those publics; and interfacing with these leaders, individual learners, and learner groups. The consequences of effective linkage with target publics should be needs identification, with the expectation that actual needs will be addressed. For educators to be reasonably assured that this will transpire, the publics within which the adult education organization functions must first be studied, analyzed, and mapped culturally, socially, economically, geographically, and politically. Particular attention must be given to groupings of people in the environment within which the organization is to direct its change efforts.

The existence of definable social groupings—families, neighborhoods, communities, and others—in human society is all-pervasive. Identity with such groupings commences at birth and extends throughout the life span. Social groupings have their origin in two social processes, namely, *stratification* and *differentiation*. These groupings are established and maintained through patterned interaction (social relationships) of members of the group and their adherence or conformity to mutually agreed upon norms and standards that result in shared goals, beliefs, values, attitudes, customs, and sentiments. For example, ethnic groups are characterized by their distinctive lifestyles. What all of this means is that the prelude to organizational linkage consists of identifying and understanding, in general, the publics or social groupings in the organization's environment.

After mapping and identification of the target publics, the next major task is to identify the leadership of these publics. This approach is based on the assumption that their leaders, either formal or informal, can accurately define the educational needs of the rank and file that comprise the target publics.

A significant element of organizational grouping of people into definable publics or social systems is the emergence of leaders who wield considerable influence on the behavior and actions of individual members, as well as the total group. These leaders acquire their influential status through reputation, heritage, and a host of other means. They tend to mirror the values, beliefs, and sentiments of their followers. Although their leadership status may be either formal or informal, leaders generally possess the authority or power to grant access to their respective group. Entree into target publics requires that adult educators identify closely with the formal and informal leadership of those publics.

Practically all of the diffusion studies to date suggest that informal leaders, in fact, often hold the key to the adoption of practices by a majority of their followers. The similarity of these informal leaders' covert and overt characteristics to the total membership of the grouping is striking. Maintenance of leadership positions in such groupings is largely contingent upon the soundness of the leaders' judgment, as perceived by their followers, in helping them safeguard and maintain their welfare. Thus, understanding the authority and power vested in informal, as well as formal, leader figures within the target publics or social groupings is vital to determining the members' needs and to securing their commitment to participate in programs focused on those needs.

Identification of target publics through mapping and identification of their formal and informal leaders leads to the next step in linkage, that is, interfacing with these leaders. Mere identification of leaders is not sufficient; rather, adult educators must consciously strive to establish communication or interface with these persons through informal and meaningful dialogue. The dialogue should be characterized by the familiar as perceived by the leaders; that is, the leaders' inputs into initial discussions should be dominant. Characterized as a listener in the initial stages of such dialogue, the adult educator should exhibit as much empathy as possible. Interfacing with leaders of the target publics entails building rapport through active, ongoing dialogue to disclose relevant educational needs of the target publics that can be translated into meaningful planned program inputs. This interfacing often leads to identification of intrinsic or felt needs that require immediate attention by the adult educator to provide visible results for the publics, thus strengthening the relationship between the informal and formal leadership and their followers.

Through progressive dialogue between the adult educator and the identified leaders, collaborative identification, assessment, and analysis of educational needs of the target public(s) become a reality. This task is ongoing; that is, ever-changing educational needs must be the focus of continuing interaction between adult educators and leaders if adult education programs are to be relevant and timely. As the bonds between the adult educator and the leaders strengthen, extrinsic needs may be discussed and acted upon.

Identification, assessment, and analysis of educational needs of distinctive learner groups is the first priority in effectively relating the adult education organization's resources to its publics. Although the immediate chore is to identify felt or expressed needs of the publics, the adult educator's long-term objective should be to increase the level of socialization of these publics, through effective educational programs, to the extent that they become knowledgeable about, concerned with, and committed to the attainment of higher-level or extrinsic needs.

The fruits of effective linkage of the adult education organization to its publics appear in the literature (Zaltman, 1973) as leading to conditions through which the target public will feel that it has a hand in initiating behavioral change. The overarching aim of linkage is to identify and link with publics to the degree that an accurate analysis of their educational needs is attained.

In summary, the planning subprocess of the conceptual programming model represents a systematic effort to combine two functioning systems, the adult education organization and its publics, into one pattern of planning that culminates in an adequate, collaborative needs identification, assessment, and analysis from which to begin the next subprocess of the programming construct: design and implementation.

Design and Implementation

Design and implementation, the second major subprocess of the conceptual programming model, has three distinct dimensions: (1) the planned program, (2) plans of action, and (3) action strategies. The *planned program* is the master plan or long-range prospectus for behavioral change toward which adult educators focus their efforts. The planned program consists of (1) a statement of the larger or macro needs, (2) a statement of macro objectives that are keyed to those needs, (3) specification of general educational strategies for achieving the objectives, and (4) specification of macro outcomes of the planned program.

Plans of action, which are short-range in nature, include specific teaching plans designed to guide the efforts of adult educators in fulfilling learner needs and attaining the long-range objectives contained in the planned program. Action strategies involved in implementing plans of action include (1) marketing; (2) procuring, developing, and using resources, both human and material; (3) monitoring ongoing educational activities; (4) reinforcing learners and teachers; and (5) using feedback to modify, as needed or warranted, teaching-learning activities to attain maximum outcomes or outputs.

Program design and implementation are logically and operationally related: logically in that both center around the critical task of structural needs of the learner; operationally in that, after establishing needs, the next phase is to translate those needs into an efficient program design.

As part of the conceptual programming model, the design and implementations subprocess is guided by certain assumptions:

> The planned program is the adult education organization's chief means of responding to the needs of its publics.
>
> The planned program is a blueprint of major behavioral changes to be effected by the adult education organization over a relatively long period of time, if improvements are to be noted in these publics.
>
> The planned program provides the adult education organization with a rationale for the allocation, deployment, and use of its resources.
>
> The planned program serves as a guide and provides direction for adult educators in deciding on strategies for coping with the educational needs of their learners.
>
> The design of plans of action guides the adult educator in systematically developing change or educational strategies to deal with the needs and objectives enumerated in the planned program within a relatively short period of time.
>
> The planned program provides the adult education organization with an excellent public relations tool.
>
> The planned program and plans of action provide the adult educator with the means needed to market them to the intended publics.
>
> The planned program and plans of action provide a base for the adult educator in identifying, recruiting, and developing resource persons to assist with the actual implementation of the planned program and its accompanying plans of action.

The design and implementation subprocess in the conceptual programming model is depicted in Table 3–3.

The design and implementation subprocess is the starting point for the planned program and extends through its actual implementation. In the design and implementation subprocess, the planned program becomes the vehicle for translating expressed needs of target publics into a meaningful and functional design. A second premise is that objectives to meet expressed needs can be treated through carefully thought-out sequential plans or plans of action. These two assumptions imply that the adult educator must function (1) as the architect in designing the program and plans of action and (2) as the facilitator in ensuring that the plans of action are effectively implemented.

TABLE 3-3   The design and implementation subprocess

DESIGN & IMPLEMENTATION

Designing the planned program	Implementing the planned program
Translation of expressed needs into macro needs.	Developing plans of action:
	Translating needs into teaching objectives
Translation of macro needs into macro objectives.	Specifying learning experiences for each teaching objective
	Developing plans for evaluating learner
Specifying general educational strategies & learning resources.	outcomes & assessing learning experiences.
	Developing & implementing strategies &
Specifying macro outcomes of the planned program.	techniques for marketing the plans of action.
	Developing & following through on plans to recruit & train leader-learner resources.
	Monitoring & reinforcing the teacher-learner transaction.

Designing the planned program to mirror the expressed needs of the target publics requires that the change agent thoroughly understand the change and curriculum development processes. The adult educator must translate the expressed or felt needs of target publics to higher-level needs that will emerge as these lower-level needs are satisfied. Such translation is essential to the performance of the adult educator's role in designing the planned program to satisfy the expressed needs of publics.

Curriculum development authorities support the notion that the design and development of the planned program is a first step in treating the educational needs of learners. The planned program provides adult educators with a master strategy both for designing learning activities that will enable these learners to experience fulfillment of their immediate, felt needs and for delineating the subsequent related behavioral tasks that must be mastered by such learners to fulfill higher-level related needs.

Several concepts undergird the design of the planned program. First and foremost, adult educators must specify the macro needs of their target public(s) in the content area within which learner needs have been expressed in adult educator-learner dialogue. The notion of "hierarchy" is useful in defining learner needs for inclusion in the planned program.

All of humankind's needs are a part of a related network or hierarchy that may not be perceived. People tend, at a given time, to feel or perceive the immediate, based on their state of socialization, with little or no knowledge about or interest in those needs that are outside their social environment and realm of perception.

For example, a homemaker's perceived need may be to learn how to prepare a cake. The need is immediate and real to the homemaker, and the adult educator should expend every effort in helping to fulfill this need. At the same time, the adult educator must view this immediate, felt need in relation to other higher-level needs that may emerge, such as the homemaker's planning and preparation of balanced meals for the family, the selection and purchase of economical foods that contain the necessary nutrients for balanced meals, and, ultimately, concern for the health and well-being of the family.

Armed with an understanding of nutritional needs, the adult educator sets about to define the "ideal" hierarchy of nutritional needs. This hierarchy begins with the homemaker's perceived immediate need (preparing a cake), then includes, in sequence, those other nutritional needs that eventually will have to be treated to enable the homemaker to make wise decisions about the preparation of balanced meals for her family. This hierarchy makes it possible to start where the homemaker is, in terms of her motivation, level of knowledge, understanding, and skills, and to plan for her orderly, continuous, intellectual growth in nutrition education. From this analysis and mental construction of a hierarchy of needs, the adult educator then can identify the macro need(s) for inclusion in the planned program.

From the specification of macro needs to be included in the planned program, the adult educator proceeds to the *formulation of macro objectives* to correspond with each of the identified needs. Higher-level, macro needs establish the distance or spread between learners' existing behavior and the ideal behavior deduced from research findings and societal expectations. The objectives hierarchy corresponding to the needs hierarchy specifies the types and levels of behavioral change to be sought in the learners. The highest level of macro need or behavior in the hierarchy is translated into a macro objective to be included in the planned program. The resulting macro objective becomes the "ideal" toward which the adult education organization's efforts are directed, and plays an important role in all future decisions related to program design/implementation.

Following specification of macro objectives, the adult educator must design and select *change* (educational) *strategies* intended to help learners achieve those objectives. Emphasis is given to identifying those strategies that will produce maximum change within the sociocultural setting of the target public. Learning strategies, as well as the effects of reference groups and aspects of the culture, are taken into account when selecting change strategies. Spicer (1952) underscores the importance of the cultural context in selecting change strategies when he notes that the method used in introducing new knowledge and technology into a culture may be the determinant of whether the people respond positively or negatively. The change strategies for achieving macro objectives must be clearly defined and included in the planned program to make the public knowledgeable about what is planned and to provide direction for the adult educator.

To focus efforts and to ensure success, the adult educator should clearly articulate the *outcomes* or outputs to be expected through achievement of the program objectives. Objectives, as previously noted, are descriptive of behavioral change sought in individuals and, cumulatively, in publics. Each objective reflects an intended behavioral change that adult educators, in collaboration with individual learners, groups of learners, and their leaders, expect will fulfill analyzed needs. The learners must have a clear concept of what they are trying to accomplish and how its accomplishment will translate into meaningful outcomes.

Successful implementation of a planned program requires that sufficient time be allotted to complete the change efforts of the adult educator and other resource persons. Allocation of time is one of the points at which the educator's expertise and experience are invaluable. The education process is slow at best. Learners must be allowed sufficient time for change to occur.

The planned program is intended to reflect the behavioral changes toward which adult educators' efforts are directed as they endeavor to respond to the needs of learners. The macro nature of the planned program mandates that the adult educator think through and develop specific incremental plans of action for its implementation. Implementation of the planned program requires that the adult educator likewise develop and effect carefully designed instructional strategies. The complexity and interrelatedness of needs outlined in the planned program do not lend themselves to immediate solution or treatment. Many high-level or macro needs require continuous and concentrated effort, over an extended period of time, before maximal behavioral change among learners can be achieved.

As indicated in the discussion of needs in the planned program, fulfillment of a macro need may entail attainment of a number of prerequisite behavioral changes among the learners. Planning for orderly and effective acquisition of these prerequisite behaviors is a major undertaking. For each macro need and, more specifically, the micro needs contained therein, sequential teaching plans or instructional units, tailored to learner needs and objectives, must be developed to guide the efforts of the adult educator in facilitating learner development. Programmed over a given interval of time, these individual but sequenced teaching plans should aid learners in acquiring the prerequisite behaviors and skills that, collectively, will enable them to exhibit the level of behavior specified in the macro objectives.

To design sequential plans of action in consonance with the needs and objectives expressed in the planned program, adult educators must ask themselves the following questions:

What are the specific learner needs encompassed within each macro need expressed in the planned program?

What behavioral change(s) must learners attain to fulfill each of the micro needs?

What learner activities should be selected and how should they be organized to facilitate learners' achievement of the desired behavioral change(s)?

What measures should be employed to assess and evaluate learner activities? How should learner progress be assessed?

The need to follow through on systematic implementation of plans of action is pointed up by several programming authorities. Plans of action are useless unless they are sequentially and methodically implemented. Tasks involved in implementing plans of action include

A carefully thought-out plan for marketing the plans of action and the planned program.

Identification, mobilization, development, and use of resources, both human and material, to implement and follow through on learner activities outlined in plans of action.

Provision for and follow-through on monitoring planned learner activities.

Provision of continuing reinforcement for the learners and teachers.

Development and implementation of a procedure that provides continuous feedback on outcomes of learner activities so that adjustments can be made in the planned program, or both, if warranted.

The design and implementation subprocess of the conceptual programming model represents the adult education organization's effort to respond effectively to the felt or immediate needs and the analyzed needs of its publics. Mastery of this subprocess leads to a discussion of the third and final subprocess of the programming construct: evaluation and accountability.

Evaluation and Accountability

Accounting for the choices and decisions made in the programming process is a major challenge for the adult education organization. To achieve this end, the organization must sustain a sound evaluation and accountability effort as an integral part of the total programming process. Several difficult and related actions must be in operation to maintain the viability of the organization while responding to the needs of its publics and society in general.

First and foremost is making explicit the values that undergird programming choices and decisions. From these values, as a second step, concentrated effort must be made to identify and describe the intended outputs or indicators of change that the organization is seeking through its planned program and shorter-term plans of action. Degree of attainment and effectiveness, as well as justification for an adult education organization's programming efforts are in the outputs of the planned program. A third step is the organization's continuing efforts to assess and evaluate the relative effectiveness of programming inputs, for example, planning decisions, identification of target publics, leader identification and involvement, needs analysis and translation, teaching-learning activities, and so forth. Finally, the adult education organization must analyze and interpret programming choices and expected outputs to its learners and their leaders and, where appropriate, to its governance body.

The evaluation and accountability subprocess is concerned with making informed judgments about the effectiveness of the planned program and plans of action based on established criteria and known, observable *evidence.* As such, the subprocess is an obvious means by which an organization can justify and account for its decisions. As a part of the conceptual programming model, the evaluation and accountability subprocess is guided by certain assumptions:

The primary purpose of the planned adult education program is to effect desirable behavioral changes in a specified public.

Outcomes/outputs of planned adult education programs can be identified and evaluated.

An adult education organization proceeds through the programming process as a series of conscious choices and decisions; it is further assumed that each decision is rational and based on values that are understood.

Management and renewal of the adult education organization depend upon continuous generation of program outputs and feedback through evaluating and accounting for program outputs.

Participation of target publics in evaluating how well their educational experiences met the planned program's objectives is both desirable and necessary.

The adult education organization has both a commitment and an ethical responsibility to account for program choices and outputs to its target publics, funding sources, the profession, and, where appropriate, its governance body.

The evaluation and accountability subprocess in the conceptual programming model is depicted in Table 3-4.

TABLE 3-4   The evaluation and accountability subprocess

EVALUATION & ACCOUNTABILITY	
Evaluation	**Accountability**
Determining & measuring program outputs.	Using evaluation findings for accounting to publics, parent organization, funding sources, the profession, and, where appropriate, the governance body.
Assessing program inputs.	
Using evaluation findings for program revisions and organizational renewal.	

The three components of the evaluation and accountability subprocess are (1) determining and measuring program outputs, (2) assessing program inputs, and (3) using evaluation findings for program revisions, organizational renewal, and accounting to learners and leaders, the organization, funding sources, the profession, and, where appropriate, the governance body.

Program output evaluation investigates the extent to which objectives were or are being attained. These outputs may be the learners' increased knowledge, changed attitudes, and acquisition of new skills. Another level of program output may be the extent to which certain practices were adopted. These behavioral outputs may be both overt and covert; that is, some outputs may be observable and measurable, while others may only be inferred.

In determining program outputs, adult educators must consider the validity and reliability of evidence used to verify attainment of specified objectives. Likewise, they need to examine initial and subsequent measures in determining program outputs. Follow-up studies on learner participants might be helpful in ascertaining the degree of permanency of the effected behavioral changes.

Ideally, sequenced teaching-learning objectives in a content or macro need area and their outputs should be additive in nature. That is, outputs of sequenced teaching-learning objectives within a need area should contribute to the major program outputs specified in the planned program objectives. Likewise, these major program outputs should contribute to the organization's objectives. This concept of hierarchy of objectives is important in the programming process.

In addition to determining the major program outputs and their hierarchical nature, adult educators make *judgments* relative to the appropriateness of those outputs in meeting needs. After careful examination, they may conclude that the outputs produced failed to contribute to fulfilling the needs and objectives identified in the planned program and in the plans of action.

Input evaluation is an assessment of all the choices and decisions made in the programming process. Particular emphasis must be given to determining the appropriateness and effectiveness of the learning activities in producing the outputs specified in the objectives.

The actual program outputs rarely, if ever, are the same as those intended or desired, because numerous variables cannot be completely controlled. Some of these variables may be referred to as *program inputs*. One major program input focuses on the organization, including its mission, philosophy, functions, structure, and processes. Other program inputs include such variables as the adequacy of the linkage effected between the organization and its target publics to identify and analyze needs, the adequacy and accuracy of the planned program in reflecting the felt and analyzed needs of the target publics, the specificity and clarity of macro objectives in relation to learner needs at all levels, time allotted, materials and supplies, the reliability and validity of factual information used, and numerous others. Adult educators must examine program outputs in relation to actual program inputs so as to recognize these variables and hence be in a better position to revise the input-output system, if needed.

The interaction among program inputs has an important bearing on program outputs. The dynamics of such program inputs as leader identification, training, and utilization; decision making; social action; planning; and the design and implementation of the teaching-learning activities may be major determinants in the teaching-learning process. A thorough understanding of the dynamics of these inputs may help adult educators to understand why certain program outputs are achieved. If the major elements in those program inputs, their packaging and delivery, can be identified for both successes and failures with regard to program outputs, adult educators will have a better understanding of the outputs achieved and how to modify program inputs to produce more desirable outputs.

The use of evaluation findings for program revision, organizational renewal, and accountability to publics, the organization, funding sources, the profession, and, where appropriate, to the governance body is the last concept to be discussed. The continuous evaluation of its planned program in relation to outputs attained or being attained is of first priority to the adult education organization. Among the several reasons for engaging in program evaluation, a major reason is to use these evaluative findings to modify or redirect program inputs, where necessary, for current or future planned program cycling. These findings may reveal that the needs of target publics require further amplification, or that the objectives need clarifying, or that the teaching-learning strategies used need to be changed or modified, or that more time should be allocated for the program.

A second major use of program evaluation findings is to examine the viability and effectiveness of the total organization. Organizational renewal in terms of mission, function, structure, or processes may be necessary for effective fulfillment of the organization's objectives.

Reporting of program results must be accurate and continuous. The adult education organization's publics must be continuously apprised of the successes *and* failures of the system; this is particularly true for learners, their leaders, and other key publics. In addition, means must be devised and implemented for reporting planned program outputs to the organization's governance body. The adult education organization must be prepared, at all times, to account to its governance body for its programs and to justify the confidence and support accorded by these policy formulators. To maintain and improve the standards of their profession, adult educators must continually examine the results of their own efforts as related to the roles expected of them as adult educator, programmer, and change agent.

THEORETICAL APPROACH IN RETROSPECT

From its inception, adult education's professionals have attempted to answer questions about programming through experience, authority, deductive reasoning, inductive reasoning, and finally the scientific approach. Certain assumptions have been required by each approach to the problem. The correctness of the answers depends on the correctness of assumptions underlying the particular approach.

Two basic assumptions undergird the scientific approach: (1) truth can be derived from observations and (2) phenomena conform to lawful and ordered relationships. Absolute truth is not the goal of scientific inquiry. Rather, the goal is theories that reliably explain and predict phenomena. Self-correction is built into the scientific approach, as every theory is considered to be tentative and may be rejected if a new theory better fits the established phenomena. The scientific approach has been employed to explain, predict, and control physical phenomena for centuries, but only recently has been employed in education. The complexity of its related educational concepts and the difficulty encountered in collecting reliable data have particularly impeded scientific inquiry in education. Nonetheless, in the recent past, the frequency of scientific inquiry in education has increased considerably and has been extraordinarily successful in both theoretical and applied research.

The conceptual programming model introduced in this chapter has both a research and an experience base. Its assumptions, concepts, and processes depict the conceptual and action steps that are undertaken by adult educators as they endeavor to plan, design and implement, and evaluate and account for planned programs to their target publics, the organization, funding sources, the profession, and, where appropriate, the governance body. This conceptual framework or macro process can be used for further study and analysis of programming in adult education. It is hoped that the conceptual programming model will stimulate adult educators to pursue research that may lead to its acceptance, rejection, or extension.

Our attention now turns to enlarging upon, analyzing, and clarifying the three major subprocesses of programming in adult education as delineated in the conceptual programming model. The first of these subprocesses, planning, is presented in Chapter 4.

REFERENCES

ARY, D., L. C. JACOBS, and A. RAZAVIEH, *Introduction to Research in Education.* 2nd ed. New York: Holt, Rinehart and Winston, 1979.

BUSKEY, J. A., and T. J. SORK, *From Chaos to Order in Program Planning: A System for Selecting Models and Ordering Research.* Proceedings of the 23rd Annual Adult Education Research Conference, Lincoln, Nebraska, April 1–3, 1982.

CUNNINGHAM, H. F., *Notes on Epistemology.* Bronx, N.Y.: Fordham University Press, 1958.

FOLLETT, M. P., "Power," in *Dynamic Administration,* ed. H. C. Metcalf and L. Urwick. New York: Harper & Brothers, 1940.

FOSTER, L., ed., *Experience and Theory.* Amherst: University of Massachusetts Press, 1979.

GETZELS, J. W., ed., *Educational Administration as Social Process: Theory, Research, Practice.* New York: Harper & Row, Publishers, 1968.

GOODE, W. J., and P. K. HATT, *Methods in Social Research.* New York: McGraw-Hill Book Company, 1952.

GUTTMAN, L., "The Problems of Attitude and Opinion Measurement," in *Measurement and Prediction,* ed. S. Stouffer. Princeton, N.J.: Princeton University Press, 1950.

HAVIGHURST, R. J., *Developmental Tasks and Education.* 2nd ed. Chicago: Committee on Human Development, University of Chicago, 1952.

HOULE, C., *The Design of Education.* San Francisco: Jossey-Bass, Publishers, 1972.

INGLE, D. J., *Is It Really So? A Guide to Clear Thinking.* Philadelphia, Pa.: Westminster Press, 1976.

INKELES, A., *What Is Sociology? An Introduction to the Discipline and Profession.* Englewood Cliffs, N.J.: Prentice-Hall, Inc., 1964.

KERLINGER, F., *Foundations of Behavioral Research.* New York: Holt, Rinehart and Winston, 1964.

————, *Behavioral Research: A Conceptual Approach.* New York: Holt, Rinehart and Winston, 1979.

KNOX, A. B., "Foreword," in *Developing, Administering, and Evaluating Adult Education,* ed. A. B. Knox and Associates. San Francisco: Jossey-Bass, Publishers, 1980.

LIPPITT, G. L., *Organization Renewal.* New York: Meredith Corporation, 1969.

MERTON, R. K., *Social Theory and Social Structure.* Rev. ed. New York: The Free Press, 1957.

NACHMIAS, D., and C. NACHMIAS, *Research Methods in the Social Sciences.* New York: St. Martin's Press, 1976.

PETERS, J. M., and C. P. KOZOLL, *"A Systems Approach to Examining Adult Education,"* in *Building an Effective Adult Education Enterprise,* ed. J. M. Peters and Associates. San Francisco: Jossey-Bass, Publishers, 1980.

POLLOCK, J., *Knowledge and Justification.* Princeton, N.J.: Princeton University Press, 1975.

ROBB, F. C., "Technology, Man, and Education." Paper presented at the 75th Annual Meeting of the Southern Association of Colleges and Schools, Miami, Fla., 1970.

SELLTIZ, C., M. JAHODA, M. DEUTSCH, and J. W. COOK, *Research Methods in Social Relations.* New York: Holt, Rinehart and Winston, 1959.

SPICER, E. H., ed., *Human Problems and Technological Change.* New York: Russell Sage Foundation, 1952.

THEODORSON, G. A., and A. G. THEODORSON, *A Modern Dictionary of Sociology.* New York: Thomas Y. Crowell Company, 1969.

TINSLEY, W. V., and M. SITTON, "Teaching Intellectual Aspects of Home Economics Through the Identification of Basic Concepts," *Journal of Home Economics,* 59 (1967), 85–88.

TOFFLER, A., *Future Shock.* New York: Random House, Inc., 1970.

VAN DALEN, D. B., *Understanding Educational Research.* Rev. ed. New York: McGraw-Hill Book Company, 1966.

ZALTMAN, G., ed., *Processes and Phenomena of Social Change.* New York: John Wiley & Sons, Inc., 1973.

ZETTERBERG, H. L., *On Theory and Verification in Sociology.* Totowa, N.J.: The Bedminster Press, 1965.

Chapter Four

Planning

Planning is a functional and integral component of the programming process in adult education. This perspective takes into consideration that many of the problems involved in defining the planning subprocess derive from a lack of specificity with regard to the meanings assigned to it in adult education and related literature (Kratz, 1971). Planning, the first of the three subprocesses of programming in adult education, as treated in this chapter, is based on (1) the five assumptions and four concepts that undergird and guide the planning process, (2) the organizational perspective and its impact on planning, and (3) the process of linking the organization to its publics.

The role of the adult education organization in programming, and subsequently in planning, was introduced in Chapter 1. Planning begins with the organization and extends through needs analysis. Thus, the approach is from an organizational aspect, extending beyond individual or group approaches to planning and problem solving, so that planning is viewed as the organization's response to the needs of its environment.

A significant number of adult educators recognize the dominant role that an organization can and does play in shaping the planning behavior of an adult educator (e.g., Knox and Associates, 1980; Schroeder, 1980). Rothman (1976) posits that both the philosophy and the objectives of an organization contribute to the development of the adult education practitioner's planning orientation and forecasting ability, citing Zald's conclusion that "needs and problems . . . are defined and shaped by the employing agency," while the adult educator's planning behavior "is determined by the structure, aims, and operating procedures of the organization that pays the bill" (p. 39).

More recently, McClure pointed out that no organization can *consistently* achieve its objectives without effective planning. In discussing the strategies of planning, McClure (1978) highlights the importance of planning to organizational effectiveness when he states that, "without goals, without plans, no rational indicator of effectiveness can be determined. Planning is pervasive; it can and should be done at all organizational levels; it can and should be done with all organizational members; and it is an ongoing and continuous process" (p. 457). Therefore, we emphasize that planning is an imperative; while the organization is important to planning, planning is equally important to the organization. Further, planning (1) provides a legitimate road map for a rational response to uncertainty and change, (2) facilitates control of organizational operations by collecting information to analyze needs and evaluate its programs and services, and (3) orients the organization to a futuristic leadership stance. Instead of reacting to problem situations only when they arise, the organization attempts to foresee and mitigate potential future problems before they become crises. This approach assumes that educational needs exist within collective problems in the environment in which the organization functions. Because organizations generally operate within definable boundaries (e.g., geographic area, community, or other sociocultural environment) and, through planning, work with the publics therein, our perspective of the organizational role is vital to our definition of planning.

ASSUMPTIONS AND CONCEPTS

As we noted in Chapter 3, planning is guided by five basic assumptions:

1. Planning is a futuristic activity.
2. The planning behavior of the adult education organization is proactive rather than reactive.
3. Planning enhances efficiency in the adult education organization.
4. Planning is sequential or stepwise, involving collecting and analyzing related information, and identifying, assessing, and analyzing needs.
5. Planning is collaborative; that is, it includes representatives of all who are affected by it.

In addition, four distinct generic concepts undergird planning: (1) planned change, (2) linkage, (3) democracy, and (4) translation. In his typology of the change process, Benne (1961) views *planned change* as involving "mutual goal-setting by one or both parties, an equal power ratio, and deliberativeness, eventually at least, on the part of both sides" (p. 6). Our point of view is that this notion of planned change, with elements of consciousness and deliberativeness, implies an exactness for organizational planning activities. The collaborative aspects strongly suggest a continuum and a sustained, collaborative effort in planning between the organization and its target publics.

The second concept, *linkage,* originated with Loomis (1959), who defines systemic linkage as "the process whereby the elements of at least two social systems come to be articulated so that in some ways they function as a unitary system" (p. 55). For example, a library and the publics it purports to serve may come to be articulated to the degree that they function as a unitary system. Schroeder's (1980) notion of adult education as a developmental process and his emphasis on the systems aspect of this process are akin to Loomis's concept; that is, the planning process involves linkage of the organization with its publics through learners' direct involvement in needs identification, assessment, and analysis.

The concept of *democracy* in planning is another important aspect. Open and free participation of learners in the decision-making process is essential to good planning, particularly in needs identification, assessment, and analysis. Benne (1961) illustrates this concept in his five "democratic norms" for the planning of change: (1) engineering change and meeting pressures for change on a group or organization must be a collaborative effort; (2) planning must be educational for participants; (3) planning is experimental and task-oriented; (4) it must be antiindividualistic; and (5) it must provide for privacy and personal development. From a conceptual point of view, these democratic norms reinforce the linkage and collaborative aspects of the organizational perspective already discussed.

The fourth and final concept basic to the planning subprocess is *translation.* This concept is based on two imperatives. The first is that the adult educator's values, knowledge, and methodology must be presented in a frame of reference that can be understood and interpreted by the organization's public. The second imperative is that the adult educator must be able to understand and interpret the social and cultural environment of the organization's public and the sociocultural characteristics of learners who are members of that public. Reciprocity in the exchange of information and acceptance of each other by the adult educator and adult learners is essential to the success of collaborative planning.

In planning, the adult educator, as change agent and programmer, is viewed as a facilitator whose principal role is that of helping adult learners examine, evaluate, and perhaps adopt new or improved behaviors that will better equip them to adapt to and cope with change in their environment. Agreement was found in the literature that performing as a facilitator in the planning or change process is difficult (Spicer, 1952; Lippitt, Watson, and Westley, 1958; Goodenough, 1963). These sources contend that adult educators' frames of reference usually are comprised of "ideal" notions of what is desirable or undesirable, good or bad, for the adult learner. In fact, these "ideal" standards and the language in which they are cast may differ considerably from those of the potential learners. Recognition and appreciation of conceptual differences, as well as conceptual agreements, are responsibilities that must be faced by both adult educators and adult learners when planning learning activities. Translating goals, beliefs, values, norms, and other aspects so that differences and commonalities can be recognized and appreciated is the adult educator's responsibility.

PLANNING DEFINED

Given the perspective, the guiding assumptions, and the concepts of the planning subprocess, which are illustrated in Tables 3-1 and 3-2, we must first provide a definition of planning that is substantial and built upon a consistent set of values. *Planning,* in this context, is defined as a rational, continuing sequence of precise educational activities carried out by adult educators, operating from an organizational base, through which the organization establishes and maintains linkage with learners and their leaders in collaborative identification, assessment, and analysis of their educational needs.

This definition of planning includes two distinct dimensions: (1) the organization and its renewal process and (2) its identification of and linkage with its target public through collaboration with target public learners and their leaders in needs identification, assessment, and analysis. Each dimension is introduced by way of distinct processual tasks. A *processual task* is defined as an orderly set of actions engaged in by adult educators in applying a concept to a particular situation, in this instance, the subprocesses of programming in adult education.

ELEMENTS OF THE PLANNING SUBPROCESS

The planning subprocess of the conceptual programming model consists of two distinct but interrelated dimensions, with accompanying processual tasks. The two dimensions are (1) the organization and its renewal process and (2) linking the organization to its publics. We turn now to a discussion of the organization and its renewal process, the first dimension of the planning subprocess, and the five processual tasks related to organizational renewal.

The Organization, Its Renewal Process, and Related Processual Tasks

Organizational renewal involves a reexamination by the adult education organization of (1) the needs of its publics and (2) its own functions, structure, and processes as related to its mission, philosophy, and objectives. Five processual tasks for the adult educator are implied here. Adult educators must acquire (1) thorough knowledge of and commitment to the mission, philosophy, and objectives of the adult education organization; (2) understanding of and commitment to the structure of the organization; (3) knowledge about and commitment to the organization's processes; (4) understanding of and commitment to a tested conceptual framework for programming; and (5) sensitivity and commitment to objective, systemic analysis. These tasks form the adult educator's working environment. And, equally important, these tasks form a dynamic that generally affects a worker's behavior.

An adult education organization exists to facilitate desired behavioral changes in its publics and its social environment, in concert with available resources. The organization is not static. Adjustments are continually being made in its functions, structure, and processes as it adapts to meet or serve the needs of its relevant publics in an ever-changing social environment.

The extent to which positive results are obtained through the programming efforts of the adult education organization is contingent upon several important factors. First among these is the extent to which the organization establishes or defines an organizational framework within which adult educators, performing as change agents and programmers, are expected to function. Adult educators need to examine, understand, and accept the functions, structure, and processes of the adult education organization through which their planned programs are generated and conducted. They must be thoroughly knowledgeable of and committed to the mission and philosophy of the organization, which provide a general framework for the behavior of its members; the objectives of the organization, which delineate the ends to be accomplished by the organization; organizational roles, which specify required responsibilities of individual adult educators and job groups in achieving the objectives of the organization; and intraorganizational relationships, which provide a basis for linking the efforts of individual adult educators and job groups in attaining maximal program impact.

A second factor in achieving positive programming results is the extent to which adult educators become knowledgeable about and skilled in management processes that will yield maximal results as specified in the objectives of the organization. Careful attention must be given to the application of supervisory practices that will facilitate achievement of the objectives of the organization, to the recruitment and development of staff resources, and to the development and utilization of a viable evaluation and accountability system.

A third factor is the extent to which adult educators understand and are committed to a tested conceptual approach for generating and effecting programs of change within their many and diverse publics. Such a conceptual framework would include basic concepts, theories, and principles of planned change derived from the behavioral sciences; linkage with target publics through leader and learner involvement in collaborative needs analysis; and the design and implementation of programs specifically tailored to the perceived and analyzed needs of these target publics.

A fourth factor of import to program success is adult educators' acquisition of keen sensitivity and commitment to objective, systemic analysis for facilitating the organization's responsiveness and renewal to meet the constantly changing needs of its publics. In a society where needs of publics and patterns of thinking, feeling, and acting are in rapid transition, the organization must be renewed by adjusting its functions, structure, and processes to accommodate adaptation to the changing social environment in which it functions.

To facilitate effective functioning of the organization in achieving its mission, continuous attention must be given to the socialization of its adult educators and the leaders of its publics. It is imperative that adult educators and lay leaders be afforded a continuing opportunity to provide inputs that will cause the organization to be more responsive to the actual needs of its publics.

Five processual tasks were advanced as possible means for adult educators to achieve understanding of and commitment to the adult education organization's functions, structure, and processes, and its renewal process.

Task 1. The adult educator must become thoroughly knowledgeable of and committed to the functions of the organization through which programs will be effected, giving particular attention to its mission, philosophy, and objectives.

The degree to which adult educators understand and identify with the basic functions of their organization is related to (1) the manner in which the mission, philosophy, and objectives of the organization are diffused among its members and their commitment is secured and (2) the opportunity provided adult educators to help the organization define and modify its educational objectives and indicate the behavioral changes sought within various target publics.

Mission, philosophy, and objectives.   The mission of the adult education organization establishes the parameters within which it is to function. Particular attention is given to the nature and distinguishing characteristics of the organization, including its origin, legal basis, clientele, reasons for existence, and types of programs to be generated. Adult educators must understand and become committed to the mission of their organization to guide their efforts in programming.

The total staff of the adult education organization must become thoroughly knowledgeable about and committed to its philosophy or "value framework" that evolves over an extended period of time. Constant effort must be expended to keep the value framework of the organization consistent, comprehensive, and workable.

The philosophy of an educational organization reflects the firm conviction that people adjust to change most rapidly in a democratic environment in which self-expression, self-direction, and self-improvement are encouraged. This democratic environment is best achieved through a program of purposeful continuing education in which people, through their own initiative, identify and solve problems directly affecting their welfare. To this end, the organization starts with people where they are by helping them to attain a more satisfying way of life. If one accepts the proposition that the philosophy or value framework of an organization influences the behavior of its members, then every educational system should develop a functioning and articulate philosophy, communicate it to its members, and take necessary action to seek commitment.

Just as adult educators must understand and be committed to its mission and philosophy, the organization's objectives or ends must be understood at all levels of the organization. The macro objectives of the organization have their origin in the contemporary needs of its publics and constitute the framework within which all decisions and actions about the organization's program must be linked.

Not only must the organization's macro objectives be understood, but organization members must understand the objectives of its various job groups. Through knowledge and understanding of the objectives of the various job groups, individual organization members can grasp the potential roles of such groups and their complementary linkage, and hence better utilize such resources in the performance of their own expected roles.

Adult educators' understanding of and commitment to the macro objectives of the organization and objectives of any constituent job groups do not result from edict. Rather, they derive from deliberate and continuous member involvement in the formulation of the objectives of the organization.

Task 2. The adult educator must understand and be committed to the organization's structure, giving particular attention to roles and relationships.

The degree to which adult educators understand and are committed to the structure of their adult education organization is related to (1) the manner in which roles of adult educators are defined and communicated to all concerned and (2) the manner in which the expected interrelationships of various organizational job groups are established and these groups know and understand them.

Roles and relationships.   The expected roles of staff members have their origin in the macro objectives of the adult education organization. The roles played by members of any organization are interrelated. Thus, if maximum results are to be attained, the activities of various staff positions and job groups must fit and mesh together in attaining the organization's macro objectives. A common problem is that too little attention is given to defining and linking roles to objectives, a factor that tends to stifle the effectiveness of members' efforts in relation to attaining the organization's macro objectives. The roles of individual positions and job groups and the interrelationships of these roles in terms of the ends sought by the organization must be clearly delineated and understood if their efforts are to be effectively focused on the macro objectives of the organization.

Most organizations typically contain varying numbers of both formal and informal groupings with their related leadership patterns, power relationships, and attitudinal patterns. Each of these groupings, although intimately related to each other and to the organization, also has an established pattern or operation. Because programming must occur at all levels of the organization, these groupings must be permitted sufficient flexibility to make and implement decisions at their respective levels of operation. Although plans are made and implemented at its various levels, these plans must be coordinated and effectively related to the overall plans of the organization.

Task 3. The adult educator must be knowledgeable about and skilled in the organization's processes, that is, supervision, staff development, and evaluation and accountability.

The extent to which the objectives of an adult education organization are achieved depends to a large measure upon the processes through which resources are identified, attained, and managed. Of crucial importance are the supervisory, staff development, and evaluation and accountability processes and practices utilized by the adult education organization.

Supervision, staff development, and evaluation and accountability.   An adult education organization may bring into its system the most competent personnel available, and provide a comprehensive and intensive personnel training program. But, unless its members are given an opportunity to function, the organization may lose much of its potential effectiveness. Adult educators must learn to share leadership and develop the capacity of colleagues and subordinates to function. Not only must leadership be exercised and a teamwork approach followed, adequate guidance also must be provided. People generally want to know if they are performing adequately and want assistance in marshaling and applying resources to achieve. The adult educator, through application of appropriate supervision styles, can contribute substantially to organizational effectiveness.

A dynamic organization is one that provides opportunities for the continuous self-renewal of its members, based on their needs, as the organization adjusts its objectives to the changing needs of its publics. Regardless of the competence of its professional personnel, the adult education organization can quickly become reified and obsolete unless these individuals are afforded continuous opportunity to engage in in-service and graduate education as part of and requisite to the changing requirements, and hence performance, of their roles. Adult educators at all levels of the organization should have the opportunity to define their training needs.

Continuing funding and support for programs are positively related to the demonstrated efficiency and effectiveness of the adult education organization. Adult education organizations have always been accountable to their relevant publics, funding agencies, and legislative bodies at the local, state, and federal levels. But there is increasing demand for accurate manifestations of output in relation to the objectives of the organization and to the efficient utilization of resources to attain desired results. Adult educators must understand the significance of evaluation and accountability and commit energy and resources to means by which the adult education organization can demonstrate to its publics, funding agencies, the profession, and, where appropriate, the governance body, that desired program results are being attained.

The evaluation system must (1) measure the behavioral changes that result, (2) provide measures of effective application of learned behavior in real life situations, and (3) provide some measure of whether or not desired changes have occurred in the social and economic patterns of relevant publics. The "proof of the pudding" is whether the program has reached its micro teaching-level objectives and the organization's macro objectives. Accountability depends on the development and utilization of evaluation systems that measure the expected behavioral changes in individuals and groups. Appropriate means must be established and utilized at all levels of the adult education organization for reporting results in a form that demonstrates the degree of effectiveness of programs.

The accountability process requires the organization to (1) identify the real needs of relevant publics, (2) develop program designs to meet those needs, (3) package program delivery systems for effective implementation, (4) develop realistic and feasible evaluative systems, and (5) establish meaningful systems through which results may be disseminated to those to whom the organization is accountable. Increased emphasis on the evaluation/accountability process can improve the adult education organization's program, the processes through which its programs are developed and implemented, and the systemic structures through which it strives to meet the needs of relevant publics.

Task 4. The adult educator must understand and become committed to a tested conceptual framework for programming.

Adult educators must be knowledgeable about and understand the total setting within which their organization's programs are generated and effected. They must acquire and utilize a tested conceptual framework that enables them to identify the needs of their publics, to obtain commitment from such publics to act, and to design and implement programs that will produce substantive changes in the learners and their social structure.

Nine program models were reviewed in Chapter 2. Not all of these models were generated through the conceptual approach to model building. As noted in Chapter 3, a conceptual programming model lends itself to further testing. Adult educators must continue to challenge and test their organization's conceptual model, employed in programming, and make needed adjustments within the organization for maximal effectiveness in planning, designing and implementing, and evaluating and accounting for the organization's programs.

Task 5. The adult educator must develop a sensitivity and commitment to objective, systemic analysis for facilitating the organization's responsiveness and renewal to meet the constantly changing needs of its publics.

Adult educators must practice constant vigilance of and develop sensitivity to the changing environment in which their organization functions. Sensitivity and commitment to the needs of the people the organization serves and willingness to change functions, structure, and processes within the accepted mission, philosophy, and objectives of the organization will ensure viability.

The general process by which renewal operates is through (1) intensive involvement of adult educators and lay leaders in developing programs; (2) intensive and open dialogue, confrontation, and coping with problems affecting the functions, structure, and processes of the adult education organization; (3) thorough understanding of past and present historical bases, programs, and clientele; (4) sensitivity to needs and the potential for meeting needs; and (5) understanding change, societal influences, and how to cope with change. Only when adult educators can objectively study themselves, the organization, the organization's program, and the environment in which they function can adjustments be made within the organization and adaptation made to the social environment for maximal effectiveness. Inclusion of the renewal element in the conceptual programming model flows out of our contentions that (1) organizational renewal is ongoing, (2) targeting and retargeting of the organization's publics is ongoing, and (3) renewal flow is concurrent with linkage throughout the planning subprocess.

The organizational renewal process flows directly into linkage with target publics, because such linkage is essential to planning. Knowles (1970) and Tyler (1971) refer to the philosophy of an organization as filtering the ultimate choice of educational needs and learning objectives, while McClure (1978) notes that "a typical mistake made by the organization when beginning the planning process is to begin immediately with statements of goals and objectives. . . . A statement of organizational philosophy must be developed to form a basis of agreement among organizational members from which goals and objectives logically can follow" (p. 459). Thus, the organization's renewal is tied to linkage with its publics and, ultimately and conceptually, to the whole of planning through needs identification, assessment, and analysis.

Linkage With Publics and Related Processual Tasks

In the conceptual programming model, linkage is basic to the entire programming process and consists of four elements: (1) study, analysis, and mapping of the organization's publics; (2) identifying target publics; (3) identifying and interfacing with leaders of target publics; and (4) collaborative identification, assessment, and analysis of needs specific to a target public. *Linkage,* in the planning subprocess, may be loosely defined as the temporary blending of two systems—the organization and its target public—into one system to achieve a common purpose.

Adult education organization programs have their origin in identified, assessed, and analyzed needs of the organization's publics. Contingent upon the perceived mission of the organization, these publics could conceivably constitute the total population or specified aggregates of people (target publics) within a designated geographic or political entity.

Determination of the needs of the adult education organization's publics is the most challenging, perplexing, and necessary task confronting the professional adult educator. Research findings on motivation, learning, and change underscore the absolute necessity of focusing the organization's programs on the identified, assessed, and analyzed needs of specific target publics if the attention, interest, and commitment of such groups toward change is to be secured. These studies further emphasize that the retention of the interest and commitment of these target publics to change will depend to a large measure upon the immediate and continued satisfaction they experience with regard to the gratification or fulfillment of their perceived needs.

Needs are determined by a multitude of psychological, social, and cultural factors. The origin and intensity of such needs are related or linked to systems of patterned interaction and processes of socialization through which humankind acquires a distinctive lifestyle. *Lifestyle* may be defined as the psychological, social, and cultural manifestation of cumulative behavior (covert and overt) that has been learned slowly and sometimes painfully throughout a person's life span in responding to stimuli encompassed in his or her social environment.

The expansiveness of the social environment and hence the degree of socialization are directly related to the experiential opportunities afforded people during their life span. Social environment includes both cultural and social forces. Culturally, lifestyle is a manifestation of learned behavior acquired in the process of growing up. It includes not only the way of making and doing things, but also the pattern of interaction with others, attitudes and values, beliefs and ideas, and feelings. Socially, learned behavior, lifestyle, and hence needs, are influenced by expectations and normative standards imposed upon a person by primacy, peer, reference, and social groupings with which that person identifies.

The import of cultural and social forces on human behavior cannot be overemphasized. To cope with needs, it is imperative that the adult educator understand how needs are linked to cultural heritage. The needs of individuals are meaningful to the extent that they perceive that fulfillment of those needs will help them achieve greater equilibrium with their defined cultural context and social environment. Too, the influence of peer and social groups on the individual's needs must be taken into account in diagnosing those needs. That is, the expectations of peer and social groups of the behavior and needs of the individual may be more dominant than any other single factor.

Intervention in the lives of people through educational programs designed and promoted by adult education organizations requires that adult educators understand the culture (way of life) of the individuals or group that they are attempting to change, and to have access (entree) into the distinctive social grouping in which such culture is maintained and nurtured.

The existence of definable social groupings in society is all-pervasive. Identity with such groupings commences with the cradle (family) and extends throughout the life span. Social groups have their origin in two social processes, namely, differentiation and evaluation. These groupings are established and maintained through patterned interaction (social relationships) of members of the group and their adherence (conformity) to mutually agreed upon norms and standards that results in shared goals, beliefs, values, attitudes, customs, and sentiments.

A significant element of such groups is the evolution of "influentials" as leaders who wield considerable influence on the behavior and actions of individual members, as well as the collective group. These persons acquire their positions of influence through reputation, heritage, as well as a host of other means. They mirror the values, beliefs, and sentiments of their followers. Their leadership positions may be of a formal or informal nature. These leaders generally possess the authority or power to grant or deny access to their respective group.

In maintaining a position within such grouping, the average person continually strives to measure up to the expectations of peers and the leadership. Such persons' intrinsic motives are oriented toward the preservation of a way of life to which they are accustomed and which makes sense to them as well as to the expectations of their peers. It is apparent from the foregoing discussion that adult educators cannot take lightly the task of relating programs to the needs of their publics.

Simply put, the content of programs designed to effect change in established behavioral patterns cannot be determined as a result of hunch or hearsay. Too, adult educators cannot assume that what is good for one sector of the public will be good for other sectors. Rather, adult educators must be able to differentiate between or map publics, their needs, the sources of such needs, and the sociocultural factors that may facilitate or impede participation of such publics in programs designed to help them satisfy or fulfill their perceived needs.

Adult educators, as change agents, must be capable of identifying the leaders of target publics and establishing effective linkage with these leaders through meaningful dialogue and the delivery of programs that will result in the immediate gratification of the intrinsic needs of their followers. Only after intrinsic needs of a given public are satisfied can the adult educator expect any success in having such publics cope with extrinsically motivated needs. That is, in the initial stages of the change process, adult educators must begin their program efforts with people where they are, rather than attempting to call their attention to needs with which they may be unfamiliar or in which they have little interest.

Adult educators must recognize that the socialization process is slow and arduous, and that it begins with the perceived needs and motives of learners in their social environment. The adult educator, the potential learners, and their leaders must be involved in the identification, assessment, and analysis of needs that will ultimately constitute the basis for an educational program.

Let us turn now to the processual tasks that contribute to the adult educator's cognitive map in understanding and implementing the linkage concept. These processual tasks deal with (1) analyzing and interpreting the social and cultural contexts of the environment in which the adult education organization functions, (2) selecting and applying conceptual tools and processes for mapping the organization's publics, (3) identifying and ordering those target publics to be served by the adult education organization, (4) selecting and applying appropriate processes for identifying the formal and informal leadership within the target publics, (5) understanding and applying the processes and strategies for interfacing with identified leaders, and (6) understanding and applying the process of promoting collaborative needs identification, assessment, and analysis with identified leaders and their followers. These linkage processual tasks consist of logical and deductive steps that give precision to planning.

Study and analysis of publics.   In the planning subprocess of the conceptual programming model (Table 3-3), the first order of business under linkage involves the study and analysis of the organization's publics, which leads to our first linkage processual task.

> *Task 1.* The adult educator must become thoroughly acquainted with and knowledgeable about the social and cultural contexts of the environment in which the adult education organization functions.

If adult educators are to establish and maintain linkage between the organization and its publics, they must acquire a comprehensive cognitive map of the organization's environment. Such a cognitive map must encompass more than a mere knowledge of political and geographic boundaries. It must include a thorough knowledge and understanding of the people who reside within the area the organization seeks to serve. Although people may be tied together spatially and in terms of a common government, numerous differences between and among people may and often do exist with regard to lifestyles, heritage, socioeconomic status, culture, patterns of interaction, and normative standards. Recognition of these differences is an essential strategy in identifying needs and ultimately tailoring planned programs to the needs of the many and different individuals, clientele groups, or publics that conceivably could reside within a given area.

Lippitt, Watson, and Westley (1958) indicate that adult educators, as change agents, must understand patterns of interaction, social differentiation, leadership and power, values and value systems, and the information base of a particular public. Bertrand (1967) supplies a set of concepts that verify our experiences, with *society* as organized groupings of people who have a common identification, substantial numbers, established relationships, and relative permanence. Within society are both social systems and social organizations.

The social systems concept is vital to our notion of planning, along with its elements and "master processes" as defined by Bertrand (1967). The elements are beliefs, sentiments, goals, norms, status role, rank, power, sanctions, and facility. The master processes within which these elements interact and are refined are communication, boundary maintenance, socialization, social control, institutionalization, and the process we have emphasized: systemic linkage.

Within the elements and master processes of a social system are concepts that provide additional analytical tools with which the adult educator can begin the complex process of understanding its social context. Other valuable conceptual tools are *social structure,* the set of fixed relationships among and within groups, and *social stratification,* the ranking of people or groups of people within the overall social system. The specific use of such concepts will be dealt with shortly.

This overview of linkage is meant to enlarge adult educators' understanding of their organization's social context. A set of conceptual tools is needed for substantial linkage, a fact that becomes more apparent as we move to the mapping process. However, our concept of linkage is committed to the facilitation of the individual's development within the social milieu. This element of individual development in the linkage concept places a heavy responsibility on adult educators in that they must be concerned with (1) individual integrity and dignity, (2) the dynamics of group behavior that affect the individual, (3) the learning process and quality of the social environment, and (4) the social trends that affect the organization's mission and philosophy (Shane and Shane, 1970).

Mapping of publics.   After thorough study and analysis of the adult education organization's publics, the next step in the linkage process is the difficult and often unfamiliar task for the adult educator, that of mapping the adult education organization's publics. Mapping is that element of the linkage process in which the adult educator, as change agent, engages for the purpose of identifying and delineating learner groups and systems to be served by the adult education organization.

> *Task 2.* The adult educator must be adept at selecting and applying conceptual tools and processes for mapping the adult education organization's publics.

In selecting the conceptual tools and processes for mapping the organization's publics, the adult educator should consider mapping as involving two logical stages. The first is giving particular attention to the defined or inferred mission of the various publics, their membership, patterns of interaction, values, beliefs, sentiments, norms, leadership, and sociocultural origins. The second logical step in mapping the adult education organization's publics is the discernment of distinctive patterns of interaction between and among people residing in the area. These patterns of interaction are reflected in social groupings that are comprised of aggregates of people bound together by common goals, lifestyles, values, beliefs, sentiments, and heritages. The behavior of these groups is generally governed and regulated by normative standards that are enforced by their membership and leaders. Entree into these groups requires adult educators to show understanding and empathy. Equally important is knowing about points of access, namely, the leadership of the groups.

The importance of knowing about and understanding the differences that exist between these groups is highlighted by the fact that their needs, and hence their readiness to participate in externally contrived programs, will vary. For example, variations in the socioeconomic status and the cultural heritage of social groupings cannot be taken lightly in designing programs for these publics. Programs planned for one particular group may not be compatible with the needs and interests of another group.

Numerous distinctive social groupings could exist within the adult education organization's environment. The identification of these groupings, based on factors such as special interests, ethnic background, socioeconomic status, religion, and culture, is paramount to the potential and probable success of adult educators in effecting programs that will yield maximal change in the patterned behavior of their publics.

One might ask why adult education should be concerned with social systems, other than via the logic of deductive analysis, since it would seem that the teacher-learner relationship is the most important factor in learning. However, positive behavioral change or new behavior is the objective of all educational efforts and, as Kelman and Warwick (1973) put it, "new behavior can gain continuity and stability only to the extent that new supports have been built around it" (p.35). An important condition for that stability is "the extent to which the new behavior is integrated into the structure of a person's social relationships" (p.35). In other words, the new learning or behavior that is facilitated by an organization's educational endeavors can best be reinforced by the social system of which the individual learner is a part.

As noted in the literature, thorough knowledge and understanding of social dynamics are essential to successful mapping of publics. Communities contain patterns of social groupings. Each group has both unique and shared beliefs and values that, observed in individual and collective lifestyles, are readily discernible, given the intellectual tools and concepts to forge linkage with these groups. To achieve such linkage, the organization must first map its publics to discern the general social context and the subsystems contained therein. Efficient mapping leads to the attainment of three goals: (1) identification of the adult education organization's target publics within the larger publics; (2) linkage with the target publics through identification of and interfacing with its formal and informal leaders; and (3) acquisition of a source of reinforcement for new ideas and practices introduced through these leaders and their followers (potential learners) in each of the target publics.

Three logical preliminary questions are likely to be, What is mapping? What are some conceptual tools that can be used in mapping publics? and Where do change agents start in their efforts to map the organization's publics? We will begin the discussion of mapping from the perspective of the organization.

Kimball (1975) defines *mapping* as a process the change agent engages in for the purpose of identifying and delineating target publics or social groupings to be served by the organization. Rhenman (1973) gives four criteria for mapping that underscore his concept of "change" organizations as proactive and adaptive to a changing environment. His criteria for mapping by a proactive organization are (1) maintaining a constant interchange with the societal context, that is, acting on and reacting to it; (2) providing alternatives to meet the problems of mapping that usually evolve from new environmental forces; (3) having the ability to discern those parts of the organization that are responsive to and responsible for mapping; and (4) having an arrangement for preserving or propagating successful experiences.

Denney's (1972) concern is with mapping service centers. He reduces the analysis of human habitation to the major elements of (1) the number of residents in a community, (2) the service area of the community, (3) the speed with which services can be delivered, and (4) the technology available to facilitate coping with the environment. His major objective is to assist planners in devising categories of service that are sufficiently flexible to determine numerous later services and the degree of specialization of such services. From the standpoint of an adult education organization, Denney's approach to mapping can be helpful in determining the distribution of services to meet educational needs of the populace.

Several authors have proffered various conceptual approaches to mapping the organization's publics. These approaches are (1) social system analysis (Loomis, 1960); (2) social stratification (Williams, 1960); (3) social differentiation (Bertrand, 1967); and (4) cultural analysis (Spicer, 1952).

A *social system* is an aggregate of people linked together in a network or system of social relationships. Its members interact according to the norms or standards accepted by the group. Their relationships and interactions are largely based on a set of interrelated roles and statuses. They are united or held together to a greater or lesser degree by a sense of common identity or a similarity of interests.

Social system analysis refers to analyzing the social structure of a group of people whose interactions are directed toward goal attainment and guided by patterns of structured and shared symbols and expectations (Loomis, 1960). Such analysis emphasizes the interrelatedness of subsystems through mutual dependencies. The manifest and latent functional or dysfunctional effects of each part of the system on other parts of the system, and on the system as a whole, are identified and delineated. Analysis, in terms of social systems, is uniquely characteristic of functionalism. *Functionalism* may be defined as the interdependence of the patterns and institutions of a society and their interaction in maintaining cultural and social unity (Loomis, 1960).

In elaborating on his concept of social system analysis, Loomis identifies nine elements and six master processes that he suggests as a powerful conceptual tool for change agents to use in identifying and analyzing social systems within the larger social structure. These elements and processes, with their definitions, are listed here to provide the reader with a perspective of Loomis's concept of social system analysis.

The nine elements of a social system are:

1. *Beliefs:* the cumulative knowledge possessed by persons who make up the system; may include superstitions or folklore, or anything that people perceive to be true.

2. *Sentiments:* affectively charged feelings possessed by members of a system that substantially influence how they respond; these feelings may be either covert or overt.

3. *Ends or objectives:* the outcomes that members of a social system expect to attain from their roles and membership in the social system.

4. *Facilities:* the means and resources available to a system for use in attaining its ends or objectives.

5. *Status roles:* the expectations that members of a system have for various positions that exist in the system.

6. *Power:* the concept of control in this system.

7. *Norms:* those defined or inferred rules that prescribe what is socially acceptable or unacceptable; one rule may be that norms regulate the behavior of members of the system.

8. *Social rank:* ranking of members of a social system according to what is rated high or low in that system; as judged by the system, overall worth determines social rank; subsystems within the larger social system also are accorded social rank.

9. *Sanctions:* certain rewards that are available to the system to secure and ensure compliance of its members.

Loomis posits six master processes for understanding a system as a dynamic, functioning entity. Comprehension of these six master processes and their definitions is essential to observing and understanding change as it is introduced into and processed by a social system:

1. *Communication:* the process by which interactions, attitudes, ideas, and emotions are transmitted among system members and by which knowledge and attitudes are formed and modified through interaction.
2. *Boundary maintenance:* the process for preserving and maintaining the identity and integrity of the system through guarding against encroachments by other systems.
3. *Socialization:* the learning and internalization of social and cultural heritages that facilitate individual integration into a social group; characterized as a lifelong process.
4. *Institutionalization:* the legitimation and subsequent internalization of certain patterns of behavior for which sanction has resulted in acceptance as right and positive.
5. *Systemic linkage:* a process by which two or more social systems temporarily form a link between one or more elements to attain mutual goals.
6. *Social control:* the process by which behaviors of the members of the system are somehow regulated to make them compatible with the functions of the system.

Social stratification, as a conceptual tool for identifying and mapping publics, is defined by Williams (1960) as "the ranking of individuals on a scale of superiority-inferiority-equality, according to some commonly accepted basis of valuation" (p. 89). Based on the premise that all societies are stratified according to certain socioeconomic and other variables, Bertrand (1967) identifies and defines seven social phenomena that collectively lead to the stratification or grouping of people in a larger social context:

1. *Income level:* per capita annual income.
2. *Occupation:* an individual's means of livelihood as well as the identification of occupational groupings.
3. *Education:* various levels of education represented in the system, the average level of education, the level most represented, and the type of education represented.
4. *Genealogy:* familial linkage.
5. *Reputation:* system members' prestige, power, leadership, friendliness, among others, as perceived by the system.
6. *Aspiration:* system members' self-concept, self-motivation, and goals.
7. *Historical development:* ascertaining the origin of some of the system's knowledge and beliefs and better understanding the system's culture.

A third conceptual tool for mapping is labeled by sociologists as *social differentiation.* This conceptual tool enables the change agent to classify the people within a system or social stratum by certain characteristics. For example, within a given public, community, system, or social class, the change agent can classify people by age, sex, and other factors. The social phenomena or criteria used are role, sex, age, ethnic background, and socioeconomic status, definitions of which follow (Bertrand, 1967):

Role: pattern of behavior, structured around specific rights and duties and associated with a particular status within the system.

Age: chronological ages categorized and grouped.

Sex: distribution and proportion of sexes represented.

Ethnic background: distribution and proportion of the differential ethnic characteristics and cultural differences associated with each.

Socioeconomic status: a form of stratification based on factors such as income, wealth, education, and social status.

Spicer (1952) and Goodenough (1963) present a convincing argument that the culture of a group or system is the most important variable in understanding how change can be introduced and implemented in that system. *Culture* refers to a body of knowledge, concepts, values, and skills that is produced by a social grouping over a long span of time and has been passed on from one generation to the next. Culture is an all-inclusive phenomenon, consisting of all the aspects of the social grouping's environment. It includes language, beliefs, attitudes, modern or primitive methods of production, the educational system, and all belongings. Culture not only consists of the artifacts and material types of possessions, it also includes sets of patterns of behaviors and attitudes that are taught by one generation and are modified by life experiences of each succeeding generation. Such patterns of behaviors and attitudes are felt to be "right" or appropriate patterns by the people who hold them (Spicer, 1952).

Cultural analysis is a conceptual tool strongly supported by cultural anthropologists as a means for understanding the behavior of social groupings in the larger social context. *Cultural analysis* may be defined as an in-depth study of a social grouping's way of life that is transmitted from one generation to another and thus forms, among other factors, a source of knowledge, beliefs, sentiments, and values (Spicer, 1952).

As a mapping tool, cultural analysis provides the change agent with insights into the reasons for behaviors, beliefs, and lifestyles of the system. It further tends to ensure the adult education organization against cultural bias that might result in the social system's rejection of the change agent, the program, and the organization. Spicer (1952) provides an illuminating perspective on the importance of cultural analysis as a tool for mapping publics in which he presents several cases where change agents and their programs were rejected by social systems because of their lack of understanding of the culture within which they were trying to work.

The dilemma facing the change agent in mapping publics involves more than a need to understand the conceptual tools discussed. Mapping also involves a high degree of skill in using the tools and knowing when to begin the process. Kimball (1975) suggests that mapping begins with change agents acquiring a broad picture of the social context in which they operate. This social context may be either large or relatively small. Within the social context, several publics, social systems, subcultures, or communities may exist. Hence, it is important that change agents use their conceptual mapping tools to identify and analyze those groupings that will become the principal target(s) in implementing the processual tasks concerned with leader identification, interfacing, and needs identification, assessment, and analysis.

Several terms may be used to define publics, including system, learner groups, special-interest groups, neighborhood, people, area or territory, and community. Consequently, it seems logical to explore what some of these terms mean and ways they might be used by the change agent.

A *public* may be defined as a group of people who (1) share common interests and identity, (2) manifest frequent or continuous interactions, and (3) are spatially distributed over a small area or a larger territory. The characteristics of a public are the same characteristics listed in Loomis's (1960) model of a social system. The change agents' orientation usually determines the "label" they assign to their public(s).

Because of the frequency with which the concept public is used in conjunction with the concept community, it seems reasonable to explore some of the definitions of a community. Early on, Loomis and Beegle (1957) defined *community* as "a social system encompassing a territorial unit within which members carry on most of their day-to-day activities necessary in meeting common needs" (p. 22). In a 1975 speech, Kimball cited Sanders's definition of *community* as "a territorially organized system coextensive with a settlement pattern in which (1) an effective communications network operates, (2) people share common facilities and services distributed within this settlement pattern, and (3) people develop a psychological identification with the 'locality symbol' (the name)" (p.1). Cary (1971) views a community as an aggregate of people, spatially related to one another, who possess common beliefs, sentiments, and goals. More recently, Park (1973) listed the essential characteristics of a community as "(1) a population territorially organized, (2) more or less completely rooted in the soil it occupies, (3) its individual units living in a relationship of mutual interdependence that is symbiotic rather than societal, in the sense that the term applies to human beings" (p. 34).

Within these four definitions of a community, at least five key characteristics can be discerned. These characteristics are (1) a group of people; (2) shared interests, attitudes, and activities; (3) common identity (agreement on a locality, perhaps a name); (4) frequent and continuing interaction; and (5) living in an identifiable territory or space that can be mapped. These five characteristics are not entirely mutually exclusive. To be a generally acceptable, universally usable treatment of the concepts public and community for adult education change agents, some additions may be in order. Nonetheless, the five characteristics listed confirm that systems analysis, social stratification, social differentiation, and cultural analysis, as discussed earlier in this chapter, are functional tools that can be used by the adult educator to identify and map publics.

Many adult educators and community development specialists advance the notion that this concept of a "general" community is analogous to the

Loomis-Beegle (1957) concept of an overall social system. This premise suggests that, within a public, community, or general social system, there probably exist a number of subpublics, subsystems, or subcommunities, or combinations thereof. Some writers on the subject prefer to label such subgroups as functional communities, communities of interest, or subsystems. Our point is to emphasize that such subgroups are concerned with a defined or inferrred function. Examples of functional subpublics or subcommunities in a larger system or public might include the following:

> *Political community:* county, township, and city governments; political organizations.
> *Educational community:* schools—primary, secondary, vocational colleges, universities; nonformal education.
> *Mass communications community:* TV, newspapers, radio.
> *Economic community:* employment, industry, business, finance.
> *Recreational and cultural community:* public parks, museums, libraries, and various such facilities; private recreation and leisure-time arrangements.
> *Supportive services community:* health facilities and opportunities; welfare efforts.
> *Social control community:* social sanction, police, courts, correction services.
> *Religious community:* churches and spiritual organizations.
> *Physical, geographical, ecological, or environmental community:* planning, development, watershed, and special functional arrangements.

These nine examples of functional publics or communities are not all-inclusive. A further division of several of these functional publics may be needed, depending on the programmatic situation confronted by the adult educator. The important point is that a certain type of public or community exists to serve each function.

An additional factor emerges in building an understanding of publics. Publics function at many levels, or in a hierarchy, whether they are general publics, subpublics, or groupings. Examining a general public may clarify this point.

Using the key characteristics or elements of a public or social system referred to earlier, one may identify a unit that might be called a family, neighborhood, community, or special-interest subsystem. At other levels, larger in size, a county or a region comprised of several counties may be identified. Continuing in this manner, a state, a nation, or the world may be defined as a public or community.

Tangipahoa Parish, Louisiana, is used to illustrate application of the mapping process. Each of the four maps in Figure 4-1 represents specific subpublics of the parish: political, mass communications, economic, and educational. Implicit in these representations is the fact that a considerable amount of overlapping exists among them. Nonetheless, the effort to delineate subpublics into categories of activities can greatly facilitate the effectiveness and efficiency of the organization's planning efforts.

Before linkage can be effected with a social system such as Tangipahoa

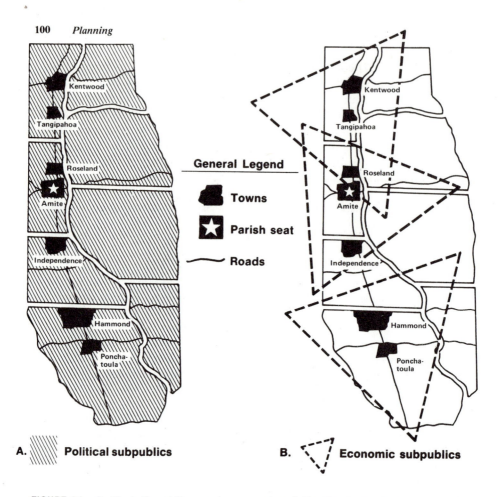

FIGURE 4-1.   An illustration of the mapping concept applied to Tangipahoa Parish, Louisiana

Parish, the adult educator must start within the broader planning subprocess. For example, in preparation for studying, analyzing, and mapping publics, the adult educator needs first to consider certain questions regarding his/her role and that of the organization: What services does the adult education organization offer? What is the stated mission of the adult education organization? What is the role of the adult educator? Which of its publics does the adult education organization wish to reach? Such questions make the processual task of mapping more specific to the situational context within which the adult education organization is expected to function.

   In this mapping exercise, the first task is to partition the larger political system (parish) into distinct, incorporated communities, wards, or voting precincts. Each of these has legal, identifiable boundaries, demonstrates the hierarchy concept, and provides a concept of the general public, that is, those

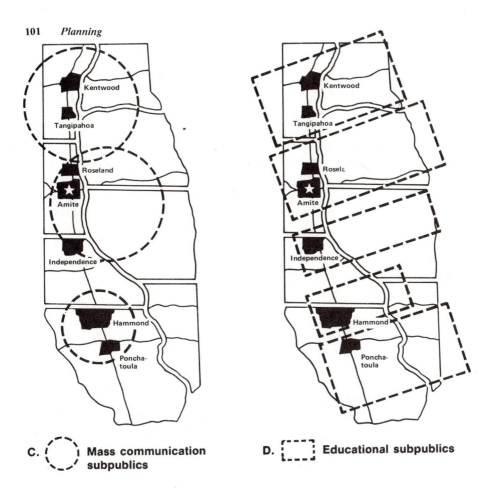

C. Mass communication subpublics

D. Educational subpublics

subpublics where the people have shared goals and concerns, call their neighborhood by name, and interact frequently.

Figure 4-1A depicts several of the political entities within Tangipahoa Parish. Within each of these political entities are both formal and informal leaders the adult educator needs to identify and interface with to gain effective access into a particular political entity.

Identification and mapping of economic subpublics is a challenging task. The economic subpublics of the parish are indicated in Figure 4-1B. An understanding of the economic subpublics within a larger system is helpful in pinpointing the type, size, and nature of economic and industrial complexes in a specific geographic area. Such information enhances the adult educator's ability to collaborate with economic and industrial leaders in offering adult education programs to their constituent worker publics.

Figure 4-1C demonstrates an effort to map the mass communications subpublics of the parish. Delineation in this case also poses problems because there are no firmly fixed boundaries. The lines enclosing the areas serviced by newspapers, radio, and television provide only arbitrary boundaries. Each of the three mass communications subpublics is serviced by at least one local newspaper and radio station. These two local media are supplemented by newspapers and radio and television programs emanating from three large metropolitan areas that are within 50–60 miles of the parish boundaries. Information about the mass communications subpublics may be helpful in deciding which to use with regard to specific adult education programs and the publics to which they are to be directed.

Figure 4-1D depicts the educational subpublics of the parish. Knowledge of these subpublics is necessary to discern among those potential target publics patterns of interaction, shared concerns and interests, and leader and power figures.

The same procedure as described and depicted in Figure 4-1 may be used in mapping other publics of interest to the adult education organization.

By way of conclusion, adult educators, in mapping their organization's publics, must display the following abilities:

> Ability to delineate the overall social context of the system or publics within which the adult education organization functions.
>
> Skill in using tested, research-based, conceptual tools of systems analysis, social stratification, social differentiation, and cultural analysis to study, analyze, and map the organization's publics and identify the target publics or subsystems within the larger system of publics in which the organization functions.
>
> Knowledge and skill in analyzing the behavior and structure of each of those subsystems identified as existing or potential target publics.

Identifying target publics.   After the adult education organization's publics have been mapped, the next step in the linkage process of planning is identification of target publics. The processual task related to this step follows.

> *Task 3.* Based on a thorough diagnosis of the organization's publics and their perceived relevance to the mission of the adult education organization, the adult educator must identify and order those target publics to be served.

The relevancy of the numerous social groupings (target publics) within the organization's environment will be determined by adult educators' perception of the mission of the organization. That is, the objectives and resources of the organization must be considered in sorting out those target publics toward which adult educators, at the operational level, should direct their efforts. This sorting out or screening process ideally should culminate in the identification and ordering of target publics. It is reasonable to assume that, as the mission of the adult education organization changes, its adult educators will redefine and reorder target publics.

Identification of target publics is followed by placing the potential target publics in priority order. The rationale for this step is both logical and practical. An organization, at best, can serve only those publics for which it has the learning resources. The actual number of publics to be served can be resolved by giving thought to the following questions: What are the mission and philosophy of the adult education organization? What does the mission imply with respect to the publics to be served? What learning resources are available to the organization? Are some of the identified publics more relevant than others to the mission of the organization? Questions like these serve to illustrate that the primary criteria for targeting its public(s) comes from the organization itself.

The mission and philosophy of the organization may specify certain publics, or they may be specified through a legislative mandate. The organization's structure and the availability of its learning resources may determine what part of the potential public(s) can be served, for example, an adult basic education (ABE) division or unit. Finally, the particular area of expertise of the adult educators may help define the public(s) they are likely to work with. These elements then are compared to what is known about the actual or potential publics to establish linkage between organizational aims and capabilities and the presumed learning needs of the target publics. Such activities should lay the groundwork for the next processual task, leader identification, by targeting specific sets of learners and by defining the degree of continuity between organizational resources and the presumed learners' needs.

Identifying leaders.   The behavior of social groupings generally is governed and regulated by normative standards that are enforced by their membership and leaders. Thus, following identification of target publics, the next logical step is to identify leaders of those publics so the adult educator can initiate contact with them.

> *Task 4.* The adult educator must select and apply appropriate processes for identifying the formal and informal leadership within target publics.

Entree into the target public requires that adult educators, as change agents, identify closely with the formal and informal leadership of that public. The necessity of this task to determining the needs of the target public and to securing their commitment to participate in programs focused on their needs is underscored by the authority and power vested in leader figures within the target public.

Practically all diffusion studies to date suggest that informal leaders hold the key to the adoption of practices by the majority of their followers. The likeness of the leaders in covert and overt characteristics to the total membership of their grouping is striking. The maintenance of positions of leadership in such groupings is contingent, to a rather large extent, upon the soundness of leaders' judgment, as perceived by the followers, in helping them safeguard and maintain their welfare.

Bertrand (1967) provides us with elements of social structure and stratification that help with specific leader identification. Rogers (1973) and Rothman (1976) stress the importance of groups as basic to all individuals and the importance of their leaders as keys to gaining entry into, communicating with, and influencing groups. So the practicality of utilizing both formal and informal leaders as linkage to groups of people is well established.

Identifying leaders with a defined public brings to mind the concept of power structure. There is general agreement that power structures exist in all social structures and that they greatly influence and are instrumental in any significant change efforts. Warren (1978) reminds us, however, that this power structure is not a single entity. Rather, it is an aggregation of numerous specific power structures operating in different areas. This discussion centers on how one goes about identifying and approaching target public leaders. It is not intended to dwell upon determinants of the power structure.

Approaches to identifying leaders. Although there are numerous approaches to identifying leaders, five are presented here that generally satisfy this requirement. These approaches, based on work by Bell and his co-workers, are cited by Freeman et al. (1970) and Tait, Bokemeier, and Bohlen (1974). Each is discussed with regard to (1) its basic assumption(s), (2) the procedures involved, (3) the types of actors involved, and (4) its advantage(s) and limitation(s). The five approaches suggested for identifying leaders are the (1) positional, (2) reputational, (3) personal influence or opinion leadership, (4) decision making, and (5) social participation approaches.

The *positional approach* to identifying leaders assumes that those who hold positions of authority actually make key decisions. This would imply that the power to influence decisions in a target public rests in the top leadership positions in formal organizations. It follows that persons who occupy these formal leadership positions in the major social, economic, political, cultural, and religious organizations in the target public actively participate in decision making. Furthermore, these leaders often control important resources that are needed for adult education programs. The success or failure of the positional approach to identifying leaders depends upon the degree to which its basic assumption is valid.

The positional approach involves selecting leaders on the basis of those who occupy identified leadership positions in formal organizations that are relevant to educational programming. Since different criteria may be needed to establish such relevance, the change agent must decide which are most useful in identifying positional leaders who can and will make a contribution to such programming.

The positional approach to identifying leaders has at least two advantages for the change agent. First, formal leaders are visible and relatively easy to identify. The change agent decides which positions are relevant to educational programming and develops a list of persons holding those positions. The second advantage is the relatively low cost of developing a list of target public leaders, although this approach to their identification has some limitations. First, some positional leaders do not exercise the power vested in the formal positions they occupy. For example, the chairperson of a county board of commissioners may not exercise the authority vested in his or her office to influence many county decisions. Second, this approach does not identify the informal leaders, that is, those persons who wield considerable influence "behind the scenes." A key influential in a civic organization may not hold an office within the organization. Further inquiry might reveal that this person exercises considerable influence in determining who is elected to office in the civic organization, as well as determining which special community projects are going to be promoted and supported by the organization. A third limitation is the difficulty often encountered by the change agent in identifying those positions with vested power or authority to influence decisions that are important to the target public.

The positional approach provides change agents an opportunity to identify some of the more influential persons in the target public who can contribute to the identification, assessment, and analysis of the target public's needs for inclusion in the planned program. It should be observed, however, that the change agent's judgment in designating positions of leadership and influence is critical to the success of using the positional approach to identify those leaders who can make a contribution to planning and implementing educational programs for adults within the target public.

The *reputational approach* to identifying leaders was developed in the 1950s as a tool for identifying community power actors. In his classic study of the power structure in Atlanta, Georgia, Hunter (1953) details the operation of power elites in social units smaller than a nation. Small groups of decision makers, with their satellite groups of intellectuals, front men, and implementers, in a real sense were a power elite.

An important assumption in the reputational approach to identifying leaders is that power to influence decisions in a target public is the consequence of reputation. This approach further assumes that leadership is too complex to be classified directly; therefore, it assesses the reputation for leadership. It also assumes that target public leaders cannot be identified solely by direct observation of who participates in public activities. Persons who operate in the background to influence program decisions also may be reputational leaders.

The procedure for identifying leaders through the reputational approach involves interviewing "knowledgeables" in the target public being studied. These knowledgeables are presumed to have broad knowledge of target public decision-making processes, and are in a position to identify those leaders who have the influence to affect a number of target public issues. Interviews with a number of these knowledgeables should reveal the reputed leaders in the target public. Identifying leaders through the reputational approach may be either a single-step or a two-step procedure.

In the single-step procedure, the knowlegeables interviewed are asked to identify and list leaders in the target public. This identification and listing is obtained by asking the "right" questions. An example of a "right" question might be, "Suppose a major policy issue, such as land-use planning, is before the public. This issue requires a decision by leaders with whom most of the people will identify and accept. Which persons would you choose to make the decision?"

In the two-step procedure, the change agent compiles lists of persons whom he or she believes are influential in the various sectors of the target public. These lists are presented to a panel of knowledgeables, who are asked to select from the list those persons reputed to have the most influence on decisions in the target public. The kinds and numbers of leaders the change agent needs to involve in the programming will determine whether the one-step or the two-step procedure will be used.

The reputational approach to identifying leaders has several advantages. It tends to identify target public leaders who function in the background, as well as those who are visible. Another advantage is that reputational leaders in a number of issue areas, both general and specific, can be identified, if these issues are included in the questions asked by the change agent. Yet another advantage of this approach is its ease of accomplishment.

Among its limitations is the question of whether the selected knowledgeables are, in fact, well informed about the target public. Another limitation is that the reputed leaders may not choose to exhibit their influence on target public decisions. Critics of the reputational approach often insist that it tends to identify leaders who have social status in the target public, but who do not participate in the actual decision making. Finally, some adult educators assert that this approach tends to identify generalized leaders and not those leaders who are needed to cope with specialized issues or problems.

The concept of the *personal influence* or *opinion leadership approach* to identifying leaders originated with Lazarsfeld, Berelson, and Gaudet (1944) in their study of the 1940 presidential election in Erie County, Ohio. According to Rogers and Kincaid (1981), the concept has undergone a number of changes. Over the past two decades, numerous researchers have sought to advance the understanding of this concept by determining the communication behaviors and social characteristics of personal influentials or opinion leaders as distinctive from those of their followers. Rogers and Kincaid (1981) define opinion leadership as "the degree to which an individual is able to informally influence other individuals' knowledge, attitudes, or overt behavior in a desired way with relative frequency" (p. 123). Personal influentials or opinion leaders may not hold formal leadership positions in the target public. Over the years, several researchers have maintained that there are as many types of opinion leaders as there are types of opinions (Lazarsfeld, Berelson, and Gaudet, 1944; Lionberger, 1960; Rogers, 1962; Rogers and Shoemaker, 1971; Rogers and Kincaid, 1981). For example, there are opinion leaders in politics, education, agriculture, fashion, sports, or other fields. These researchers indicate that each social stratum has its own opinion leaders.

The personal influence or opinion leadership approach assumes that there are "respected" persons in each target public to whom some people look for advice and information and who, through such consultations, influence the behavior and actions of these people. These "respected" persons cannot be identified solely by direct observation of who participates in various target public activities.

Rogers and Shoemaker (1971) advance several generalizations about the differences between personal influentials or opinion leaders and their followers. According to these authors, personal influentials or opinion leaders, as compared to their followers, can be characterized as having greater exposure to mass media, greater social participation, higher social status, and being more innovative. In characterizing personal influentials or opinion leaders and how they differ from their followers, one should observe that, because these leaders value their role in the community, they generally support and conform to its norms, an attitude that is essential to the maintenance of their leadership status.

Differing approaches may be used in identifying personal influentials or opinion leaders. Rogers and Shoemaker (1971) describe the first as the *sociometric* method, in which all or a representative sample of the people in the community or target public are polled to determine whom they go to for advice and information. Simple, direct questions are used to determine those persons most often used as sources of advice and information. The second and more direct method involves using a *selected group of informants* to designate personal influentials or opinion leaders. A direct question is asked of the informants, such as, "Who are the leaders in this target public?" The third method is referred to as the *self-designating* method. In this approach, reputed leaders are asked a series of questions to determine the degree to which each perceives himself or herself to be an opinion leader.

The personal influence or opinion leadership approach has several advantages. First, it identifies persons who have access to and control the communication network of their followers. Second, it provides clues about the existence of specific cliques in a target public. Knowledge of such subgroupings can greatly facilitate the work of the change agent. Third, because of its effectiveness in pinpointing influentials in the decision-making process regarding needs identification, this leadership approach is both efficient and economical.

Among the limitations of this approach is the prevalent question of whether the identified personal influentials or opinion leaders are active or passive in their communications behavior. Passive leaders may oppose or make no effort to support those needs that a majority of the public feels should be included in an adult education program. To overcome this obstacle, the change agent must identify and focus attention on these passive leaders, a pursuit that may require considerable time and effort.

The basic assumption underlying the *decision-making approach* to identifying leaders is that influence is acquired through contributing to and participating in decision making in the target public. Involvement in decision making is the criterion for recognizing and identifying leaders.

In the decision-making approach, a number of instances are selected that are presumed to represent those target public decisions made within a specified period of time. These decisions are studied and analyzed through various public media, minutes of meetings, personal interviews, or other sources to determine the names of persons who were cited as involved in the decisions. Through this approach, the change agent can assess actual rather than reputed behavior. Study and analysis of a variety of decisions, from their beginning through their implementation, may reveal the role that these decision makers performed at each stage of the issue. Such analysis may help the change agent to determine the extent to which the leaders who made decisions on each issue also actively participated in their implementation.

Leaders identified through the decision-making approach are active or instrumental in community issues. Analysis of several decisions may establish whether these decision makers are *generalized* leaders or *specialized* leaders. Since the decision-making approach focuses on identifying actual behavior rather than reputed influence, the identified leaders are highly visible.

This approach to identifying leaders has the advantages of pinpointing (1) actual behavior or influence, rather than reputed influence; (2) the actual overlap of influence from one issue to another; and (3) the decision maker's role at each stage of the action. A disadvantage of this approach is that it requires considerable time and may be expensive. Further, the decision-making approach fails to identify (1) those leaders who function in the background to influence public decisions and (2) those who wield sufficient influence to keep controversial issues from emerging into open confrontation.

The fifth and final approach to identifying leaders is the *social participation approach*. The assumption underlying this approach is that influence on target public decisions is acquired through membership and holding office in voluntary organizations. In this approach, each individual's participation in voluntary organization activities is combined into an individual index or score to denote degree of social participation. Those persons with the highest social participation scores are then identified as leaders. This approach involves determining which members of the target public participate in the action phases of almost all programs in a community or target public.

An important advantage of the social participation approach is that it identifies persons who actively participate in target public organizations, action groups, and public programs. Further, this approach may identify younger members of the community or target public who are actively participating in voluntary organizations and who aspire to leadership positions.

The social participation approach to identifying leaders has some limitations. First, it identifies only those persons who actively participate in target public organizations, action groups, and public programs, and not those who operate behind the scenes. There also is the question of the extent to which these active participants are the actual decision makers on key community or target public issues. The social participation approach has the added disadvantage of being time-consuming and possibly costly for the change agent. Further, the change agent may discover that some of the currently active decision makers in community or target public affairs may hold memberships in voluntary organizations but are neither active participants nor officeholders in those organizations.

As a hypothetical case, suppose you, as a change agent, wish to mobilize leader participation to alter the basic local power structure as you perceive it. Or, suppose you are not really sure of the type of leadership you wish to mobilize? Perhaps you want reputational leaders, but not those who operate behind the scenes. Which approach should you use?

Again, as in mapping, the question focuses on where one begins. As in mapping, we suggest that leader identification begins with the organization. From the organizational perspective, the change agent, as provider, appears as one who is willing to work with identified volunteer leadership to bring about change. The idea is to meld the provider system with the potential user system. The basic assumption about leadership, then, is one of reasoning that the values held by identified leaders reflect the beliefs and values of the public they serve as leaders.

Thus, we contend that neither of the five suggested approaches to leader identification, by itself, possibly can serve in every case to link the adult education organization to its publics and to identify real needs. We, therefore, suggest an eclectic attitude on the part of the change agent, and urge a combination of these approaches or a combination of elements of each approach to reach the desired objective of the specific instance. As an example, let us consider a literacy program. Perhaps, for continued funding purposes, it is essential to secure the support of recognized community leaders. But it is also important that the change agent make contact with informal leaders among the illiterates who can help legitimize the program to the target publics they represent. In this case, a strictly positional approach is likely to accomplish only part of the task of effective linkage. For the change agent operating from an organizational base, the positional approach is a minimum to attain the type of linkage desired.

We contend that the positional approach may be used in combination with elements from the four remaining approaches. In this way, if the change agent is sophisticated in the use of personal interviews and questionnaires, information might be obtained about a variety of leadership roles. A few questions might elicit information about people with reputations as knowledgeables. For example, "Who knows the most about how people in the community feel about Issue X?" A few other questions might relate to decisions from either a historical or an advocacy perspective; that is, they would elicit information either on leaders who have helped mold past decisions or on others, such as newspaper editors, who influence decisions by taking an advocacy role.

A final note: the change agent should always be interested in those who participate in social issues and social events, and should consider an active or vicarious involvement in those same issues and social events. This is to say that a good planner, seeking good linkage, should allocate some time and resources toward target public affairs from a participatory standpoint.

The identification of leaders of target publics is not sufficient. Linkage with target publics will not begin until or unless effective interfacing with these leaders has been established.

> *Task 5.* The adult educator must have knowledge and understanding of the processes and strategies for interfacing with the identified leaders of the target publics.

After the leaders have been identified, the change agent must consciously strive to establish communication with these persons through informal and meaningful dialogue. Such dialogue should be characterized by the familiar as perceived by the leader(s). That is, the inputs of leaders into initial conversations should be dominant. The change agent is characterized as a listener in the initial stages of such dialogue. The change agent should strive to exhibit as much understanding and empathy as possible.

Only after a "positive" two-way relationship is established should the change agent begin to interject external information inputs into the dialogue. Such dialogue should not be restricted to a single meeting. Ideally, the dialogue would be continued through the period of time required to establish a meaningful relationship between the leader(s) and the change agent.

The Beal et al. (1966) model, referred to in Chapter 2, has an element of participation that sustains the planning subprocess in the conceptual programming model. The steps in the Beal et al. model show continuing interaction with leaders. The conceptual programming model advocates a precise involvement of leaders in public programs, a trend apparent since the 1960s. As Bermant, Kelman, and Warwick (1978) brought out, the value preferences and choices inherent in social intervention are most likely to establish conflict points over four primarily ethical concerns: (1) choice of goals, (2) definition of the targets of change, (3) choice of means to implement change, and (4) assessment of the consequences. The principal effect of interfacing with these leaders is to resolve, in advance, many of the potential problems that might arise. The discussion of the mobilization of group leaders by both Rogers (1973) and Rothman (1976) is in keeping with this ethical commitment to program planning.

The assumptions underlying an ethical and precise involvement of community leaders in public programs echo the spirit of both organizational pluralism and the democratic process that can combat elitism. Certain aspects of group dynamics provide a psychological boost to participation by all persons involved in a social change. Finally, the sense of organizational renewal can be paralleled by community renewal through citizen (learner) participation.

From the perspective of program planning as part of the conceptual programming model, interfacing with leaders of target publics has two immediate ends. First, interfacing with and mobilizing these leaders is a key to building the element of trust that is essential to program planning. Next, from this trust and from our assumptions about the underlying community values these leaders represent, collaborative educational needs identification, assessment, and analysis can be conducted.

Involving leaders and learners in planning. Each processual task delineated thus far has contributed to the next processual task, which is considered the most important in the planning subprocess—promoting collaborative identification, assessment, and analysis of the learning needs of the organization's target publics. The general idea is that the adult educator, as programmer, in collaboration wth identified leaders of the target public(s) and their followers (potential learners) becomes intensively involved in a study of the situation to identify, assess, and analyze the educational needs of those publics. This process then becomes one of the organization's primary tasks in designing a program to meet those educational needs.

> ***Task 6.*** The adult educator must understand and be skillful in the application of the process of promoting collaborative needs identification, assessment, and analysis with target public leaders and their followers.

Through informal and meaningful dialogue with the leaders of a target public, the immediate perceived needs of the public represented by the leaders should come into focus. The immediate efforts of the adult educator should be directed toward generating programs focused on those felt needs that will result in almost instant payoff to the target public. Results perceived by the target public to be meaningful in satisfying their needs should enhance their state of readiness and receptiveness to considering external information that has a bearing on nonperceived needs. That is, the stage should be set for adult educators to begin channeling program inputs into the dialogue with the leaders and the followers that will cause them to translate extrinsic needs into felt needs.

The identification, assessment, analysis, and ultimate fulfillment of needs of distinctive target publics are of first priority in effectively relating the resources of the adult education organization to its publics. However, a long-term objective should be to increase the socialization of these different groups through effective educational programs to the extent that they become knowledgeable about, concerned with, and committed to seeking solutions to problems or needs that transcend the boundaries of individual groups and affect the welfare of the general public. Ideally, this stage of socialization will result in the linkage of leadership systems of target publics that will facilitate concerted effort on the part of the several publics in effecting needed changes that are outside the capability of a single group.

We have approached linkage with leaders primarily from a utilitarian, practical point of view; that is, they are useful "connections." However, there is an even deeper rationale for involving leaders and learners in adult education program planning. Several authors illustrate diverse support for such involvement (Schutz, Baker, and Gerlach, 1958; Knowles and Knowles, 1972; Long, Anderson, and Blubaugh, 1973).

Schutz, Baker, and Gerlach (1958) contribute a model of group development that is relevant to the conceptual thread being developed. They see three basic stages in group development: (1) inclusion, (2) control, and (3) affection. The first stage, *inclusion,* occurs when individuals feel that they are a part of the group in question; the second stage, *control,* occurs when these individuals have a great need to assume control of group growth. Both of these stages are relevant in that they imply involvement of individuals in planning their own learning, most particularly in the group context focused upon here. The third stage, *affection,* is positive feelings developed by the group members.

Knowles and Knowles (1972) also give us general principles of group development, particularly the observation that people are committed to goals in proportion to their degree of participation in determining those goals. An additional principle is that groups can be viewed as instruments for change, if (1) both "changers" and those who will change feel similar senses of group membership, (2) the group attraction outweighs the discomfort of a change, and (3) the group members share the same need perception. These three principles are vital in involving social system leaders and learners in a continuous identification, assessment, and analysis of systemic needs since, if needs are shared and learners and their leaders support an educational change, the chances are enhanced for effective behavioral change among the learners.

The process advocated by Long, Anderson, and Blubaugh (1973) includes several approaches to community development that are similar to the planning concept embraced in the conceptual programming model. Three of these are worth focusing on: (1) the community approach, (2) the information self-help approach, and (3) the special-purpose, problem-solving approach.

The *community approach* aims at broad-based participation, which includes sharing in decisions about goals and interests; that is, participation that is analogous to the advocated leader involvement. The *information self-help* approach begins with individual or group concern about some deficit or need in community living. This move toward community development can arise potentially from the interaction of a change agent and community leaders, as in the conceptual programming model. The information self-help approach definitely involves an educational program subsequent to determination of a community need. The *special-purpose, problem-solving* approach also begins with problem identification, a step vital to needs analysis in planning. All three of these approaches are predicated upon involving formal or informal (or both) community leaders in planning for change.

Adult education literature provides the final conceptual contribution here. Kempfer (1951) sounds a theme that will carry through this discussion of involving learners and their leaders in planning when he writes: "Skill in bringing adults into the process of identifying their educational needs and interests is an earmark of outstanding directors of adult education. . . . The most advanced kind of program planning . . . is that which makes identification of need an integral part of the educative process'' (pp. 62–63). Thus, we see that needs identification is the most important facet of adult education, and that is the aim of the detailed set of *processual tasks* related to planning, as approached in the conceptual programming model. The interaction with social system/community leaders/learners should provide the adult educator with a set of educational needs that might be met within the parameters of the mission, philosophy, and teaching resources of that educator's organization.

Adult education literature corroborates the elements of planning identified and discussed thus far. The several programming models detailed in Chapter 2 provide some points of similarity to the planning subprocess of the conceptual programming model that are worth citing.

The Beal et al. (1966) model parallels the conceptual programming model in several aspects. Those authors advocate extensive analysis and utilization of local social systems and their leaders to identify needs and to legitimize and diffuse social action. Lippitt, Watson, and Westley (1958) provide a set of ideas complementary to those of Beal and his co-workers. Their process of planned change begins with developing a need for change out of self-perception or group perception of a problem (this parallels the concept of "a felt need"). This type of need development is elemental in the change agent–systemic leader interaction. Also, one can see the process described by the Lippitt group as one of socialization in which, through ongoing interaction and problem solving, the change agent and his or her clients build a relationship of trust. The latter enables, first, identification of felt needs and, subsequently, less immediately conscious needs, all of which are potentially resolvable through educational means.

Houle (1972) and Kidd (1973) add concurrent thoughts about where to start in adult education programming. Houle implies in his programming model that the learners' interests are the focus of planning in adult education; that one should start with the learners' thoughts and concerns. Kidd advocates starting with learners' current interests, to *engage* them, so that less immediate interests might be met later. All of these approaches reinforce our notion of planning activities that are aimed squarely at analyzing the educational needs of target publics so that appropriate planned programs can be designed and implemented.

The concept of needs.   In the conceptual programming model, the general idea is that the adult educator, the identified target public leaders, and their followers become intensively involved in collaborative identification, assessment, and analysis of the educational needs of those publics. This collaborative effort is one of the primary tasks in planning to meet educational needs.

In speaking to the concept of needs, several questions arise that must be addressed: What is meant by needs? Who determines needs? What are some approaches to determining needs?

The literature is replete with definitions related to the needs concept. Tyler (1971) defines a *need* as the difference between the present condition of the learner and an acceptable norm. Maslow's (1970) hierarchy of needs is often cited by authors in their discussion of the needs concept. According to Maslow, needs may be arranged from the lowest and most fundamental to the highest. Within this hierarchy, a higher-level need is not activated until the individual has attained some level of satisfaction of the need(s) below it. Maslow's hierarchy of needs, from the lowest to the highest, includes (1) survival, (2) safety, (3) belonging, (4) recognition, (5) achievement, and (6) self-actualization. On the whole, an individual cannot satisfy any higher-level needs until preceding needs are satisfied. Maslow proposes three principles of operation for these needs: (1) gratification of the needs on each level, starting with the lowest, frees a person for higher levels of gratification; (2) those persons in whom a need has been satisfied are best equipped to deal with deprivation of that need in the future; and (3) healthy persons are those whose basic needs have been met so that they are principally motivated by the need to actualize their highest potentialities.

Havighurst (1952) equates needs with developmental tasks that occur within the several stages of life, ranging from infancy and early childhood to later maturity. A *developmental task* is defined as one that arises at or about a certain period in the individual's life, successful achievement of which leads to happiness and to success with later tasks. Conversely, failure leads to unhappiness for the individual, disapproval by the society, and difficulty with later tasks. Havighurst suggests that three forces influence developmental tasks within the several stages of life: (1) physical maturation, (2) cultural pressures of society, and (3) personal values and aspirations of the individual. The manifestation of Havighurst's treatise on needs is that certain developmental tasks come with great urgency during the several stages of life; at these stages, motivation to learn is intense and education becomes extremely important and effective. Havighurst refers to these stages as *teachable moments*. Hence the "teachable moment" becomes an important concept in the needs identification, assessment, and analysis processual task in the planning subprocess of the conceptual programming model.

Combs (1962) posits that the basic need of all human beings is to *strive for adequacy*. People seek not merely the maintenance of a *perceived self* but the development of an *adequate self,* a self capable of dealing effectively and efficiently with the necessities of life, both now and in the future.

Emerging from these definitions of needs is the notion that needs of a person or a group of persons who make up a target public are the cumulative effects of a host of psychological, social, cultural, and physiological factors.

Thus, needs can be defined as a deficiency, imbalance, lack of adjustment, or gap between the present situation and a set of societal norms believed to be more desirable. Needs imply a gap between *what ought to be* and *what is.* Leagans (1964) and Tyler (1971) illustrate the gap as follows:

WHAT OUGHT TO BE —Desirable situation

Gap   = Need   —Difference

WHAT IS   —Actual situation

What is is determined by collecting and studying pertinent information about the existing situation. Such information must be carefully collected, analyzed, and interpreted by the adult educator and leaders and learners of the target public. In general, people are concerned about their current situation. The adult educator, in collaboration with leaders of the target public and their followers, can use properly selected and interpreted information to analyze needs, to stimulate interest among the target public, and to arrive at alternative courses of action to fulfill these needs. Specifically, information must be gathered that relates to (1) current trends and projections, (2) physical factors, (3) people (what they perceive their needs to be), and (4) public issues and policy.

Care should be taken to select data that can be analyzed and presented and that are relevant to the needs of the target public. In most instances, the following questions can be used by the adult educator and leaders and learners to identify, collect, analyze, and present the kind of data to point up the significance of a situation for a given problem area or need:

Does a need really exist?
What is the basis of the need?
How widespread is the need? How many persons are affected by the need?
What is the relative importance of the need? In what way is this a social or economic need (or both)?
How do people feel about the seriousness of the need?
What are the potential consequences to the people if no effort is made to fulfill or meet the need?

Information that merely describes the current situation in a target public does not make a program; it only describes the existing situation. The findings of studies and surveys can only describe the situation; they cannot result in a program.

Adult educators need to take another step, that of deciding what ought to be or is expected by the target public, while at the same time being cautious to assure that the level of what ought to be is within the learners' capabilities.

The nature and extent of the need should point up the importance of the problem; the wider the gap between what ought to be and what is, the greater the problem.

The what-ought-to-be level can be determined from social norms, research findings, and value judgments by adult educators and the leaders of target publics. Research may disclose, for instance, that the use of selected, recommended practices in family resource management can result in considerable savings for families. These families or target publics may not be knowledgeable about such practices. The difference between the practices being followed by the families and the recommended practice mirrors the need.

The needs of a target public are determined through situation analysis: by finding their present situation, their possible situation, and the ideal situation. The *present* situation means *what is*; the *possible* means *what could be;* the *ideal* means *what ought to be.* To identify needs on which to focus the planned program, one must analyze the present situation, determine possibilities, and choose the ideal. Objectives should be set that focus on changing the target publics' behavior to the possible and the ideal. Analysis of data and collaborative decision making about needs that involve target public leaders and their followers (the learners) are the keys to needs identification and selection.

Publics must be led to recognize the importance of the difference between their current situation, the possible, and the ideal. To become motivated to change, target publics also must place value on achieving the ideal. The crux of the problem in changing the target public's behavior is the innate, passive resistance to change prevalent among publics. Resistance to change is not altogether natural resistance, however. Spicer (1952) maintains that "people resist changes that appear to threaten basic securities; they resist proposed changes that they do not understand; and they resist being forced to change" (p. 18). When the target public views their present situation as adequate and they do not recognize any need for change, the astute adult educator will immediately explore ways to motivate individual members of the target public. Individual members of the target public must become motivated to the degree that they recognize the need to change and place value on attaining the change.

McMahon (1970) classifies needs into two broad categories: (1) *felt* or immediate needs and (2) *unfelt* or analyzed needs. All needs must become "felt" to serve as motivating forces. Reported research indicates that various publics often are not aware of many of their most important needs; that is, publics often have significant needs that are unfelt. It is not enough to design programs based entirely on what people feel their needs are since these may not represent their most important needs. Adult educators also must identify those important needs the target publics fail to recognize and plan educational activities to convert these into felt needs. Without this further step, programs will be less important, tending to focus on immediate interests rather than on basic, long-term needs.

Careful decisions must be made about the selection of needs to be included in the planned program. These decisions must relate to the present, the possible, and the ideal situations. Ultimately, they must become decisions about acceptance of items to be included in the planned program. These are major decisions, not only because the future of the target public and their situation will be influenced, but because extensive resources will have to be committed. Needs are central to the commitment of adult education resources. Indeed, these needs are translated into the objectives of the planned program.

In making decisions about what to include in a planned program, the adult educator should keep in mind that the needs (economic, social, or psychological) of the target public constitute the support on which rests the success of adult education. Collaborative synchronization of needs as the target public and their leaders see them with those perceived by the change agent is an important responsibility of the change agent. Any procedure that assures focus of the planned program on both felt and unfelt needs is a "good" procedure.

Diagnosing needs.   Diagnosing needs is a complex and challenging undertaking in the program planning process. A major concern is reaching agreement on who should have the principal role in diagnosing educational needs of a target public. Several questions regarding this situation need to be addressed, including: Should needs be diagnosed solely by the learners or by the change agent? Or, should needs be diagnosed jointly by the learners and the change agent? What are some of the dangers of the change agent diagnosing target public needs without the active involvement of leaders and learners in that public? Should the change agent prescribe and package programs for the intended learners?

The action proposed in the conceptual programming model is that of an active partnership between the change agent and the leaders and learners in the target public in a collaborative effort to identify, assess, and analyze the learners' needs and to develop an educational program or learning activities that are intended to help the learners meet those needs. This approach differs from the practice followed by many adult education organizations and change agents in determining needs and developing programs for target publics. A common practice among many adult educators and their organizations has been first to define what they felt to be the target public's needs and then offer a prescribed program such as a lecture series, workshop, conference, or a course. As a result of this top-down process, publics have adversely viewed both the predetermined need and the prescribed program. As a consequence, the intended public has rejected the "defined need" and its proposed solution.

Superimposing programs on publics sometimes is associated with the mission and philosophy of the adult education organization. Often national, state, and even county-level organizations package and encourage the application of "canned" programs, without investigating the need for tailoring them to meet local needs. An example is the tendency of some community colleges and university extension divisions to develop and market courses without seeking inputs from those persons toward whom the courses are directed.

The target publics and their leaders make the final judgment about educational needs and what will fulfill those needs. In most instances, adult learners' participation in an educational program is voluntary. Even in mandatory learning situations, such as labor education classes or professional renewal programs sponsored and conducted by employers, the final decision of whether or not to become actively involved in the learning process rests with the adult learner.

The adult educator is the facilitator, resource person, and arranger in most voluntary teaching-learning or "change" situations. The role of the adult educator in change situations is that of interfacing with learners and their leaders in collaborative needs identification, assessment, and analysis, as well as in the actual implementation of the planned program. This role is not too different from that of astute political leaders who make every effort to anticipate and keep in touch with the needs and feelings of their electorate.

Lippitt, Watson, and Westley (1958) stress that the change agent must exhibit considerable objectivity in working with publics, warning that change agents sometimes tend to assume they know what is best for their publics. This "all-knowing" role can seriously hamper the teaching-learning relationship between the change agent and the learner.

Atwood (1967) aptly summarizes some thoughts as to the importance of involving adult learners in identifying and analyzing their own educational needs:

> The rationale for a sound diagnostic procedure in adult education seems to rest upon one very basic question—that learning experiences for adults should be designed to meet what they perceive to be their real needs.
> If one accepts this basic assumption, the importance of a diagnostic procedure or a basis for planning becomes readily apparent. The procedure must be one that leads to the [collaborative] identification of real educational needs by the public affected [and the adult educator]. (P. 3)

Approaches to diagnosing needs.   There are many ways by which the adult educator can obtain information about a target public's needs. Among these approaches are continuing interfacing with leaders of target publics, listening, surveys, community studies, checklists, questionnaires, and the use of census reports or other compilations of pertinent data. Diagnosing the educational needs of target publics is a continuing process that may vary in its degree of success in resolving problems. Boyle (1981), for example, concludes that effective approaches to identification of these needs and interests is a continuing challenge for many adult educators.

Interfacing with leaders of the target public in diagnosing needs has been used successfully by a number of adult education organizations, for example, the Cooperative Extension Service, community colleges, community development groups, and health-related educational organizations. Most adult educators recognize that they must first interface with the leaders of target publics to gain acceptance, legitimation, and support from their followers. Once these leaders have been identified, the adult educator must then determine who among them are the best spokespersons for the target public. Experience has shown that many leaders represent specialized interests and can or will speak only for a specific interest group. Some leaders of a designated public will insist that they speak only for themselves.

Faced with this dilemma, the adult educator is forced to contact a large number of reputed leaders and, in some cases, their followers. An adaptation to this approach is the formation, use, and maintenance of advisory committees made up of a representative cross section of persons reputed to be leaders of the target public. These may be standing committees or they may be ad hoc groups that are dissolved after the special program has been launched. Representativeness is the key in forming an advisory committee that can truly speak for the public in enunciating their educational needs. Advisory committees for the purpose of identifying, assessing, and analyzing educational needs are widely used by the Cooperative Extension Service, community colleges, community development organizations, and health-related adult education groups.

A second method used in the diagnosis is the change agent's effective use of the interpersonal skill of *listening*. Target public leaders and their followers (potential learners) have information and suggestions that the change agent needs to hear and analyze. Much can be learned about the educational needs of the public through listening. Boone, Dolan, and Shearon (1971) advise that:

> The identification of the leaders of their public by change agents is not sufficient; rather, they must consciously strive to establish communication with these persons through informal and meaningful dialogue. The dialogue should be characterized with the familiar as perceived by the leaders. That is, the inputs of leaders into such conversation(s) should be dominant. The change agent is characterized as a listener in the initial stages of such dialogue. The professional should strive to exhibit as much empathy as possible. Only after a "positive" two-way relationship is established should the change agent begin to interject external information into the dialogue. Such dialogue should not be restricted to a single encounter, but ideally should be considered through the period of time required to establish a meaningful and continuing relationship between the adult educator and his public(s). (P. 9)

The third method used in diagnosing needs is the *survey approach*. The survey is perhaps the most common approach used by adult educators to identify the educational needs of their target publics. Considerable know-how is required to design reliable and valid survey instruments. In designing a survey instrument for use in a community or target public, attention needs to be given to

> The purpose and nature of the survey to be conducted.
>
> The scope and breadth of the survey.
>
> Costs to design and conduct the survey.
>
> Identification of key "leaders" or "target public knowledgeables" from whom input must be obtained in the design and conduct of the survey.
>
> Design, preparation, and pretesting of the survey instrument.

Identification and selection of potential respondents.

Conduct of the field work.

Analysis of the data collected and preparation of a report.

Development and implementation of a plan to interpret the findings of the survey in collaboration with the leaders of the community or target public in which the survey was conducted.

Despite its inherent limitations, the survey can be useful. According to McMahon (1970), the most serious limitation of the survey is the gap between the respondents' interest, as shown in a positive response, and the motivation and commitment required for participation in the learning activity. In his discussion of reliability problems associated with the survey method, McMahon reminds us that a response expressed on a survey instrument is only an opinion expressed at a particular point in time. A favorable response to a series of questions is not necessarily a commitment on the part of the respondent to act in a certain way or to support a certain issue, when and if it again comes to the respondent's attention. McMahon gives as an example that, after the facts (e.g., finances, costs, location) surrounding an issue are made known to the respondents, some who expressed a favorable attitude toward the survey questions associated with the issue may oppose its specific features. He further suggests that, in designing a survey instrument, adult educators should use straightforward, specific questions.

A target public survey conducted without the knowledge of and inputs from their leaders most probably will be useless in the change process. The change agent must involve target public leaders in design and administration of the survey instrument, interpretation of the findings, and explorations of their implications.

A fourth method used in diagnosing the educational needs of a target public is the *community/target public study*. A critical concern here is the availability of funds and resources to design and conduct such a study. McMahon (1970) identified seven interrelated dimensions of a community that should be examined if programming is to be aimed at meeting the needs of the public. These seven dimensions are not mutually exclusive and, in most instances, are overlapping. He further emphasized that, to ensure understanding and acceptance of such a study, leaders in both the community and in the target public must be involved in all decisions related to its conduct, its design, the method to use in collecting data, analyzing the data collected, and interpreting the findings.

The following seven dimensions of a community should be studied in collaboration with leaders, if planning is to be directed toward diagnosing and meeting local needs:

1. *The population:* change agents and leaders of target publics must understand the community. They need to know about the human and physical resources that make up the community. Who are the people in the community? What are some of their

personal characteristics? How homogeneous/heterogeneous are they in terms of characteristics?

2. *The institutional structure of the community:* this dimension refers to the organized social relationships most people create to help meet their needs.

3. *Social stratification:* a concept used to describe the way people within a social aggregate are ranked and layered into classes, based on socioeconomic status and other "prestige" variables.

4. *The value system:* factors that are given high priority in the community.

5. *Informal social relations:* relationships, generally informal, that are developed and nurtured within the community structure. Through this network of interactions and informal relationships, informal leaders emerge who wield considerable influence in the community.

6. *Power structure:* key persons within the community who control and can make things happen in the community.

7. *Ecology:* the spatial distribution of people in the community; divisions of the community with respect to social and economic functions; transportation, housing areas and patterns, school districts.

Christenson and Robinson (1982) also consider the community study method as a means to identify target public needs. They suggest the systems concept be used as a guide for constructing a study to probe community needs and strongly support the concept of involving leaders and learners in all aspects of the process.

The *checklist technique,* which is relatively simple to administer, is recommended for use in diagnosing a public's needs (Knowles, 1952; McMahon, 1970; Warren, 1978). Suggested checklist response items include types of businesses, educational needs and facilities, cultural opportunities, recreational facilities, and the physical appearance of the community.

Perhaps the most extensive set of checklists for studying and analyzing a community or target public was compiled by Warren (1978). The elements of the target public Warren deals with are its background and history; economic life; community organizations, institutions, and agencies; government and politics; communications network; and intergroup relations. Again, data generated can be meaningless unless the potential learners and their leaders are involved in administering the checklists and analyzing and interpreting the data.

A fifth approach to data collection in diagnosing needs is use of *census or other survey reports.* Census data are a rich source of information about political and legal groupings of people. These data can be summarized and compared by ten-year intervals to depict trends in personal, social, and economic characteristics of people. Other reliable sources of data about defined publics are population centers on university campuses, state departments of human resources, chambers of commerce, and local planning commissions. Data from these sources generally are more current than census data. Ideally, the leaders of target publics should have a role in interpreting these data.

In every human and physical situation there are always (1) the facts, (2) people's understanding of the facts, (3) people's attitudes or value judgments about the facts, and (4) people's actions or reactions related to the facts. Probably the most forceful attitudes people have are those related to what ought to be and ought not to be in their situation. Hence, people tend either to approve or disapprove facts, as they see them, in relation to some desirable new situation. Understanding and acceptance of factual information is directly related to the degree to which the people have been involved in collecting and interpreting these data. The process of merging useful technology from physical and biological sciences with that of the behavioral sciences and applying this to the problems of planned change is, therefore, the essence of adult education and the context in which people's needs play the major role.

PLANNING IN RETROSPECT

The planning subprocess in programming is defined and discussed as a deliberate, rational, continuing process of educational activities the adult education organization directs at identifying its target publics and their leaders, linking with those publics through interfacing with the leaders and the learners in collaborative identification, assessment, and analysis of educational needs. Through this process, the organization is maintained and renewed.

Four basic concepts support planning:

1. *Planned change:* the idea that education is a rational, goal-directed, collaborative effort between adult educators and adult learners and their leaders to bring about measurable differences in behavior or structure.
2. *Systemic linkage:* conscious recognition that the organization must articulate functions or structures congruent with those of the public (system) being served to the end that, in some fashion, the two operate as a single system.
3. *Democracy:* represented by the collaborative and egalitarian involvement of educators, leaders, and learners in planning for change.
4. *Translation:* the notion that the adult educator's values, knowledge, and methodology must be presented in a frame of reference that is interpretable to adult learners.

Steps in the planning subprocess flow from the application and integration of these concepts. The first, the context for all planning, is an analysis of the organization and its renewal process, in which the organization continuously examines its structure and activities, and the needs of its publics, so that it does not depart from its original mission. The second step is linkage, in which the organization articulates its functions, structure, and processes with those of the target public to the degree that the two operate temporarily as a single system. This step must be carried out within an understanding of the social context or formal articulation of the functions, structure, and processes of the social system.

The actual linkage of the adult education organization with its target public(s) or learner system(s) is achieved by the change agent through

1. Studying, analyzing, and mapping the publics within the organization's environment to become acquainted with and knowledgeable about the social, cultural, and political "geography" within which the organization functions.
2. Identifying the target public(s) or learner system(s) to be involved in planning.
3. Identifying and interfacing with both formal and informal leaders of the target public(s).
4. Collaborating with the leaders, learner groups, and individual learners in an egalitarian approach to identifying, assessing, and analyzing educational needs of the learners.

This final phase of the linkage process epitomizes the third basic concept of the planning subprocess: democracy.

The importance of the planning subprocess of programming to an objective and accurate identification, assessment, and analysis of expressed needs of target publics cannot be overemphasized. In Chapter 5, we will describe how the adult education organization ought to respond to these needs through the design of a planned program and its actual implementation.

REFERENCES

ATWOOD, M., "The Diagnostic Procedure in Adult Education," *Community Teamwork,* 19 (March 1967), 1–5.

BEAL, G. M., R. C. BLOUNT, R. C. POWERS, and W. J. JOHNSON, *Social Action and Interaction in Program Planning.* Ames: Iowa State University Press, 1966.

BENNE, K. D., "Democratic Planning and Human Engineering," in *The Planning of Change,* ed. W. G. Bennis, K. D. Benne, and R. Chin. New York: Holt, Rinehart and Winston, 1961.

BERMANT, G., H. C. KELMAN, and D. P. WARWICK, *The Ethics of Social Intervention.* New York: John Wiley & Sons, Inc., 1978.

BERTRAND, A. L., *Basic Sociology: An Introduction to Theory and Methods.* New York: Appleton-Century-Crofts, 1967.

BOONE, E. J., R. J. DOLAN, and R. W. SHEARON, *Programming in the Cooperative Extension Service: A Conceptual Schema.* Misc. Extension Publ. # 72. Raleigh: North Carolina Agricultural Extension Service, 1971.

BOYLE, P. G., *Planning Better Programs.* New York: McGraw-Hill Book Company, 1981.

CARY, L. J., *Community Development As a Process.* Columbia: University of Missouri Press, 1971.

CHRISTENSON, J. A., and J. W. ROBINSON, JR., *Community Development in America.* Ames: Iowa State University Press, 1982.

COMBS, A. W., Chairman, *Perceiving, Behaving, Becoming: A New Focus for Education.* ASCD 1962 Yearbook Committee, Association for Supervision and Curriculum Development. Washington, D.C.: National Education Association, 1962.

DENNEY, H., *Decongesting Metropolitan America.* Columbia: University of Missouri Extension Division, 1972.

DURKHEIM, E., *The Division of Labor in Society.* Glencoe, Ill.: The Free Press, 1964.

FREEMAN, L. C., T. J. FARARO, W. BLOOMBERG, JR., and M. H. SUNSHINE, "Locating Leaders in Local Communities: A Comparison of Some Alternative Approaches," in *The Structure of Community Power,* ed. M. Aiken and P. Mott, New York: Random House, Inc., 1970.

GOODENOUGH, W. H.,   *Cooperation and Change.* New York: Russell Sage Foundation, 1963.

HAVIGHURST, R. J.,   *Developmental Tasks and Education.* 2nd ed. Chicago: Committee on Human Development, University of Chicago, 1952.

HOULE, C.,   *The Design of Education.* San Francisco: Jossey-Bass, Publishers, 1972.

HUNTER, F.,   *Community Power Structure.* Chapel Hill: University of North Carolina Press, 1953.

KEMPFER, H.,   "Identifying Education Needs and Interests of Adults: A Summary of an Evaluative Study," *Adult Education,* 2 (1951), 32–36.

KIDD, R. J.,   *How Adults Learn.* New York: Association Press, 1973.

KIMBALL, W. J.,   "Understanding Community." Presentation at Short Course for Intensive Training for Non-Metropolitan Development, Lincoln, Nebraska, and East Lansing, Michigan, April and September, 1975. Michigan Cooperative Extension Service, Michigan State University, East Lansing, Mich., 1975.

KNOWLES, M. S.,   "Your Program Planning Tool Kit," *Adult Leadership,* 1 (1952), 12–21.

_____, *The Modern Practice of Adult Education: Andragogy versus Pedagogy.* New York: Association Press, 1970.

KNOWLES, M. S., and H. KNOWLES,   *Introduction to Group Dynamics.* New York: Association Press, 1972.

KNOX, A. B., and Associates.   *Developing, Administering, and Evaluating Adult Education.* San Francisco: Jossey-Bass, Publishers, 1980.

KRATZ, R. N.,   "Education Planning Literature Review." Exchange Bibliography, Nos. 243–244, Council of Planning Librarians, Monticello, Ill., 1971.

LAZARSFELD, P. F., B. BERELSON, and H. GAUDET.   *The People's Choice; How the Voter Makes up His Mind in a Presidential Campaign.* New York: Buell, Sloan, and Pearce, 1944.

LEAGANS, J. P.,   "A Concept of Needs," *The Journal of Cooperative Extension,* 2 (Summer 1964), 89–96.

LIONBERGER, H. F.,   *Adoption of New Ideas and Practices: A Summary of the Research Dealing With the Acceptance of Technological Changes in Agriculture With Implications for Action in Facilitating Such Changes.* Ames: Iowa State University Press, 1980.

LIPPITT, R., J. WATSON, and B. WESTLEY,   *The Dynamics of Planned Change.* New York: Harcourt, Brace & World, Inc., 1958.

LONG, H. B., R. C. ANDERSON, and J. A. BLUBAUGH,   *Approaches to Community Development.* Iowa City, Iowa: NUEA and American College Testing Program, 1973.

LOOMIS, C. P.,   "Systemic Linkage of El Cerrito," *Rural Sociology,* (March 1959), 54–57.

_____, *Social Systems.* Princeton, N.J.: D. Van Nostrand Company, 1960.

_____, and J. A. BEEGLE, *Rural Sociology.* Englewood Cliffs, N.J.: Prentice-Hall, Inc., 1957.

MCCLURE, C. R.,   "The Planning Process: Strategies for Action," *College and Research Libraries,* 39 (1978), 456–466.

MCMAHON, E. E.,   *Needs—Of People and Their Communities and the Adult Educator.* Washington, D.C.: Adult Education Association of the USA, 1970.

MASLOW, A. H.,   *Motivation and Personality.* New York: Harper & Row, Publishers, 1970.

PARK, K. E.,   "Human Ecology," in *Perspectives on the American Community,* ed. R. Warren. Chicago: Rand McNally & Company, 1973.

RHENMAN, E.,   *Organization Theory for Long-Range Planning.* New York: John Wiley & Sons, Inc., 1973.

ROGERS, E. M.,   *Diffusion of Innovations.* New York: The Free Press, 1962.

_____, "Social Structure and Social Change," in *Processes and Phenomena of Social Change,* ed. G. Zaltman. New York: John Wiley & Sons, Inc., 1973.

ROGERS, E. M., and D. L. KINCAID,   *Communication Networks: Toward a New Paradigm for Research.* New York: The Free Press, 1981.

ROGERS, E. M., and F. F. SHOEMAKER,   *Communication of Innovations: A Cross-Cultural Approach.* 2nd ed. New York: The Free Press, 1971.

ROTHMAN, J.,   *Promoting Innovation and Change in Organizations and Communities: A Planning Manual.* New York: John Wiley & Sons, Inc., 1976.

SCHROEDER, W.,   "Typology of Adult Learning Systems," in *Building an Effective Adult Education Enterprise,* ed. J. M. Peters and Associates. San Francisco: Jossey-Bass, Publishers, 1980.

SCHUTZ, R. E., R. L. BAKER, and V. S. GERLACH,   *Stating Educational Outcomes.* New York: Van Nostrand and Reinhold, 1958.

SPICER, E. H.,   *Technological Change.* New York: Russell Sage Foundation, 1952.

TAIT, J. L., J. BOKEMEIER, and J. BOHLEN,   *Identifying the Community Power Actors: A Guide for Change Agents.* North Central Regional Extension Publication 59. Ames: Iowa Cooperative Extension Service, 1974.

TYLER, R. W.,   *Basic Principles of Curriculum and Instruction.* Chicago: University of Chicago Press, 1971.

WARREN, R. L.,   *The Community in America.*   3rd ed. Chicago: Rand McNally & Company, 1978.

WILLIAMS, R.,   *American Society.* New York: Alfred A. Knopf, 1960.

Chapter Five

Design
and
Implementation

The activities in the second subprocess of programming, design and implementation, may be viewed as a transition from the abstract to the concrete, from diffuse to focused activity, and from aggregate to individual efforts. In this transition, the thinker becomes the practitioner as the focus shifts to action-oriented, service-delivery steps that derive from prior planning based on theory and practical experiences. The design and implementation subprocess has as its primary focus the organization and activation of a purposive educational response to needs identified, assessed, and analyzed in the planning subprocess. Design and implementation includes three distinct but interrelated dimensions: (1) the actual design and development of the planned program, (2) sequenced increments or plans of action for carrying out the planned program within designated time periods, and (3) formulation and execution of general educational strategies in implementing the plans of action and, ultimately, the planned program. Also provided for are specific means for evaluating program outcomes.

In this chapter, as in Chapter 4, we will begin with the assumptions and concepts associated with the design and implementation subprocess, followed by a broad definition of program design and implementation. The processual tasks associated with the subprocess will be identified and stated. We will also see how, in the design and implementation subprocess, organizational systems and resources are brought to bear on individual behaviorial change and how further interfacing between adult educators and learners and their leaders is approached.

The planning subprocess yields a set of raw data regarding learning needs of a specific public. Still required is precise ordering of those needs so they can be met through appropriate educational experiences that are within the purview of the organization's mission and its available resources. Thus, the intellectual link between the planning and the design and implementation is the transition from *inductive* collection and analysis of information on learning needs to the *deductive,* logical efforts of the adult educator to translate those needs into a rational and manageable educational design. This is the pattern of most adult education activities: the adult educator collaborates with learners and their leaders in identifying, assessing, and analyzing expressed needs and then assumes the professional responsibility for designing and implementing a planned program of suitable and acceptable learning experiences.

As examples, we see a technical college administrator starting with a general plan to provide training for new industrial supervisors; working through specific needs, objectives, and educational strategies; and translating those into a particular set of curricular offerings. Or, there is the community schools' coordinator attempting to translate the findings of a survey of the local district's need for adult basic education into an evening program tailored to the learning needs and characteristics of a working population. Or, a local self-reliance agency confers with inner-city church leaders to identify their parishioners' energy-related needs, then extends audio-visual tutorial materials and self-help training efforts to assist affected householders in finding ways to insulate their homes.

The list of examples in which the total programming process described here could be applied is endless.

ASSUMPTIONS AND CONCEPTS

A definitive set of assumptions and concepts underlies the program design and implementation subprocess. Because learning experiences that result from these efforts focus ultimately on the individual learner, our primary assumption is that all educational activity is aimed at bringing about individual behavioral change. Even when some impact on social or cultural structures or systems is intended, education operates at the individual level, and social change occurs through cumulative, individual behavioral change.

As noted in Chapter 3, the design and implementation subprocess is guided by eight basic assumptions:

1. The planned program is the adult education organization's principal means of responding to the needs of its target publics.
2. The planned program is a blueprint of major behavioral changes to be effected by the adult education organization over a relatively long period of time, if improvements are to be noted in these publics.
3. The planned program provides the adult education organization with a rationale for the allocation, deployment, and use of its resources.
4. The planned program serves as a guide and provides direction for decisions on strategies for coping with the educational needs of learners.
5. The planned program provides the adult education organization with an excellent public relations tool.
6. The design of plans of action guides the systematic development of change strategies to deal with the needs and objectives enumerated in the planned program, within a relatively short period of time.
7. The planned program and plans of action provide the adult educator with the means needed to market them to the intended publics.
8. The planned program and plans of action provide a base for the adult educator in identifying, recruiting, and developing resource persons to assist with the actual implementation of the planned program and its accompanying plans of action.

The intent of behavioral change is to broaden the individual's behavioral repertoire so that associated needs, both felt and analyzed, can be met. We assume that needs are met through directed action, with that action arising from individual output from the point of view of both the educator and the learner.

Human behavior, human society, and human concerns are all complex; human needs are assumed to be similarly complex. The imposition of logical, orderly, and sequential structure in sets of needs and in programming subprocesses promotes efficiency and completeness in meeting needs. The logical processes required are analysis and decision making. A necessary intellectual component is the translation of needs into positive behavioral outcomes or outputs. Organizational and learning structures facilitative of attaining those outcomes must be established, maintained, and utilized in a manner both adapted and adapting to the social, economic, political, legal, and technological environment in which needs are discovered.

Responsibility for providing the learning structure required for attaining behavioral change objectives belongs to adult educators and the various components of educational systems, both formal and informal. Adult educators are expected to have special expertise in the deductive skills of translating analyzed needs into objectives aimed at specific behavioral change outcomes. They also are expected to be skillful in designing change strategies that will produce the outcomes specified in the objectives.

Human behavior develops throughout the life span. The design of change strategies and learning experiences requires intellectual command of such development in cognitive, affective, and psychomotor behavior. The craft of instruction derives from the individual educator's observational acuity in recognizing signs of such development.

DESIGN AND IMPLEMENTATION DEFINED

Given the undergirding perspective, basic assumptions, concepts, and processes, a conceptual and operational definition of design and implementation must be provided. The subprocess involves translating the identified and analyzed learning needs of target publics into meaningful and cogent designs and developing effective teaching-learning strategies for their implementation. The program design and implementation subprocess has three interrelated dimensions, namely, (1) the planned program, (2) plans of action, and (3) action strategies for implementing plans of action and the planned program.

The *planned program* is a master prospectus or plan for change toward which adult educators focus their efforts. The planned program consists of (1) a statement of macro needs, (2) a statement of macro objectives that are keyed to the macro needs, (3) specification of general educational strategies for achieving the macro objectives, and (4) specification of macro outcomes of the planned program.

Plans of action, which are short-range in nature and logically sequenced, include specific teaching-learning strategies designed to guide the adult educator in fulfilling learners' needs and attaining the objectives contained in the long-range planned program. Implementation of a specific plan of action entails action strategies in which the adult educator engages to assure that the plan is carried through to successful completion. These action strategies are (1) marketing; (2) procuring, developing, and using the necessary, available resources, both human and material; (3) monitoring ongoing teaching-learning transactions; (4) reinforcing learners and teachers; and (5) using feedback to evaluate and, if needed, to revise teaching strategies or learner experiences, or both, to attain maximum behavioral change in the learners.

The order of program design and implementation, as depicted in the conceptual programming model in Chapter 3, can be seen in the basic flow of its two major dimensions. The first dimension is to design a planned program: a written statement of identified and assessed learning needs, parallel and connected; educational objectives and strategies designed to meet those needs; and evaluation strategies to be used in assessing educational outcomes or behavioral change. The learning needs included in this planned program statement are macro, in the sense that they imply relatively long periods of time to fulfill, large segments of target publics, extensive resource commitments, and a generally broad scale of educational strategies. The second dimension is to implement the planned program through sequenced, hierarchical, short-range plans of action, utilizing the same components as in the planned program but, in this instance, targeting the analyzed needs. Plans of action focus on shorter time periods and general, individual teaching-learning activities. They imply sequential and specific teaching-learning activities, within a clearly defined and relatively short time period, which are monitored and evaluated to ensure maximum behavioral change.

These relationships are depicted schematically in Figure 5-1. Macro and micro levels of description and general educational strategies, as explicated in the planned program and the plans of action, are compared in Table 5-1.

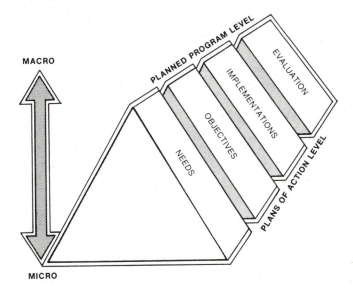

FIGURE 5-1. Hierarchies of needs, objectives, implementation (strategies and mechanisms), and evaluation parallel each other. Each hierarchy has both macro and micro levels.

TABLE 5-1.   Comparison of macro (planned program) and micro (plans of action) levels of description

Characteristic	Level of description	
	Macro	Micro
Time frame	Longer (extended period of time)	Shorter (1 year or less)
Scale	Broad (superordinate)	Narrow (subordinate)
Level of effect (target audience)	Aggregate (group, community)	Individual
Resource commitment	Relatively greater	Relatively less
Agent	Organization	Individual
Nature of effect intended	Community/social change	Individual behavioral change
Mechanism	Strategic level	Teaching level (tactical)
Evaluation focus	Planned program	Individual learner
Time order of completion	Later (cumulative)	Earlier (sequential)
Organizational level of decision-making	Higher levels	Lower levels
Information sources	External (environment)	Internal (downward flow)
Processes in programming	Higher level (primary)	Lower level (secondary, tertiary)
Priority for action	Higher (earlier)	Lower (later)
Origin	Inductive (from observation)	Deductive (from generalizations)
Statement form	Generalized (global)	Specific (focused)
Complexity	Complex	Simple

ELEMENTS OF THE DESIGN
AND IMPLEMENTATION SUBPROCESS

Based on the foregoing definition of program design and implementation, the subprocess may be viewed as consisting of three distinct but related dimensions, with accompanying processual tasks. The three dimensions are (1) the planned program, (2) plans of action, and (3) action strategies.

The Planned Program and Related Processual Tasks

The planned program can be described as the delineation, derivation, and ordering or designation of priorities for macro educational needs, objectives, and strategies. Gross's (1976) definition of *program* is quite acceptable within the context of design and implementation: "A program is a sequence of future actions to which a person, unit, or organization is committed" (p. 230).

The long-range planned program flows from organizational linkage with publics and operates within the larger context of organizational renewal. The planned program, in turn, forms the context for elaboration of shorter-term, more focused plans of action that encompass hierarchies of micro needs and objectives and related activities to involve the individual learner. The planned program and its processual tasks provide a framework within which actual teaching strategies and learning experiences can be deduced.

At progressively finite levels of analysis and effort, we can think in terms of "triplets": organizational mission/structure/renewal; long-range objectives/strategies/program evaluation; plans of action/teaching strategies and learning experiences/monitoring. The parallel is obvious. The introductory section of this chapter provides the overall rationale for program design, the sequencing of educational experiences to maximize learning. The planned program is a way of anticipating and coping with change, seen in the expression of felt needs by target groups and in collaborative needs identification and analysis. Included are both current needs for change and needs from change developing across time. However, as Hirst (1975) puts it, "once more we must realize that a global term [like felt needs] cannot be the source of specific educational objectives" (pp. 286–287). The implication is that organized, deductive, objective-producing activities are required if one is to progress from generalized needs of target publics to specific learning objectives and outcomes/outputs, via carefully chosen, constructed, and implemented teaching-learning strategies. This thread weaves throughout both the planned program and the plans of action.

This view of a planned program is consistent with modern thought in curriculum development. Wiles and Bondi (1979) state that the "promotion of purposeful change requires organization" (p. 33) and that a curriculum provides a "road map by which change can be anticipated and followed" (p. 40). That "road map" flows from a logical sequence of actions by the adult educator; that is, educational goals are based on values, educational objectives derive from these goals, and learning opportunities are based on objectives. This sequence parallels Tyler's (1971) four curriculum organization questions, cited in Chapter 2 and reintroduced later in this chapter, and is mirrored in the conceptual flow presented here.

The advocacy of planned programs does not derive solely from theoretical and practical considerations in education; it also is consistent with broader trends. The past 60 years or more have been a time of growing concern about rational planning in business, in government, and in education. The tasks involved in that notion of planning overlap and are cognate with the planned program processual tasks to be discussed here. The use of planning units has increased rapidly in business and government; detailed descriptions of planned activities are required to receive federal grants and contracts; and systems such as management-by-objectives (MBO) have been developed to provide a rational framework for planning and program activities. Decreasing availability of resources and concomitant emphasis on accountability for the disposition of resources reinforce the importance of planning beyond its immediate worth.

We value efficiency and low cost/benefit ratios. Long-range planning promotes both.

Programming in adult education is a long-range process, explicitly so in its intent to effect social change through change in individual behavior. The anticipated long-range impact of programming is expressed in its values, aims, and goals. So, if an organization is focusing on individual and aggregate long-range social effects, farsighted, ongoing programming is both a logical and a responsible endeavor. Further, adult education organizations and individual change agents must have a sense of what lies beyond current felt needs, in the form of elaborated higher-order, future-oriented needs based on projections of trends and broader social, political, legal, economic, and other perspectives. Felt needs are an effective and sensible starting point, but the change agent must develop a sense of the "next steps" to provide a basis for exploring and assessing further needs via interfacing with target public leaders and their followers.

Again we note that felt needs may be addressed more or less directly, depending on what those needs are. An important aspect of the educator's job, perhaps the pivotal aspect, is the capability to perceive relationships among expressed needs and to envision relationships to needs that might be present but are not expressed. "Next steps" in this sense implies elaborating hierarchies that embody felt needs and demonstrating relationships to both higher-level (broader) and lower-level (narrower) analyzed needs. The adult educator's contributions of expertise and experience to long-range planning include the ability to project a timetable for reaching particular goals: broader aims typically require longer periods of time than narrower aims. Accurate judgment of the time required to attain particular goals is crucial to long-range planning, for such judgment sets the time dimensions of "long range."

A further aspect of timing is the assessment of starting points. *Needs assessment,* in a broad sense, seeks an answer to the question, What are the existing skills and abilities within the target public, relative to their needs and objectives? In essence, long-range planning takes into account not only "where we want to go," that is, some specifiable goal, but also "how far we have to go," a statement implying knowledge about the learners' initial status. An analogy may help.

If someone we wish to help tells us he needs to make a trip to New York City, it is easy to specify the goal—arrival in the "Big Apple." But we will have great difficulty in planning his route and travel schedule and in making all the related decisions—how much time he should allow for the trip, what he should take with him, whether he will need to make intermediate stops, and so forth—unless we know where he is starting from. It makes a great deal of difference in our planning if he sets out from Portland, Maine, versus Portland, Oregon!

A trip has three components: a starting point, a destination, and a route of travel between the two. An educational program/plan has three analogous components: a diagnosis of existing behaviors, a specification of intended behavioral change objectives, and a plan of educational experiences required to

bring about the desired outcome or change. Clearly, the amount of time required for a trip depends on the distance to be traveled and the complexity of
the route. In the same fashion, the form and content of a planned educational
program depend on the discrepancy or gap between existing and desired learner
behaviors and on the number, type, content, and complexity of teaching-learning
activities to be engaged in to attain the desired learner behaviors.

Having a "feel" for the direction in which the program is heading also
is helpful to the individual change agent. Such feeling can give meaning to day-
to-day activities and can provide expectations of what actions will be necessary
in the immediate future. Beyond that, striving for the ideal underlies all social-
action programs, an ideal generally expressed in organizational philosophy.
Working toward an ideal can be a motivating force in itself, for both organizational affiliates and clients, and can be made explicit in a planned program.

In the conceptual programming model, the design of a long-range planned
program involves several processual tasks. The intent here is to show, through
six such tasks, the internally consistent logic in the sequence of needs/objec-
tives/strategies and the rational design/framework being constructed. These
processual tasks deal with (1) translating analyzed needs into macro needs, (2)
formulating macro-level objectives, (3) formulating general change or educational strategies, (4) identifying intended outcomes for each macro objective,
(5) establishing a timetable for completion of each program strategy, and (6)
providing for evaluative information gathering.

> *Task 1.* The adult educator must translate the expressed needs into macro needs
> of the target publics in the content areas within which learner needs have been
> identified in adult educator-leader-learner collaboration. The macro needs so
> specified form the base for constructing a needs hierarchy.

Within the context of designing the planned program, the initial processual task
of translating analyzed needs into macro needs is the thread back to the prior
planning subprocess. The expressed needs identified, assessed, and analyzed in
the planning subprocess provide the basis for generalizing to high-level macro
needs. The macro needs become the focus of the planned program.

Earlier, the rationale for processual task 1 was explicated: expressed needs
are the logical, practical and learner-engaging place to start with any adult education program; learning is part of human development, which proceeds in generally definable stages; those stages require programs that parallel and
incorporate developmental sequences; and a needs hierarchy is a *translation* of
desired learner development into terms useful for programming. Note that expressed needs are a diagnostic starting point from which, depending on the nature
of the particular need, higher-order or lower-order needs, or both, are deduced.

Tyler's (1971) work in curriculum development becomes relevant at this
point. He provides theoretical support for the link between the planning and
the design/implementation subprocesses by emphasizing that curriculum development begins with analyzing the needs that stimulated the decision to develop

a curriculum. This emphasis demonstrates not only the linkage between needs analysis and designing adult education programs; it points to the need for analysis. One approach to analyzing learning needs is to develop a needs hierarchy from knowledge of means by which and sources from which such needs emerge and how they must be successively met.

The pattern of needs assessment and subsequent analysis and ordering is acknowledged in several of the adult education programming models discussed in Chapter 2. All of the models presented there explicitly state that needs are, in a functional sense, the basis of the actual educational program. Beyond that, and even though their tactics differ, several of the authors of these models present a process or strategy for analyzing needs so that they might be translated into educational mechanisms (Lippitt, Watson, and Westley, 1958; Beal et al., 1966; Freire, 1970; Knowles, 1970).

The translation called for in processual task 1 proceeds in two directions. Beginning with felt/expressed needs, the next step is to fashion around such needs both higher-order needs that encompass the felt needs and lower-order needs that lie between the felt needs and the higher-order needs. The simple example in Figure 5-2 may be helpful to illustrate this point.

Suppose we are confronted with an expressed need such as "consumers need to be more careful shoppers." Assessment and analysis, which must be a collaborative effort between the organization and the target public and its leaders, may show that this expressed need actually is a reflection of a broad macro need to develop the consumers' ability to make informed decisions in the marketplace. Such decisions may provide increased satisfaction and yield the greatest economic return on funds expended. Consequently, the planned program may center on providing financial management concepts and techniques for "making effective purchase decisions." By analysis, the expressed need, "being a careful shopper," is related to an array of more specific needs, that is, the abilities to (1) differentiate between wants and needs in making decisions in the marketplace; (2) recognize reliable sources of information that can be used in comparing the features, quality, and costs of products; (3) compare qualities, prices, warranties, installation and maintenance requirements, and credit costs for cost effectiveness of products; (4) interpret payment options available in purchasing products and the economic benefits and risks associated with each option; and (5) exercise their rights and responsibilities as consumers in the marketplace. Typically, the expressed/felt need is an intermediate-level need, reflecting larger-scale, longer-term concerns. Such needs are resolvable through focused, narrow-scale, short-term but cumulative, sequential learning experiences.

This first processual task in designing a planned program is unique in that emphasis is placed on translating expressed and analyzed needs into macro needs. These macro needs form a hierarchy of needs. The hierarchy describes ongoing human and program development, helps build the structure for ultimate program design, and conceptually orders the ideal needs implicit to the organiza-

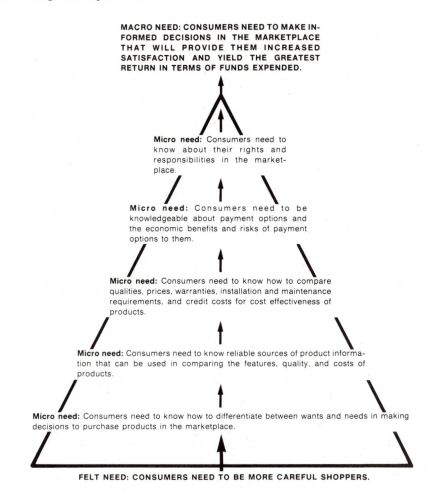

MACRO NEED: CONSUMERS NEED TO MAKE IN-FORMED DECISIONS IN THE MARKETPLACE THAT WILL PROVIDE THEM INCREASED SATISFACTION AND YIELD THE GREATEST RETURN IN TERMS OF FUNDS EXPENDED.

Micro need: Consumers need to know about their rights and responsibilities in the market-place.

Micro need: Consumers need to be knowledgeable about payment options and the economic benefits and risks of payment options to them.

Micro need: Consumers need to know how to compare qualities, prices, warranties, installation and maintenance requirements, and credit costs for cost effectiveness of products.

Micro need: Consumers need to know reliable sources of product information that can be used in comparing the features, quality, and costs of products.

Micro need: Consumers need to know how to differentiate between wants and needs in making decisions to purchase products in the marketplace.

FELT NEED: CONSUMERS NEED TO BE MORE CAREFUL SHOPPERS.

FIGURE 5-2. A hierarchy of needs in consumer resource management

tion's philosophy and objectives, while meshing the organization's mission with community/social realities.

> ***Task 2.*** The adult educator must formulate, for each macro need, the macro objectives that specify the learner behavior sought in fulfilling macro needs of target publics. Macro objectives reflect the ultimate (terminal) behavior change desired in the learner.

Processual task 2 flows from processual task 1 of specifying macro needs and constructing a hierarchy for corresponding micro needs, and employs the same logic. The need for an organized structure for growth through learning is implied here. The adult educator, as a change agent and programmer, has the responsibility for translating the needs hierarchy into educational objectives. The structure that evolves is a corresponding hierarchy of objectives. This hierarchy of objectives accents the macro objective at the top of the hierarchy, with descending subordinate micro objectives. At the pinnacle of the hierarchy is the macro objective, while at the base of the hierarchy is the lowest-level micro objective keyed to the felt need. Arranged between the lowest micro objective and the macro objective are sequential, ascending level micro objectives. Bloom et al. (1956); Krathwohl, Bloom, and Masia (1964); and Tyler (1971) give credence to the hierarchical approach to specifying objectives that have their origin in the corresponding hierarchy of needs.

The programming models advanced by Knowles (1970), Houle (1972), Kidd (1973), and Boyle (1981) all recommend developing objectives as the initial step in designing programs, with varying methods of selecting, formulating, and arranging objectives. Hirst (1975) also supports the production of objectives to correspond with each of the needs contained within the hierarchy. It is of interest that these five programming authorities stress that learning needs must be translated into objectives to design educational programs for adults.

The conceptual programming model advanced by the author emphasizes that the focus of the planned program is the macro need and its accompanying hierarchy of micro needs, along with the corresponding macro objective and its hierarchy of micro objectives. These two hierarchies provide the rationale for selecting, developing, and employing specific educational change strategies directed at achieving each of the objectives in the hierarchy. The stated objectives must be (1) consistent with organizational mission, (2) within the limitations of available resources, and (3) practical within the capabilities of intended learners. Determining the capabilities of intended learners is perhaps one of the most important and complex tasks in the entire programming process, for this is another point at which the organization must interface with target publics as individual learners and learner groups. For this reason, if no other, it is important to understand both the general context and the specific milieu within which objectives are to be derived. Earlier, a series of assumptions and concepts pertaining to program design and implementation was laid out. The primacy of behavioral change was emphasized at that point.

The derivation and statement of objectives require that the adult educator resolve issues such as the type and level of behavioral changes that are possible, that are probable, that are practical, and that are desirable, given the macro objective. Setting objectives is a serious, important, and difficult undertaking, a task that has occupied the best minds in education for decades. Figure 5-3 illustrates how a hierarchy of objectives can be constructed from the hierarchy of needs depicted in Figure 5-2.

For each need (macro or micro) identified in Figure 5-2 at least one corresponding objective has been formulated (Figure 5-3). The macro objective clearly states that the ultimate aim is to have consumers acquire the ability to

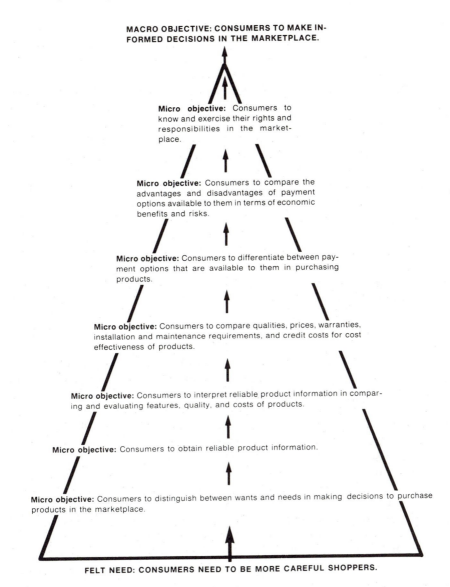

MACRO OBJECTIVE: CONSUMERS TO MAKE IN-
FORMED DECISIONS IN THE MARKETPLACE.

Micro objective: Consumers to
know and exercise their rights and
responsibilities in the marketplace.

Micro objective: Consumers to compare the
advantages and disadvantages of payment
options available to them in terms of economic
benefits and risks.

Micro objective: Consumers to differentiate between payment options that are available to them in purchasing
products.

Micro objective: Consumers to compare qualities, prices, warranties,
installation and maintenance requirements, and credit costs for cost
effectiveness of products.

Micro objective: Consumers to interpret reliable product information in comparing and evaluating features, quality, and costs of products.

Micro objective: Consumers to obtain reliable product information.

Micro objective: Consumers to distinguish between wants and needs in making decisions to purchase
products in the marketplace.

FELT NEED: CONSUMERS NEED TO BE MORE CAREFUL SHOPPERS.

FIGURE 5-3. A hierarchy of objectives in consumer resource management

make informed decisions in the marketplace. Ascending levels of micro objectives are for consumers to know how to (1) differentiate between wants and
needs in making decisions to purchase products in the marketplace; (2) obtain
reliable product information; (3) interpret product information in comparing
features, quality, and costs of products; (4) compare qualities, prices, warran-

ties, installation and maintenance requirements, and credit costs for cost effectiveness of products; (5) differentiate between payment options that are available to them in purchasing products; (6) compare the advantages and disadvantages of payment options in terms of economic benefits and risks; and (7) know and exercise their rights and responsibilities in the marketplace. Achievement of these objectives by the consumers should result in their being more careful shoppers.

Given the example of a hierarchy of objectives (Figure 5-3), it is fitting at this point to examine a larger theoretical picture of objectives. Tyler's (1971) concept spells out the major issues in selecting and formulating objectives; yet, in approaching his contribution to formulating objectives, one must consider his entire curriculum-building framework. Within that framework, Tyler organizes curriculum building around four now familiar questions that were cited in Chapter 2 but are repeated here for the reader's convenience:

1. What educational *purposes,* i.e., objectives, should the school (organization) seek to attain?
2. How can learning experiences be *selected* that are likely to be useful in attaining these objectives?
3. How can learning experiences be *organized* for effective instruction?
4. How can the effectiveness of learning experiences be *evaluated?*

Tyler's sources of educational purposes are the learners themselves—"What do they want in education?"; contemporary life—"What skills for living are required?"; subject specialists—"What content is to be taught?"; the organization's social philosophy—"Whom shall we believe and follow?"; and the psychology of learning—"What works, and why, in learning?" The influence of these sources has been ratified by a number of curriculum development experts testifying to the correctness of Tyler's insights.

In the rational approach to curriculum development, setting objectives is seen as specifying educational ends, which then help focus on appropriate means to those ends. For Tyler (1971), the elements of *behavior* and *content* are essential to stating objectives. Much thought also has been given in educational literature to *learning objectives,* their rationale, and the range of specificity in their statement.

The basic problem in developing objectives is to achieve precision in describing desired behavioral change. As Hirst (1975) puts the rationale for educational objectives, "Talking about the pursuit of growth and the satisfaction of needs must not blind us to the need to formulate, in detail, what objectives constitute growth and what precisely it is that pupils need" (p. 286). Hirst's comment is entirely consistent with the behaviorally based view to which we subscribe.

So, one function of objectives is to delineate behavioral growth or change. Objectives provide bases for selection and organization of learning experiences, give direction, define goals for accomplishment, relate educational input and learning output, and make the specific process of learning mutually comprehensible for all involved.

Behavior is one element in Tyler's framework for objectives. Again, the literature supports the need to state educational objectives in behavioral terms. Gagne (1972) capsulizes this point of view: "One assumes that the general purpose of instruction is learning on the part of the student. . . . Therefore, . . . one should attempt to identify the outcomes of learning as something the student is able to do, following instruction, which he was unable to do before instruction" (p. 394). Gagne is saying that the focus must be observable action on the part of the learner, congruent with our assumption of learning as behavioral change.

Beyond that basic assumption, and the range of functions previously described, Saylor and Alexander (1974) see behavioral objectives as allowing more precise individualization of instruction and as "the only meaningful basis for evaluating the outcomes of instruction" (p. 173). This is an important insight. Instruction ultimately succeeds or fails at the level of the individual; thus, in instructional situations, one must respect individual needs, individual capabilities, and individual motivations. Consequently, we must evaluate progress toward objectives on the basis of individual achievement of individual objectives. Group, social, community, and other aggregate, macro objectives are attained through cumulative individual achievement.

Realities of finite time and limited human, financial, and material resources frequently do not permit a thoroughgoing commitment to individual instruction. Indeed, such instruction is a luxury that programs rarely can afford. Yet, we acknowledge a commitment to individual instruction when stating objectives, which typically begin with "The student will be able to. . . ." Individualization is a rarely attainable ideal, a commitment to which even group-oriented instruction is directed.

Educational literature deepens the concept of the actual statement of objectives (e.g., Saylor and Alexander, 1974; Golby, Greenwald, and West, 1975; Wiles and Bondi, 1979). In addition to the elements of behavior and content, consideration must be directed to performance conditions; performance criteria; observable, measurable specificity; statement from the learner's point of view; and, finally, precision in those statements.

A basic methodological problem here is how to state objectives both precisely and functionally. This is where we must turn to the contributions of Bloom et al. (1956) and Krathwohl, Bloom, and Masia (1964) in developing taxonomies that help adult educators cope with the methodology of the design/implementation subprocess. The classification of educational objectives is hierarchical—simple to complex and concrete to abstract.

The assumptions and implications of the hierarchical approach are far-reaching. To begin with, the statement of specific instructional objectives occurs within a larger, deductive hierarchy of organizational mission, philosophy, and objectives (Wiles and Bondi, 1979), which is identical to the flow of the conceptual programming model. In their discussion of the hierarchical approach to objectives, Krathwohl, Bloom, and Masia (1964) suggest that a readiness relationship exists between those objectives lower in the hierarchy and those higher in it. This is an important statement: it specifies the *developmental* nature of such hierarchies. We have already stated that programming objectives must reflect expected growth. Hence, hierarchies of objectives are the intellectual realization of growth stages within any educational context.

This discussion of processual task 2 has been lengthy, because the task of developing macro (terminal) objectives and, subsequently, a hierarchy of subordinate objectives is both essential and demanding. The task serves as a bridge from assessed macro needs to corresponding macro objectives, which, in turn, will become the structure for program operation. As shown in the preceding description, the elements of processual task 2 derive from basic curriculum development theory and process, and they provide a logical structure for growth.

> *Task 3.* The adult educator must formulate general change (educational) strategies for assisting target publics in attaining behaviors specified in the macro objectives.

Processual task 3 follows a pattern already established: formulating general educational strategies logically flows from the immediately preceding task of setting objectives and lays the groundwork for its parallel task, selecting specific learning experiences, in designing plans of action. Also, task 3 has its own practical logic. Administering a program requires the adult educator first to define the general strategy by which the organization is to help the target public change (learn).

To understand processual task 3, attention needs to be given to defining the concept of strategy and its application to the planned program. A *strategy* is a carefully designed plan or scheme of learning activities to achieve the macro objective and its subordinate micro objectives. A macro objective and its subordinate objectives are illustrated in Figure 5-3. In the case of consumer behavior, the change agent has the option of selecting from among a number of learning activities in his or her attempt to help consumers acquire the ability to make informed decisions in the marketplace. First, the learning experiences for each micro objective encompassed in the hierarchy of objectives are carefully selected. When considered as a whole, these learning experiences/activities constitute a "change" strategy.

Arranging the learning experiences/activities into an overall change strategy requires particular attention. That is, they must be ordered and sequenced so that they reinforce one another to create awareness, stimulate interest, provide information, and ultimately encourage behavioral change or adoption of new behavior by the learner, group of learners, and perhaps the system. Radio announcements and television spot announcements may help consumers become aware of a need or problem; newsletters, demonstrations, and pamphlets may stimulate interest; and publications and other printed materials may provide information on the problem. Neighborhood and community meetings and demonstrations could be used to encourage behavioral change or adoption of new behavior among the consumers. The objective is to design a strategy that is functional in producing both individual and group behavioral change and can be communicated to the target public.

Delivery strategies for educational services take many forms, from one-to-one tutorial or advisement methods to large-scale formal classes and all sorts of educational settings in between. Choice of appropriate strategies is keyed to specified objectives, but certainly has to take into account the historical antecedents of services delivery (e.g., what forms of instruction have been found acceptable to the target publics in the past?), social contexts and sponsorship (family groups, neighborhood associations, social action groups, among others), locations (e.g., churches, school buildings, community centers, or individual homes), and other factors that may affect both participation in and the effectiveness of whatever instruction is offered.

Cross (1981) provides an extensive review of factors that contribute to participation in adult learning opportunities, along with a list of barriers to participation. In choosing broad strategies for adult instruction, both types of factors must be taken into account. To some degree, motivations for participation are reflected in needs expressions. Perhaps more importantly, as many of the barriers to participation must be removed as can be arranged. Cross speaks of *situational barriers*—costs, time requirements, and competing responsibilities; *institutional barriers*—length of programs, attendance requirements, convenience of scheduling, and lack of availability of information; and *dispositional barriers*—attitudes toward education and self-respect.

Alert programmers will take into consideration all three types of barriers. They will interpret and analyze barriers in light of accumulated knowledge about the target public(s), and will construct overall educational experiences that minimize barriers to participation while maximizing effectiveness of instruction.

When delineating change strategies to achieve this goal, adult educators must comprehend and weigh appropriately both general and specific information about the community: awareness of factors facilitating and hindering participation and options for educational service delivery. Only then can they reach a judgment on the complexity of anticipated efforts with the target public.

Selection of general educational strategies is a major means by which the mapping and needs assessment steps are tied to educational marketing efforts. The "product" to be delivered has to be related to "consumer" needs and, similarly, has to be "packaged and delivered" in a manner acceptable to the consumer.

Examples abound. Adult basic education is unlikely to be a major product of a university but may be a central activity in a neighborhood community schools program. Improved farming techniques can be taught effectively through the Cooperative Extension Service, but would be an unlikely topic for a church's educational program. Child-rearing methods might be entirely appropriate to a young homemakers' club, but would not fit well into a technical college's continuing education program. Instruction in personal hygiene might take different forms in rural versus urban settings.

To repeat, pragmatically, the educational strategies chosen reflect objectives derived from analyzed needs, knowledge of social contexts, and sensitivity to marketing requirements. These factors are blended with more theoretical orientations toward instructional strategies that are based on principles of curriculum development. Educational strategies are attempts to answer a relatively broad question: What approaches to learning, in given social and physical environments, are most likely to lead to the achievement of specified objectives?

Other authors share a common thread in their orientation to change; they have stages of development and "stopping points" at which the larger picture is examined. They also respect the view that criteria for choosing approaches to educational change are definable, useful, and necessary.

For Lippitt, Watson, and Westley (1958), the stage of working toward change requires a progressive delineation of the problems, routes, and goals involved, a task roughly parallel to the development of a planned program. Beal and his group (1966) and Freire (1970) put forward a similar process of definition and redefinition that characterizes the conceptual programming model, although this model is more formal and complex.

One final thread in selecting change strategies must be attended to. In the earlier discussion of planning, attention was directed to the particular sociocultural organization of target publics. That same type of attention resurfaces here. Because macro needs are defined out of and in terms of the sociocultural milieu of potential learners, and because macro objectives are defined and ordered out of socially relevant macro needs, the general educational strategies here also must take into account that entire social world. Educational strategies chosen should fit into learner lifestyles and social group norms and expectations. The powerful influence of those social elements is recognized and accepted.

> *Task 4.* Intended outcomes must be identified for each macro objective. Macro outcomes should delineate the social-aggregate change intended, based on cumulative attainment of lower-order objectives.

Objectives, as previously noted, are descriptions of intended behavioral change in individuals and, cumulatively, in social groups. Each objective reflects an intended behavioral change (individual or group) that adult educators expect will fulfill individual and, by extension, group/community needs. In the sense the term is used here, intended outcomes are more reasonably applied at the group/community level, while at the same time reflecting individual behavior.

For instance, the earlier example of a communitywide need for improved economic behavior, as suggested in an expressed need for people "to be more careful shoppers," could be elaborated to mean enlightened economic behavior within the community. What might be the outcomes of fulfilling these needs?

On the individual level, we might look for evidence that shoppers compare prices when shopping, as one result of their educational activities. But on other levels, we might see broader indicators: fewer personal bankruptcies, fewer mortgage foreclosures, reduced personal debt, all correlated with improved economic behavior. At the same time, other trends may appear, not necessarily as direct results of learning experiences but as secondary or indirect effects or outcomes: fewer incidences of crime, marital problems, truancy, juvenile delinquency, accompanied by greater numbers of young people finishing high school and going on to college or vocational schools.

The point is that adult educators, in cooperation with learners and their leaders, make projections as to the intended outcomes of proposed educational activities. Judgment clearly is required here: Will the probable outcomes of these activities solve group/community problems identified earlier? If not, what other problems might these probable outcomes solve and how important are they? Does the proposed educational strategy require revision? If so, of what sort? Certainly, social change agents have not always been as responsible or as perspicacious as they might have been in anticipating outcomes. Note Tyler's (1971) principle that a given educational activity may have multiple outcomes: responsible change agents attempt to forecast as many of those outcomes as they can. Spicer's (1952) casebook is a source of many interesting examples of how seemingly minor technological innovations have altered rather radically the conduct of life in cultures around the world.

Tentatively answering outcome questions forms the base for more formal, future evaluation and accountability efforts, and feeds into them. More will be said about evaluation and accountability in Chapter 6, but certainly a requisite first step is to be clear about what we anticipate will happen.

> *Task 5.* The adult educator should estimate the time required to complete each component of program strategy. Those components requiring longer time periods should be incorporated into the long-range planned program. Those requiring shorter time periods should become parts of appropriate plans of action.

Time is the one resource that is in absolute, fixed supply. The judicious use of time is a crucial management responsibility. By its very nature, planning acknowledges the passage of time and the fact that activities will occupy time. Making accurate forecasts of where activities are to take place, when resources will have to be made available, when information for decisions will be required, and when decisions will have to be reached are the essence of management. Thus, no programming can occur without considering, in at least broad terms, the time needed to execute the program being planned.

We have proposed here that needs, objectives, and the activities associated with them are organized hierarchically. Smaller scales of effort typically are tied to shorter time requirements; broader scales of effort generally require more time. This is common sense. What may be less obvious is that the scales of effort are nested and interdependent, sequential, and correlated.

Many planners in government and business use the PERT system, a graphical method that portrays time spatially and is highly useful for pinpointing critical steps of subprocesses, and thus potential bottlenecks, in the accomplishment of projects. In another area altogether, pharmacologists speak of "rate-limiting steps," the points in complex physiological systems that set boundaries on the output of those systems. The analogies are direct.

In any multilevel, multicomponent system, some objectives can be accomplished more quickly than others. Specific allocations of time are dictated by orchestration of resources (human, financial, and material) for the most efficient accomplishment of objectives.

This discussion makes a rather arbitrary but nonetheless useful distinction between planned programs and plans of action incorporated within planned programs. We thereby recognize that different levels of activity require different time dimensions and, additionally, postulate the cumulation over time of local, small-scale efforts into larger-scale, more global efforts.

> *Task 6.* The adult educator must provide for evaluative information gathering, based on stated objectives and focused on decision-making processes regarding need fulfillment and organizational renewal.

The process of writing objectives and selecting educational strategies is not complete until some evaluative mechanism has been worked out. As suggested in Table 5–1, macro evaluation typically occurs at the planned program level. In some sense, evaluation at that level is part of a management control system, the channel through which information about the operation of the program, as a whole, is fed back to organizational administrators. Information at this level might include impact assessments, as well as participation reports and cost figures. Adaptation of administrative regulatory procedures in the service of efficient progress toward program objectives is based on such feedback. A component of the whole stream of macro evaluation information, and the most important one, is progress toward attainment of learning micro objectives (plans of action) by individual learners. Administrative response to failure to achieve micro objectives might include counseling and coaching instructions; shifts in allocations of human, financial, or material resources; or review of aspects of the planned program and plans of action.

Feedback derived from evaluating program outcomes is critical to organizational renewal and in maintaining and strengthening workable linkages with target publics. Consequently, while specifications of data collection and reporting methods can be deferred for later elaboration in plans of action, it is important to keep in mind that allowing for evaluation is a necessary aspect of long-range, strategic planning. Criteria to be used in evaluation will be suggested by the form of stated objectives. Mechanisms for incorporating evaluation results are needed, and should be planned for. Evaluation itself consumes time and resources, which also must be planned for.

In most organizations, authority to allocate resources is concentrated near the top of the organizational hierarchy. Resources, in this sense, flow *downward* through the hierarchy, with information about the effective use of resources collected nearer the base of the hierarchy. Such information, and its interpretation, flow *upward* through the hierarchy. Criteria for evaluation are related to objectives. Just as there is a hierarchy of objectives, there are levels or a hierarchy of related criteria and "valuing" judgments. These two flows, of resources down and information up, form a *feedback loop* that is in constant operation. The feedback loop adjusts and adapts the service-delivery mechanisms to changing environmental circumstances. The necessity for establishing this loop may be ignored in programming only at the risk of a progressive loss of organizational adaptation and adaptability and a consequent diminution in efficiency and effectiveness in meeting program objectives.

An excellent demonstration of the perceived worth of evaluation to the programming process can be seen in the model advanced by Beal and his co-workers (1966). These authors stress, continually and explicitly, the need for evaluative checks, with a looping metaphor at every step in social change efforts (see Table 2-1).

Plans of Action and Related Processual Tasks

The second dimension of the program design and implementation subprocess is designing plans of action. Plans of action mirror the process of designing the planned program, with the difference that allocated times for completions are shorter and specific objectives more narrowly stated. *Plans of action* may be defined as specific teaching strategies and learning experiences to guide the adult educator in fulfilling macro needs through attaining macro objectives contained in the planned program. These plans of action delineate and order (1) micro needs, (2) micro objectives, (3) teaching strategies and learning experiences, and (4) specific plans for evaluating change in learners' behavior (outcomes) and assessing learning experiences. The set of processual tasks related to plans of action shares the same intellectual roots and uses the identical deductive methodology of the planned program but with more specificity. Where the planned program involves long-range planning, plans of action specify, in sequence, the educational needs, objectives, and strategies to be activated and completed within a much shorter, designated period of time.

The processual tasks involved in designing a plan of action follow the same pattern as those in designing the planned program: needs/objectives/strategies/evaluation. And that pattern grows out of three familiar and distinctive sources. Again, Tyler (1971) provides an overall, rational, curriculum-building methodology; Bloom et al. (1956) and Krathwohl, Bloom, and Masia (1964) provide their hierarchical approach to the specification of objectives; and human developmental frameworks, such as Maslow's (1970), contribute to the processual task pattern.

This inductive-deductive methodology is defined and described in Chapters 1 and 3. What must be clearly understood is that logical thinking, coupled with experience and expertise, connects the derived micro needs with the overarching macro needs, and similarly for objectives.

An analogy may be useful. An architect designs a building that, to be constructed, must be considered in terms of component systems working together. In constructing the building, the entire structure is approached by its component parts. Thus, there may be one subcontractor who works on the building's framing and masonry, another on plumbing, yet another on the wiring, and still another on the heating and ventilating system. Each of the subcontractors has to see that appropriate materials and workers are brought together at the right times and places such that each subsystem can be constructed. Each subcontractor has a separate set of plans or blueprints to follow, all keyed to the master plan (program) of the general contractor.

To illustrate the generalization further, let us suppose a city agency having the mission of city beautification contacts a neighborhood homeowners' group. In the process of talking with the leader of the group, the need to improve the landscaping of neighborhood properties is expressed. When the homeowners' needs are analyzed, the city educational programmer perceives that this is an intermediate-level need implying a more macro need (perhaps a "need" to beautify homeowners' property) and more micro needs; that is, improving landscaping will entail learning about lawn care, planting flowers, and so forth. These, in turn, may be broken down into smaller "chunks." The macro need for property beautification, at the same time, may be seen as allowing the deduction of other related unexpressed needs, for example, dwelling maintenance that, in the programmer's experienced judgment, also will have to be addressed.

Components of the programming process can be identified in the flow of this example: the organization's mission, a target public, an expressed need, analyzed needs at macro and micro levels. A planned beautification program will include the major analyzed macro needs and others that may arise. For instance, property beautification may involve interim decoration, a completely different direction for learning, and could easily spill over into areas such as a neighborhood "community watch" or efforts to rehabilitate surrounding commercial and residential areas.

Plans of action are derived from the planned program in terms of intermediate steps toward long-range, macro objectives. For example, in the situation described, a first-year plan of action might focus on landscape design, lawn planting and care, and tree or shrubbery planting. A second plan of action could address activities such as lawn and shrubbery disease control, pruning and other maintenance efforts, and choice of ornamental flowers. Each plan of action incorporates a series of sequential activities aimed at achieving macro objectives. In essence, the derivation of micro objectives is a kind of "task analysis" to identify, in a larger framework, which skills are required.

Examples of this same theme occur in almost everyone's daily experiences.

One learns to play a sport by practicing fundamental skills of dribbling, passing, shooting, and by running through patterned drills until the component acts become integrated into a skilled performance. The same idea occurs in learning to play a musical instrument: how to sit, how to hold the instrument, fingering patterns, scales, and others. In more cognitive areas, learning to read depends on the development of basic perceptual skills, the identification of letters and words, the connection of sounds to visual patterns, and so forth.

In deriving micro objectives, programmers draw on their training and expertise to develop lists of component skills that cumulatively build to the achievement of larger objectives. The process requires observational acuity, ability to see and decompose patterns, recognition and accommodation of variances in individual performance, and highly tuned, logical capabilities, all brought to bear on a well-defined problem area.

As implied by the design of a planned program, one practical concern here is how to meet the ongoing learning needs of any given public or organization. The planned program develops a forward-looking general framework for meeting those needs. A plan of action makes that framework more specific and details actual learning experiences that will meet specific needs within a specified time.

The processual tasks in plans of action, enumerated and supported, are meant to answer four basic questions:

1. What are the felt and analyzed learner needs encompassed within each macro need outlined in the planned program? How can the micro needs be arranged into a hierarchy?
2. What behavioral change(s) must learners exhibit to fulfill each of the micro needs contained within the macro needs? How can these be incorporated into a hierarchy of teaching objectives keyed to the micro needs?
3. What learner experiences should be selected and how should they be organized to facilitate learner achievement of the desired behavior stated in each micro objective?
4. How should learner progress be assessed and what measures should be used to evaluate learner activities?

These questions form the core for this explication of plans of action and the accompanying four processual tasks.

Task 1. The adult educator must delineate, order, and sequence into a logical hierarchy the micro needs of learners encompassed within each macro need.

First, Saylor and Alexander (1974) set us firmly in the context of curriculum development with this comment: "We define curriculum as a plan for providing sets of learning opportunities to achieve broad goals and related specific objectives for an identifiable population served by a single school center" (p. 6). The material presented so far has brought us to the point of having broadly defined needs, objectives, teaching strategies and learning experiences, and an evaluation plan. This first task, and the succeeding three tasks, definitely extend themes within the realm of curriculum development that will lead to the statement of specific objectives and the selection or creation of corresponding sets of teaching strategies/learning experiences.

How do we make the translation accurately and effectively between macro needs and objectives and micro needs and objectives so that the desired learning occurs? The Bloom-Krathwohl taxonomies and the Tyler rationale represent the application of precise, rational analysis to curriculum design. Both employ deductive logic.

Processual task 1 flows out of the initial task in designing the planned program, just as that task of stating macro needs was linked with the preceding analysis of needs. The argument for this particular curriculum development step is already familiar, having been described earlier; that is, expressed needs are the basis for designing teaching strategies and learning experiences; meeting those needs implies intellectual growth of the learner; a hierarchy of needs orders that growth into manageable, practical, and appropriate sequences; and concrete design of sequential teaching strategies and learning experiences can best be achieved through such hierarchies.

The primary difference here is the *level* of focus. At the teaching-learning level, the aim is to provide definite learning experiences within a specific time period. Providing an ordered sequence for micro needs sets a starting point for learning, gives a structure for short-term and long-term intellectual growth, and designates an ending point for plans of action and the planned program.

> *Task 2.* The adult educator must formulate teaching-learning micro objectives for each micro need deduced from macro needs specified in the planned program.

As in the processual tasks for the planning subprocess, the next step in designing plans of action is to go logically from micro needs to micro objectives. The rationale and methodology are the same, but at a micro level: a micro objectives hierarchy structures anticipated growth, helps in the choice of teaching strategies and learner experiences, and provides the framework for program evaluation. In stating micro objectives, we must consider both content and desired behavior; objectives provide both specific direction and guideposts for implementation; and taxonomic concepts such as those of the Bloom and Krathwohl groups are useful tools for stating objectives that enable the learner, ultimately, to go from the simple to the complex and the concrete to the abstract.

Micro or teaching objectives, along with macro or planned program objectives, specify the behavioral changes to be effected in the learners. The point was made that a statement of objectives promotes mutual teacher-learner comprehension of instructional intents. Micro objectives detail specific changes in behavior, aimed at individual learners and, via those learners, only secondarily at groups.

There is, furthermore, a marketing involvement implied here. Stated micro objectives describe in detail what the plans of action encompass at the level at which they will be consumed by learners. If the plans of action are to be effective, the micro objectives must be acceptable or "salable" to individual learners.

Micro objectives are statements of behavioral change intended to fulfill individual learners' micro needs. In this sense, stating micro objectives requires sensitivity, skill, and acumen, for it is at this level that the planned program is "fine-tuned" for peak efficiency. Most important is that the learners clearly understand how and why the teaching objectives relate to their felt needs.

A two-dimensional design of sequenced micro objectives, clearly and concisely stated, appears in Figure 5-4. The purpose of the design is to accentuate the different content and behavioral aspects of the micro objectives shown in the hieriarchy of consumer objectives (Figure 5-3). The consumer resource management program is aimed at the development of five types of consumer behavior among adult learners. The first type of consumer behavior to be developed is the learners' understanding of important facts and principles; the second type is familiarity with dependable sources of information, that is, places to which the adult learners, as consumers, may go for information on various aspects of consumer resource management. The third type of behavior is the learners' ability to interpret data with regard to all the decisions they may have to make in purchasing products in the marketplace. The fourth type of behavior is the ability to analyze and evaluate consumer goals, values, wants, and needs; consumer information; types of products available; and features of products, including qualities, prices, warranties, installation and maintenance costs, and

Content Aspect of the Objectives					
Consumer Resource Management	**Behavioral Aspect of the Objectives**				
	1. Understanding of important facts and principles	2. Familiarity with dependable sources of information	3. Ability to interpret data	4. Ability to analyze and evaluate	5. Ability to apply
A. Consumer Goals, Values, Wants, and Needs	X	X	X	X	
B. Types and Reliable Sources of Consumer Information	X	X	X	X	
C. Types of Products Available	X	X	X	X	
D. Features of Products: Qualities, Prices, Warranties, Installation and Maintenance Costs	X	X	X	X	
E. Available Payment Options (Credits)	X	X	X	X	X
F. Consumer Rights and Responsibilities	X	X	X		X

FIGURE 5-4.   Illustration of a two dimensional chart in stating sequenced micro objectives to be included in plans of action for a program in Consumer Resource Management

payment options. The fifth type of behavior is the learners' ability to apply their rights and responsibilities as consumers in the marketplace.

This two-dimensional design emphasizes that the teaching-learning micro objectives in consumer resource management must be arranged in a sequenced manner that ultimately will lead to the learners acquiring the ability to make informed decisions in the marketplace. The specification of five types of consumer behavior to be developed further suggests the need for learning activities that will provide those consumers with an understanding of important facts and principles in consumer resource management; increased familiarity with sources of consumer resource management information; increased ability to interpret, analyze, and evaluate consumer information with regard to decisions to be made in the purchase of products; and practice in the application of consumer rights and responsibilities in the marketplace.

This two-dimensional design has three important aspects. First, it serves to call the programmer's attention to the importance of the content aspects of teaching-learning micro objectives. The purpose of the program is viewed as developing behaviors in several content areas encompassed in consumer resource management, including goals and values, types and sources of consumer information, product availability, features of products, payment options, and consumer rights and responsibilities. Second, the two-dimensional design demonstrates the interrelatedness of the behavioral and content aspects of teaching-learning micro objectives. The relationship of a specific behavioral aspect to a particular content affected is denoted in Figure 5–4 by an "X." For example, the design illustrates that consumers need to understand important facts and principles with respect to *all* of the content areas. And third, the two-dimensional design aids the programmer in designing incremental plans of action to implement the planned program. It also provides clues about learning activities and the type of evidence that still needs to be presented for adult learners to conclude that they have acquired the behavior specified in each of the teaching-learning micro objectives.

Task 3. The adult educator must select and organize, for each micro objective, learning experiences that will facilitate attainment of the behavior specified in the objective.

Gress and Purpel (1978) provide a technological perspective, complementary to the selection and organization of learning experiences, through a redefinition of curriculum implementation to cover this processual task, that is, converting the curriculum design into specific instructional activities. The next issue is how to put this perspective into operation to deal with the two basic curriculum problems: (1) distinguishing teaching strategies and (2) providing economy and efficiency in learning, characterized by multiple experiences, within short periods of time.

After formulating micro or teaching-level objectives, the adult educator is faced with the task of defining and designing the learning experiences to be provided for each micro objective. Essentially, adults learn through experiencing, that is, through their reactions to the environment and responses to environmental requirements. There may be only one teacher in the learning situation, there may seem to be only one set of external situations, but there are as many learning experiences as there are learners participating. This phenomenon places considerable responsibility on the adult educator who, acting as instructor, must either set up multifaceted situations that are likely to evoke the desired experiences for all learners, or vary the experiences in the hope that at least one will be meaningful to each of the learners. When selecting learning experiences, the adult educator needs the answer to two questions: (1) What will lead to attainment of the given objective(s)? and (2) How can teaching strategies and learning experiences be designed to facilitate learning? The following generalizations about learning may be helpful to adult educators in selecting appropriate learning experiences.

It might be said that, unless an adult learner is motivated, no learning will occur. Many adults are aware of their educational deficiencies, but they may not be aware that their deficiencies could be reduced or eliminated. Until there is a perceived need to change, desire to change, and belief that change is relevant and possible, the adult tends not to change.

Motivation may be extrinsic or intrinsic. If adults participate in an educational program because someone else feels it is important for them to do so, the underlying motivation is termed *extrinsic*. When adults themselves feel that participation in learning experiences is important, the underlying motivation is termed *intrinsic*. Although people can and do learn effectively with extrinsic motivation, intrinsic motivation is more effective in the continuation of learning and its retention over a long period of time.

Learning also is more effective when the material being learned is meaningful to the learner. The importance of this generalization should not be overlooked. To be effective, learning must be related to something that is meaningful to the adult learner. Goals must be set and the pursuit of these goals must be organized by the learner, not by the instructor. As adults learn how to set their goals, to proceed toward those goals, and to recognize that they are progressing, learning will become more meaningful and desirable.

Self-activity is the most easily visualized of the learning areas, but probably the least understood. For learning to occur, there must be active participation by the learner; that is, the learner must think through the material, question, discuss, rethink, do something with the subject matter. In learning psychomotor skills, practice is provided as a matter of course. Self-activity also must be provided for learners to acquire intellectual skills in the cognitive domain. Learners need practice in solving problems and utilizing or applying the intellectual skills learned.

There is no substitute for practice in learning. Thus, the educator needs to ask, What do these adults need to learn? What are the skills they must practice before they can perform at a designated level of proficiency? Because spaced or distributed practice brings about the most effective learning, the adult educator must plan what is to be learned and in what period of time. The subject matter can then be divided into units and practice periods can be spaced or distributed, thus contributing to the effectiveness of the learning experience and the quality of learning that occurs.

A primary concern in dealing with adult learners is relearning. In conversation, the impression is given that learning is similar to veneer on a table; the phrase, "add to one's knowledge," often is used. This sounds as though one learns and subsequently adds "layers" of knowledge. Instead, if effective learning is to occur, what has been learned previously needs to be related to new learning. There must be recognition of prior experiences so that the new learning can be explored as it relates to what the learner already knows. *Relearning* involves changes in the learner's feelings about a subject, views on the importance of that subject, and understanding of the subject.

Readiness relates to the probability that the student will learn in a given situation. Readiness is the stage in the learner's development when learning comes easily, effectively, and without disturbance. This notion is drawn from Havighurst's (1956) concept of developmental tasks. A developmental task stems from pressures of three basic sources: the individual's (1) physical development, (2) psychological development, and (3) cultural environment. Degree of readiness determines whether or not the adult learner will grasp basic skills and progress toward success in other developmental tasks. The astute adult educator should be alert to the learner's readiness and provide for its enhancement and utilization in learning.

The individual learner is an integrated whole that learns, feels, behaves, and thinks as a total organism. Thus, learning experiences should be structured that provide for and encourage that integrated whole. Adult learners seek equilibrium; at the same time, they seek to achieve. As they recognize a need and it becomes meaningful to them, adult learners seek to meet that need. These are goal-oriented individuals who establish and seek goals as the setting provides.

Generalizations relating to individual differences among learners refer to their capacity, maturity, and aspirations. Content and materials must be adjusted to fit the individual learner. Level of achievement in learning is affected by the learner's level of aspiration or performance expectations. Many adults may not aspire to change their level of performance because they feel they can perform only in the way to which they are accustomed. At the other extreme and just as unrealistic is the learner whose expectation level is too high; this can be shattering. Part of the role of the adult educator is to help learners to be realistic about personal performance expectations.

Learning proceeds best for adults when they are cognizant of their learning achievements, strengths, and weaknesses. Further, when adults know their learning status and progress, they can and will modify their behavior more successfully to achieve their objectives.

The adult learner needs opportunities to experiment with self-directed approaches, to make mistakes and correct them. Each person has a unique pattern and rhythm of growth. To the degree that the adult educator adapts the subject matter to the individual learner's maturity and level of behavior, speed and ease of learning will be enhanced. Because each learner brings his or her own personality and experiences into the learning situation, the adult educator will want to take into account individual backgrounds and experiences. The learning experience will be affected by the degree to which these backgrounds and experiences are recognized and provided for.

Three criteria can be used to organize a group of learning experiences: continuity, sequence, and integration. *Continuity* refers to the major curriculum elements. This criterion emphasizes the fact that adult learners need recurring and continuing opportunity to recall and practice the behavior stipulated in an objective. Provision must be made for such recall and practice. *Sequence* emphasizes the importance of having each successive experience build on the preceding one, while leading the learner more broadly and deeply into the content involved. This criterion emphasizes progressive levels of development with each successive learning experience. *Integration* emphasizes the horizontal relationship of learning experiences. Learning experiences should be so organized as to help adult learners acquire an increasingly unified view of and relate their behavior to the elements dealt with. The foregoing notions about selecting and organizing learning experiences are in agreement with established adult learning theory.

There is no formal algorithm for selecting and organizing learning experiences; it is a task that has not been, perhaps cannot be, reduced to a formula. However, because educational programs must be tailored to specific publics according to their culture and values, the adult educator needs to develop a proper learning climate within which these adult learners are sufficiently comfortable to enjoy the full benefits of the designed learning experience. The conceptual programming model suggests patterns of decision making and some types of criteria. Ultimately, however, successful learning experiences hinge on individual adult educators bringing science and art to bear in particular instructional settings.

Task 4. The adult educator must plan for assessment of learner progress in achieving the behavioral change or outcome specified in each micro objective and for rigorous evaluation of experiences provided for learners to acquire the intended behaviors.

One thread that runs throughout the conceptual programming model is that of a logical, deductive methodology; that thread is especially conspicuous in this assessment/evaluation task. Objectives flow from needs; objectives are stated in behavioral terms to denote level of anticipated intellectual growth or change; and assessment/evaluation flows from the behavioral objectives and the learning experiences provided.

As in other aspects of program design and implementation, the programming models presented in Chapter 2 support the assessment/evaluation task as the "next step" and as involving both behavioral outcomes and the learning experiences themselves. Tyler (1971), for one, provides general evaluation guidelines (discussed fully in Chapter 6). The core of evaluation for Tyler is assessing the degree to which learning experiences produce desired behavioral change, providing continual monitoring throughout the learning activities, and collecting valid evidence about teaching strategies and learning outcomes. Although evaluation is one of the elements of evaluation and accountability, the third and final subprocess of the conceptual programming model, it must be anticipated and planned for throughout the programming process, primarily via the three stages of defining, ordering, and sequencing objectives.

Evaluation at the micro objectives level is concerned with determining whether or not a given objective has been reached with a particular learner, following participation in a specific learning experience. Mager (1962) discusses the traps into which educators can fall in evaluating learner progress. Congruent with the deductive methodology of this entire presentation is that assessment of individual learner progress toward the achievement of a micro objective is tied logically and consistently to the objective in terms of behavioral output to be measured, conditions under which assessment is made, and so forth. Tyler's (1971) suggestion of a behavior-content grid, as illustrated in Table 5-1, provides a potentially powerful technology for maintaining such consistency. Examples provided by Bloom et al. (1956) and Krathwohl, Bloom, and Masia (1964) further refine that approach.

A breakdown in the deductive pattern of thinking and analysis that leads from organizational analysis, to nurturance of community linkage in needs identification and analysis, through the challenging planning process, and on into program design and the implementation of plans of action would be a reflection on the professionalism of the adult educator as change agent and programmer and on adult education in general. Yet, it seems frequently to be the case that evaluation in decentralized field settings is left to the devices of the individual field practitioner, who performs under local stresses that can be understood only incompletely at other levels of the organization, and who may have limited resources and motivation to engage in rigorous evaluation procedures. At the same time, these data are the droplets that must be accumulated to produce the flow of information essential for organizational renewal through adaptation to change in its environment. And the field practitioner is in the best position to collect these data.

The foregoing is intentionally strongly stated. In the programming process, we speak of "closing the loop" with evaluation and feedback. Our contention is that, without effective mechanisms to implement renewal, the organization becomes progressively less well adapted to its environment and, like the dinosaur, eventually will become extinct. The beginning point in collecting good information is at the teaching-learning interface. Emphasis on such feedback must be incorporated into the plans of action. The importance of the evaluation steps should be the watchword for field practitioners.

Action Strategies and Related Processual Tasks

Implementing plans of action, at its simplest, can be defined as the activation of all elements contained in the plans of action through efforts of the adult educator as a facilitator of learning. Many of the authors already examined provide support for one or more of the five processual tasks involved in implementing a plan of action: marketing strategies, resources for implementation, monitoring, reinforcement of learners, and feedback.

> *Task 1.* The adult educator must utilize various strategies and techniques in marketing both the planned program and the plans of action.

The practice of marketing a product usually is perceived as being solely the province of business organizations. However, adult educators have been engaged in that practice for many years, without using the specific word marketing. In adult education *marketing* can be defined roughly as gaining acceptance of, consensus upon, or participation in any given educational venture. This can include both "selling" the program to community leaders and recruiting learners.

Marketing texts refer to a number of concepts useful for adult educators. While only a few of these are mentioned briefly here, it is becoming increasingly clear that marketing activities will claim more and more of adult educators' attention as time passes. The principal reasons for this prediction are, first, adult education program activities compete directly for the time and effort of potential participants, both among themselves and with multiple entertainment and recreational outlets. Second, decreasing personal finances among potential clients means that decisions to participate are increasingly difficult to make.

The latter point brings out the idea that, in general, the market represents an economic arena in which value is exchanged for value. In the case of adult education, the participant exchanges time, effort, and money, along with cognitive and affective energy, for presumably improved cognitive, affective, or psychomotor skills. Often, the decision to participate in an educational activity may mean the sacrifice of scarce time, limited energy, and finite monetary resources that could as easily be allocated for other goods or services. The marketing problem for adult educators, then, is to produce a product, for example, a set of objectives that the potential adult learner will view as worth such a sacrifice—in other words, to produce a value worth the exchange.

Marketing specialists speak of "market mix," a term intended to suggest that the decision to enter into the market or to participate in marketing transactions is multifactorial. This collection of factors has come to be known as the four P's: program, price, promotion, and place. Each of these factors has an impact on an individual's decision to participate in a proffered educational activity or experience. Let us consider briefly each of these independent factors.

The basic assumption regarding *program* is that potential consumers of the adult education program will participate only when the program offered matches their current or anticipated needs. Knowles (1970) stresses the assumption that adult learners are "now"-oriented: educational activities are selected on their capability for fulfilling immediate needs. By extension of these assumptions, one builds a program through community and participant-oriented research into felt/expressed needs.

The planning subprocess and the design dimension of the design and implementation subprocess of the conceptual programming model directly address this aspect of marketing. The planning subprocess entails mapping publics to discover relevant cultural, political, economic, and other constraints and influences on social systems by which such systems may be delineated (see Chapter 4, Planning). Target publics and their leaders and followers are identified and are engaged in identifying and analyzing those publics' expressed needs. These needs then are used in the design dimension to construct a planned program intended to fulfill those needs; that is, the educational "product" is explicitly designed with the identified and analyzed needs of a target public in mind.

With regard to *place*, a social system, a community, a public generally occupy a geographical region. The "marketing mix" concept suggests that the economic exchange intended can occur only when the potential consumer comes into contact with the product.

In the case of an educational program, the best marketing strategy is to locate the program services delivery as close as possible to the location of the target public. This location has both a physical and a temporal aspect: the central notion is that the program must be easily accessible to members of the target public. If it is too far away, obviously, the location is wrong. Although the wide availability of personal automobiles and public transportation affects this relationship, it must be noted that many target publics—the poor, the elderly, the handicapped, mothers of young children—may not easily avail themselves of educational opportunities if they are physically difficult to get to.

A parallel case can be made for temporal "place." A program scheduled during the work hours of members of its target public may as well be on the moon for its practical availability. A further aspect of place is the layout or arrangement of physical facilities. In a sense, these factors are part of the program "product." The acceptability or appeal of the program will depend directly on the acceptability or appeal of the facilities, especially in the case of some special groups such as the elderly or the handicapped. Finally, the match of place with adult learner characteristics, expectations, and self-concept or role perception is worth mentioning. We noted earlier that mismatches between program objectives and sponsoring or hosting agencies are possible, with a predictable, negative effect on participation. A similar generalization holds here: participants interested in adult basic education, for example, are probably more comfortable going to class in a community center rather than a school building.

Setting *prices* for educational programs is perhaps the area in which the most confusion exists. Yet, this is one of the most obvious determiners of participation. There is a large literature on price setting to which the reader should turn for more sophisticated guidance than can be offered here. A few generalizations will have to suffice.

In many settings, pricing policies are determined beyond any control of the programmer. In North Carolina, for instance, the fee charged for continuing education courses in the state's community colleges is fixed by the state legislature. In other settings, the presence of tax, grant, or other subsidies complicates the picture.

Price theorists cite three basic approaches to price setting. The first, *full-cost pricing,* takes full costs, direct and indirect, plus some typically fixed "profit" or "markup" percentage and prorates that figure over some estimated volume of production or sales. In an educational setting, this may be an appropriate method. A major limitation is that the number of adult learners usually is not known in advance. An alternative is to set a minimum enrollment such that costs are recouped.

A second approach is *going rate* pricing, the assumption being that by making one's price match the "going rate" among competitors, one will draw at least a proportionate share of the market. Since costs among competitors are likely to be fairly close, a reasonable return might be expected. A difficulty for educational programs is a complex system of subsidies that influence costs in unknown ways among competitors: matching the going rate, without the same subsidies, may mean incurring a loss.

The final approach to pricing is *marginalism*, based on the notion that, as price goes up, participation goes down. However, revenues go up with price, to a point, and then decline. Revenue is unit price multiplied by participation. Clearly, the pricing strategy here is to maximize revenue by setting the price at the point where the peak occurs. The real problem is getting reliable information on the effect of demand versus price, so marginalism is difficult to put into practice.

A reasonable middle road might be to set program prices (1) initially on the basis of full cost, then adjust for any subsidies or (2) on the going rate or perceived ability of the target public to pay. For some types of items there is an appeal in higher price, although quality frequently lags behind. At the same time, higher prices effectively reduce the "true" target public, so both factors need to be kept in mind. One typically hopes to maximize participation; price of the program obviously bears on participation, but in complex and convoluted ways.

No program succeeds unless information about its availability, context, and benefits is communicated to the members of the target public. *Promotion* or advertising of programs, services, or products takes many forms. Although no specific recipes for success can be given, some helpful guidelines are offered.

First, one must think through the promotional campaign. The primary task is to establish an objective, for example, to enroll ten new mothers and fathers in a Parent Effectiveness class. This marks where the campaign is headed. Next, describe the target public of the campaign; this resembles the mapping step mentioned earlier, yet, typically, has a narrower focus because the objectives of the program are narrower. Next, list the benefits of the program for the target public—what improvements they might expect in their lives. Note that, for many people, to be told "you will learn" has much less appeal than to be told "you will become able to." The benefits cited must be supported by credible arguments and other information, so the next step is to list these. Finally, describe on paper for yourself a tone or manner for the campaign; for example, the tone of a Cadillac advertisement is quite different from that for a Chevrolet. The tone should be consistent with what you know about the target public.

Promotional media include radio, television, newspapers, flyers, posters, even billboards. The approach here is to select those most likely to reach the public you want to serve, balanced against the expense involved.

As a rule, word of mouth is most effective, and the best advertisement is a satisfied client. Linkages into the community also can be exploited effectively as means to promote programs.

In summary, the marketing mix begins and ends with a detailed knowledge of the target public and its needs, as described under the planning subprocess in Chapter 4. Factors of program, place, price, and promotion all hinge on this knowledge. Consequently, we can give no better advice than to perform the linkage development and needs identification, assessment, and analysis steps particularly well.

> *Task 2.* The adult educator must identify, mobilize, develop, and utilize resources, both human and material, to implement and carry through effectively the adult learning experiences enumerated in the plans of action.

Once plans of action have been designed, the adult educator's attention must turn to decisions that will have to be made to implement the plans. Learning activities associated with each plan of action must be carefully studied and analyzed to determine learning experiences to be offered and teaching strategies to be used. Having selected those to be used, decisions must be made about resources that will be needed to assure successful follow-through in their implementation. Decisions also must be made about the time element for each learning experience. Succeeding decisions will include the schedule for specific learning activities, the location, the type of meeting facilities needed for learning activities; the procurement or preparation of learning resource materials; and the use of local resource persons, usually leaders, to assist with promoting and organizing activities and, in many instances, in the actual teaching. All of these are important decisions to be made and actions to be implemented that may affect either favorably or unfavorably the impact of the plans of action or teaching-learning activities.

Because scheduling of learning activities can have a major effect on participation, several factors should be considered. Experience has shown that, in most instances, a large segment of the target public will be fully employed persons who, unless their employers permit participation during working hours, can attend classes only during evening hours. Thus, the employment status of target publics and their work schedules are important considerations in scheduling decisions. Seasonal factors, particularly in rural and rural nonfarm areas, need to be considered. Farm audiences usually can participate more fully during late fall and winter months. Early rather than later evening hours for classes generally are preferred by adults.

Determining the location or place for learning activities also requires careful thought by the adult educator. Most writers on the subject suggest that, to provide maximum access, programs should be offered at a location as nearly central to the target public as possible. Efforts to establish learning sites in or near industries that employ potential learners often entail making contacts with the administrators of these businesses or industries. Adult educators have experienced considerable success in persuading such administrators to provide meeting space and related resources for learning activities in the plant or in the industrial facility.

Once the sites/locations have been determined, the next task is to select the type(s) of meeting facilities needed for the planned learning activities. The major goal is to select facilities that are comfortable for adults and conducive to learning. Various meeting facilities might be considered, including homes, community centers, church buildings, school meeting places, as well as a host of others. Whatever the choice, care should be taken in selecting facilities that are conducive to adult learning.

The adult educator must make decisions about the resource materials to be used in the several learning activities of the plans of action. Such materials may be purchased or developed by either the adult educator or talented local resource persons. Considerable creativity will need to be exhibited in selecting or preparing materials that are relevant to the specific learning activities and the educational needs of the target publics. A number of commercial firms prepare and offer for sale resource materials for adult learners. The adult educator probably will have access to catalogs published by adult education commercial firms that may be useful in selecting learning materials.

In many instances, the adult educator, as the only professional change agent in a community, county, or other form of social system, faces educational needs situations that might involve any number of learning activities and potential adult learners. To deal with this dilemma, the adult educator must solicit the help of volunteers in the neighborhood, community, or system to assist with promotional and organizational work, as well as with the actual teaching. Although this identification and recruitment of volunteer leaders can extend the adult educator's efforts in a number of ways, some preparation is necessary.

Each learning activity must first be analyzed to determine the competencies that will be needed to assure its implementation. Most communities and larger social systems contain an abundance of highly qualified lay leaders and other resource persons. To locate these resources, the target public first must be surveyed to identify the number and type of potential volunteer leaders and resource persons available to assist in conducting adult learning activities. These potential resource persons should be approached by the adult educator and asked if they will assist with specific adult learning activities. Once resource persons have been identified and recruited, the adult educator must concentrate on training and equipping them to assume specific roles.

Well-planned volunteer leader training programs can contribute much to these volunteers' effectiveness in promoting and organizing adult education program activities, as well as the actual teaching. Volunteers can be rich sources of knowledge, know-how, and experience. Actually, many of these resource persons can be identified during the time that the adult educator maps publics, selects target publics, and interfaces with the leaders of those publics and their followers in needs identification, assessment, and analysis activities.

Task 3. The adult educator must make provisions for ongoing monitoring of planned learner experiences.

Once learning is activated, the next processual task is to develop and implement a systematic approach to observing, studying, and monitoring the learning activities. Astute adult educators will adopt a participant-observer role to keep abreast of the ongoing learning activities.

The objectives of this monitoring processual task are (1) to ensure that learning activities are implemented as intended and (2) to be available to leaders, teachers, and other resource persons for assistance on programming matters, as needed. In this sense, adult educators become "managers" in carrying out various parts of the plan of action. Monitoring ongoing learning activities means that adult educators, as managers, develop and implement a system for keeping in touch with volunteers, teachers, and other resource persons as they carry out the learning activities.

To monitor a system or network of planned learning activities and the actions of those involved in their implementation requires an effective and open two-way communication system between adult educators and the implementers, whether teachers, organizers, or others. Continuous interaction between adult educators and these implementers is essential to the successful implementation of planned learning activities. The feedback obtained from leaders and resource persons provides information on which to base informed and timely decisions about any needed learning activity adjustments or modifications. It is important and sometimes crucial that adjustments or modifications in an ongoing learning activity be made as quickly as possible to assure maximal behavioral change.

In functioning as monitors and managers of the network of learning activities included in a plan of action, adult educators perform several leader-manager-teacher roles. First, they must be knowledgeable about the planned learning activities and the sociocultural environment in which these activities are being carried out. Second, they need to understand the strengths and limitations of the local leaders and resource persons involved in the organizing, promoting or marketing, and actual teaching of these learning activities. Third, adult educators must exercise the interpersonal skills needed to create an open, two-way communication system with the many persons assisting with implementing the various aspects of the planned learning activities. Fourth, they must establish and maintain a monitoring system for observing ongoing learning activities. Such a system includes periodic visits to the sites of learning activities, conferences with those carrying out the learning activities, telephone calls, and a host of other mechanisms. Fifth, adult educators must know how to process, evaluate, and use the feedback obtained from leaders as a base for program change and adjustment decisions, as needed. Sixth, they must be adept at making good, practical decisions about learning activities and their intended outcomes.

In summary, adult educators function as managers and monitors in establishing and maintaining an effective two-way communication system with the leaders and resource persons who are involved in carrying out planned learning activities, that is, plans of action. Maintenance of such a system helps to assure the attainment of maximal change impact on learners. It is at this stage in the programming process that adult educators' tutorial craftsmanship becomes crucial to its success.

Task 4. The adult educator must provide for continuous reinforcement of the learners and the teachers.

Behavioral change efforts undertaken by individual learners, groups of learners, and systems of learners require considerable input on their part in attempting to understand and respond to the proposed change. As pointed out earlier in this chapter, some relearning by those affected usually is required. That is, learners have to cope with and contrast their familiar ways of behaving to a different way of behaving. This process often is perplexing and frustrating to those who are attempting to change their behavior. Further, in most change situations, the adult learners involved are busy persons for whom learning new ways of behaving is secondary to earning a living and performing other crucial adult roles. The point being emphasized here is that the "change" process in adult education is difficult for both learner and teacher and often very slow. To help them persist in this type of situation, those who are attempting to learn need some type of feedback. Lippitt, Watson, and Westley (1958), Kidd (1973), and Knowles (1970) conclude that behavioral change occurs most effectively when adult learners are given feedback about their performance, along with support and encouragement for their efforts.

Whose role is it to provide continuing feedback and reinforcement to adult learners? Most adult learning activities involve both an adult educator and resource persons such as leaders, organizers, and teachers at the action level. It would seem that all these persons should use every opportunity to provide feedback to the learners. Adult educators, who often function as managers and strategists, should carefully prepare volunteer leaders and other resource persons in how to recognize and reward adult learner performance. The performance of this role by the volunteer or other resource persons requires a thorough understanding of adult learners and their needs, as well as knowledge about strategies for structuring behavioral change situations for these learners to provide motivation and experience satisfaction.

Adult educators, when interacting with learners, should capitalize on every opportunity to support the change efforts of volunteer leaders and teachers by providing feedback and reinforcement to the learners. In like fashion, volunteer leaders and other persons who often organize and actually teach in planned learning activities, need to experience satisfaction in the performance of their difficult and demanding task. It is the adult educator's responsibility to provide feedback to these persons concerning their performance.

The importance of the reinforcement processual task to effective programming is highlighted in learning theory. Learning proceeds with greater ease for adult learners when they are aware of their strengths and weaknesses. Adult learners' response to a change situation is affected by their perceptions of their degree of success in achieving the new behavior and its relevancy to their lifestyles. When adult learners know their status and are made aware of their progress, they more successfully modify or change their behavior to achieve their objectives.

> *Task 5.* Adult educators must maintain a sensitivity to the need for and a willingness to adapt or redirect learner experiences as monitoring, feedback, and their own observations expose the need for such change.

This final processual task related to plans of action points up the importance of keeping teaching strategies and learning experiences geared to adult learners' perceived needs. Considerable flexibility is needed to act promptly in modifying or changing learning activities when situations warrant. Adult educators who have implemented a long-range planned program know various circumstances inevitably may lead to alterations in the original design. Learners' needs may shift within a content area; unique group characteristics may render original teaching strategies or learning experiences, or both, inappropriate. Further, anticipated resources for learning activities may not materialize.

A key factor in implementing and carrying out plans of action is adult educators' sensitivity to and understanding of what is transpiring with regard to the change situation. Well-informed adult educators will promptly grasp problematic situations and respond positively and effectively with regard to modifying learning activities or other aspects of the planned program and the overall programming process.

Periodic evaluations of the ongoing plan of action should provide an assessment of each learning activity in the plan of action and indications of the adequacy of the learning activity in effecting positive behavioral change in the adult learners, within their sociocultural context. In addition to providing an opportunity to replan and make adjustments for any inadequacies, such evaluations should suggest "next step" actions. Lippitt, Watson, and Westley (1958) and Beal et al. (1966) concur with this approach to learning activity modifications through monitoring and feedback.

DESIGN AND IMPLEMENTATION
IN RETROSPECT

The design and implementation subprocess is the starting point for the planned program and extends through its actual implementation. The subprocess has as its primary focus the actual design, development, and implementation of a planned program as a purposive educational response to expressed needs identified and analyzed in the planning subprocess. Design and implementation has three distinct but interrelated components: (1) the translation of analyzed expressed needs into hierarchies of needs and objectives, (2) sequenced increments or plans of action for executing the planned program within designated periods of time, and (3) formulating and executing educational strategies for implementing plans of action and, ultimately, the planned program.

Adult educators are expected to translate the felt/expressed need of the target public that has been identified and analyzed in collaboration with learners and their leaders into a hierarchy of high-level (macro) related needs. The expressed need becomes the entry-level or threshold need at the base of the hierarchy. The macro needs are included in the planned program and become the major focal point of the adult educator's change efforts over an extended period of time. Macro needs lead to the formulation of parallel macro objectives, plans of action, general educational strategies, and specification of expected outcomes, all of which are included in the planned program. Plans of action become the means for implementing the planned program.

In designing plans of action, the adult educator gives attention to those micro needs included in the needs hierarchy that was generated in arriving at the macro needs to be included in the planned program. These sequenced, lower-level micro needs become the basis for designing incremental, sequenced plans of action. For each micro need, micro or teaching objectives are formulated and appropriate learning experiences are selected and organized. Plans for evaluation are designed to measure outcomes of each teaching objective and to assess the adequacy or efficacy of the learning experiences.

Actual execution of the individual plans of action requires rigorous surveillance and follow-through by the adult educator. Action strategies involve (1) marketing the plans of action; (2) identifying, mobilizing, developing, and utilizing human and material resources; (3) ongoing monitoring of the planned learning experiences; (4) making provision for and providing reinforcement for the learners and teachers; and (5) using feedback to modify or redirect learning experiences, as warranted.

The third and final programming subprocess in the conceptual programming model is evaluation and accountability, treated in Chapter 6. This subprocess sets forth the framework for decisions to be made by adult educators in evaluating and accounting for the outcomes/outputs of the planned program.

REFERENCES

BEAL, G. M., R. C. BLOUNT, R. C. POWERS, and H. J. JOHNSON, *Social Action and Interaction in Program Planning.* Ames: Iowa State University Press, 1966.

BLOOM, B. S., M. D. ENGLEHART, E. J. FURST, W. H. HILL, and D. R. KRATHWOHL, *Taxonomy of Educational Objectives. Handbook I—Cognitive Domain.* New York: David McKay Company, 1956.

BOYLE, P. G., *Planning Better Programs.* New York: McGraw-Hill Book Company, 1981.

CROSS, P. K., *Adults as Learners.* San Francisco: Jossey-Bass, Publishers, 1981.

FREIRE, P., *Pedagogy of the Oppressed.* New York: Herder and Herder, 1970.

GAGNE, R., "Behavioral Objectives? Yes!" *Educational Leadership,* 29 (1972), 394–396.

GOLBY, M. J., J. GREENWALD, and H. WEST, eds., *Curriculum Design.* London: Croon Helm, Ltd., 1975.

GRESS, J. R., and D. S. PURPEL, eds., *Curriculum: An Introduction to the Field.* Berkeley, Calif.: McCutchan Publishing Company, 1978.

GROSS, B., "Administrative Planning," in *Public Administration: Concept and Case,* ed. R. J. Stillman. Boston: Houghton Mifflin Company, 1976.

HAVIGHURST, R. J., *Adult Education and Adult Needs.* Boston: Center for the Study of Liberal Education for Adults, 1956.

HIRST, P., "The Nature and Structure of Curriculum Objectives," in *Curriculum Design,* ed. M. J. Golby, J Greenwald, and H. West. London: Croon Helm, Ltd., 1975.

HOULE, C., *The Design of Education.* San Francisco: Jossey-Bass, Publishers, 1972.

KIDD, R. J., *How Adults Learn.* New York: Association Press, 1973.

KNOWLES, M. S., *The Modern Practice of Adult Education: Andragogy versus Pedagogy.* New York: Association Press, 1970.

KRATHWOHL, D. R., B. S. BLOOM, and D. B. MASIA, *Taxonomy of Educational Objectives. Handbook II—Affective Domain.* New York: David McKay Company, 1964.

LIPPITT, R., J. WATSON, and B. WESTLEY, *The Dynamics of Planned Change.* New York: Harcourt, Brace & World, Inc., 1958.

MAGER, R. F., *Preparing Instructional Objectives*. Palo Alto, Calif.: Fearn Publishers, 1962.

MASLOW, A., *Motivation and Personality*. New York: Harper & Row, Publishers, 1970.

SAYLOR, J. G., and W. M. ALEXANDER, *Planning Curriculum for Schools*. New York: Holt, Rinehart and Winston, 1974.

SPICER, E. H., ed., *Human Problems in Technological Change*. New York: Russell Sage Foundation, 1952.

TYLER, R. W., *Basic Principles of Curriculum and Instruction*. Chicago: University of Chicago Press, 1971.

WILES, J., and J. BONDI, *Curriculum Development: A Guide to Practice*. Columbus, Ohio: Charles E. Merrill, 1979.

Chapter Six

Evaluation and Accountability

Evaluation and accountability, the third and final subprocess in the conceptual programming model, pose some of the greatest challenges, yet enjoy only broad agreement among experts as to context and general approach. Explication of the conceptual programming model has included several references to the necessity for continual evaluation and feedback, beginning with the design dimension of the design-implementation subprocess and continuing through the implementation dimension. Now it is time to consider what the evaluation or judgment and decision-making dimension and the accountability or reporting dimension of this third and final subprocess mean in the context of programming.

Certainly, evaluation "closes the loop," providing feedback to the organization and the target public, and thus logically follows teaching-learning activities. But it might easily have been addressed first, in the sense that evaluation is the most basic element of programming. From another perspective, the programming process has been alluded to as continuous and cyclic: evaluation is the step that joins cycles of program activity, which provides for continuity. In a more typical view, evaluation *follows* activity.

Several factors combine to make evaluation a challenging undertaking. First among these is the variety of definitions that have been proposed for the concept. Suffice it to say, only the broadest consensus, spiced with liberal amounts of conflicting opinion, exists on what evaluation is.

A second obstacle to evaluation is that multiple definitions and conceptual perspectives suggest a range of technical, methodological, and interpretive alternatives. It matters a great deal, for example, whether one selects a naturalistic, descriptive approach versus a quantitative, hypothesis-testing approach to how a given evaluation will be planned, implemented, reported, and used.

Finally, most students, observers, and practitioners of evaluation would concur that evaluation is just plain hard to do well. Several reasons for this can be pinpointed. Specification of what to measure is often difficult because evaluation relates to all sorts of complex issues: values held by evaluators, administrators, learners; philosophical allegiances; purposes, both known and unknown; and so forth. Even given some agreement on what to measure, implementing measurement is frequently complicated by lack of availability or applicability of appropriate instruments, by less-than-desirable reliability and validity of selected measuring devices, by sampling problems, by inapplicability of statistical techniques, and the like. Interpretation of planned program outcomes/outputs is usually less than straightforward due to uncontrollable, confounding, and intervening variables. Similarly, generalization suffers due to some of these same factors, plus the nonrecurring nature of situations, each of which may involve different learners, different teachers, and different contexts.

The most useful approach to evaluation often appears to be more qualitatively or clinically oriented and less research-directed, in that the decisions made are based on limited and sometimes inadequate information. What we hope is that decision makers, given a framework for evaluation, will become aware of the areas in which their information may be either highly subjective or insurmountably limited and in which, consequently, their decisions are only "best guesses."

ASSUMPTIONS AND CONCEPTS

As noted in Chapter 3, the evaluation and accountability subprocess is guided by six basic assumptions:

1. The primary purpose of the planned adult education program is to effect desirable behavioral changes in a specified public.
2. Outputs/outcomes of planned adult education programs can be identified and evaluated.
3. An adult education organization proceeds through the programming process as a series of conscious choices and decisions. It is further assumed that each choice and decision is rational and based on values that are understood.
4. Management and renewal of the adult education organization depend upon continuous generation of program outputs and feedback through evaluation and accountability.
5. Participation of target publics in evaluating how well their educational experiences met the planned program's objectives is both desirable and necessary.
6. The adult education organization has both a commitment and an ethical responsibility to account for program choices (inputs) and outputs to its learners, funding sources, the profession, and, where appropriate, its governance body.

The evaluation and accountability subprocess is based on three concepts. These are (1) determining and measuring program inputs, (2) assessing program inputs, and (3) using evaluation findings for program revisions, organizational renewal, and accounting to the target publics, funding sources, the profession, and, where appropriate, the governing body.

EVALUATION

The many views found in the literature on evaluation begin with varying definitions of the term. Among the definitions of evaluation offered by various authors are

> The process of determining the extent to which objectives have been attained in evaluation (Thiede, 1964, p. 29).

> Program evaluation is the determination of the extent to which the desired objectives have been attained or the amount of movement that has been made in the desired direction (Boyle and Johns, 1970, p. 70).

Educational evaluation is the process of delineating, obtaining, and providing useful information for judging decision alternatives (Stufflebeam, 1971, p. xxv).

The process of evaluation is essentially . . . determining to what extent the educational objectives are actually being realized by the curriculum and instruction (Tyler, 1971, pp. 105–106).

Program evaluation is the process of judging (or a judgment as to) the worth or value of a program. This judgment is formed by comparing evidence as to what the program "is" with criteria as to what the program "should be" (Steele, 1970, p. 8).

It [evaluation] is simply the determination of the goodness, worth, or value of programs (defined as systems of social interaction with both experiences and outcomes) (Forest, 1976, p. 167).

Grotelueschen (1980) provides additional perspectives on evaluation. These include (1) comparing actual performance with performance standards, (2) providing data inputs for assessing alternatives for decisions, (3) comparing effects with analyzed needs, (4) allowing audience values versus program merit judgments, and (5) seeking expert opinion or critical review of programs.

The foregoing definitions and perspectives illustrate the range of thinking and the variety of responses to what evaluation is; and they are potentially confusing. In anticipation of such confusion and to focus the discussion, we will provide an operational definition of evaluation and an accompanying set of processual tasks. However, it will be useful first to identify six intellectual *themes* essential to an accurate definition of program evaluation:

1. *Rationality* and *order* are premises designated as underlying and permeating the whole programming process as depicted in the conceptual programming model.
2. The *organizational context* and the *sociocultural context* in which evaluation functions form the environment for, a focus into, and a beneficiary of the concept.
3. Evaluation is an *ongoing process* that has its roots in (a) the planning subprocess and its preliminary data and (b) the design and implementation subprocess.
4. Evaluation, like planning, takes place at *multiple levels* of programming activity.
5. *Decision making*, based on judgments of planned program worth, is the central function in evaluation,
6. *Judgments* require the complementary notion of criteria against which critical judgments about planned programs are made, the central question being, What is good?

These six intellectual themes indicate the broadening of the evaluation concept that has evolved since Tyler (1971) initially defined the term in 1950. More specific concerns in planned program evaluation that will be examined as this discussion progresses are how program inputs, context, and processes relate to program outputs; how efficient a program is; how suitable it is; and its overall importance.

The principal product of programming, as examined so far, is a set of teaching-learning micro objectives incorporated into one or more sequenced plans of action. The micro objectives so stated are phrased in terms of individual behavioral change. We have contended all along that the ultimate work of programming depends totally on individual learners' behavioral change brought about by their participation in judiciously selected and organized learning experiences, facilitated by professionally prepared educators.

The teaching-learning micro objectives are described as being the result of a deductive, analytical chain leading back through hierarchies of objectives, hierarchies of needs, and, as primary input information, felt needs identified, assessed, and analyzed collaboratively with leaders and learners in the target public. Satisfying those felt needs and related analyzed needs depends on the attainment of specified macro objectives. The basic units of such macro objectives are sequenced micro objectives at the teaching-learning interface. Overall success of the planned program will be revealed first in the achievement of individual objectives: no program implemented at the individual learner level (and no educational program can be implemented in any other way) succeeds unless micro objectives at that level are attained. Program evaluation, then, begins by examining progress toward meeting micro objectives. The consequences of such an examination are that the entire programming process and the organization from which the programming originates also must be examined. An analogy might be helpful here.

Most manufacturing companies have a quality control department. That department has the responsibility for examining samples of finished products to determine if they meet acceptable standards for sale. If the finished product is unsatisfactory, where might one look for the problem to be corrected? Clearly, it could be at any point of the manufacturing process. One logical approach to locating the source of the problem would be to examine each manufacturing phase, in reverse order, from finished product back toward raw materials. Our suggestion is that evaluation of programming should take a parallel approach. First, we ask whether our stated micro objectives were achieved. Then, depending on the answer, we examine the adequacy of other phases of the programming process, for example, macro objectives or needs assessment and analysis. A series of questions about programming can be constructed to facilitate such assessment; we will turn to those presently. The fact that programming occurs in an organizational context brings up the notion that a planned program's success depends on its context at least as much as on the efforts that are carried through in delivering the program.

To return to the manufacturing analogy, the quality control department, in attempting to isolate the source of defective products, might conclude that certain aspects of the manufacturing milieu, such as the layout of the plant, or the supervision of employees, or employee practices, or management arrangements, were responsible for poor product quality, rather than some aspect of the manufacturing process itself. In adult education organizations, somewhat similar questions can be asked about the decision-making process, personnel relations, management policies and practices, or other facets of the organizational environment. The point here is that beginning an evaluation at the "product" or "outcome" level leads directly back to examination of processual tasks and the organizational environment.

One may reasonably assume that few organizations are perfectly organized, structured, or operated for their intended function in a given environment. A major goal of program evaluation is to provide information or feedback that can be used in organizational renewal, that is, an organization's efforts to improve its functions and adapt to its environment. Feedback, in the "quality control" sense, is the only apparent means by which such adaptation can occur. Gordon Lippitt (1976) defines *feedback* as "the return of a portion of the output of a system, process, etc., to its input in such a way as to modify the input, frequently for purposes of control" (p. 8).

Adaptation of function to environment would be expected to promote organizational efficiency, in the sense of cost per unit of service delivery, thus leading to more services delivered within a given budget. When tax monies or any other funding source are used to support adult education programs, efficiency of operation is a major goal. Efficiency depends on organizational adaptation, which depends on feedback, which depends on assessment of program outcomes or *evaluation*.

The conceptual flow of evaluation reverses that of the total programming process; that is, evaluation begins with plans of action outcomes. Starting at this level, we ask whether or not teaching-learning objectives were realized. If not, we examine the objectives, the learning experiences provided, and the monitoring and reinforcing activities. Were the objectives appropriate for the learners involved? Were they stated in measurable terms? Were adequate resources made available? Was there a clear relationship between needs and objectives; that is, was the deduction skillfully done? Was our marketing effort appropriate and effective? All these questions reflect on the processual tasks of plans of action and action strategies. Next, we examine the long-range planned program in much the same fashion, particularly considering the logical, deductive methodologies used to identify, assess, and analyze needs; specify and state macro needs; translate macro needs into macro objectives; specify general educational strategies; and make general plans for evaluating outcomes.

Planning, the first subprocess in programming, provides the foundation for later tasks. If we discover discrepancies from anticipated outcomes or outputs, it is possible that the fault lies all the way back in the planning subprocess. Perhaps we erred in needs analysis: did we misunderstand or fail to communicate the input of leaders and their followers, for instance? Or, perhaps, errors in judgment occurred in elaborating analyzed needs from expressed/felt needs. Then, again, did we identify the appropriate target public leaders to query? Did we do a thorough job of mapping and setting priorities of target publics? All these questions can and should be raised as evaluative issues.

Finally, we come to the organization itself. If teaching-learning objectives were not met, was it because the organizational mission, philosophy, functions, structure, and processes were mismatched with the task at hand? Were the objectives within the mission of the organization? Did the organizational structure facilitate or hinder attainment of the objectives? Certainly, these questions reflect on the organization's adaptation or adaptability to its environment and suggest avenues for organizational renewal based on the outcomes of the organization's programming efforts.

In describing their social action model, in which feedback loops are a major constituent, Beal et al. (1966) make an important point for all programming efforts, one which we reiterate here. Before continuing the discussion of this model, however, it would seem appropriate to speak to the feedback loop concept; that is, a *feedback loop* is the path through a feedback system from input to output and back to input. Thus, feedback is a two-way communications system. According to G. Lippitt (1976), Bradford maintains that individuals need accurate information about the difference between what they are trying to do and how well they are doing it. They need to be able to use this information to correct or change their actions, to steer themselves. This looplike flow of information is discussed by Pfiffner and Sherwood (1960): "Essential to feedback is the notion that the flow of information is actually having a reciprocating effect on behavior. That is why the term *loop* is frequently associated with feedback. This circular pattern involves the flow of information to the point of action, a flow back to the point of decision with information on the action, and then a return to the point of action with new information and perhaps instructions" (p. 299).

Returning to the Beal et al. (1966) model, these authors perceive programming as a macro feedback loop in which evaluative results (assessments of program outputs) are used to revise, refine, and renew the program and the programming process. But nested within the macro loop are a series of micro feedback-evaluation loops, in which the adequacy of each programming step is assessed through discussion among program personnel and with target public leaders; through monitoring ongoing activities, particularly with participant clients; and through continual observation and updating of information from the target public as a whole. These micro loops are depicted as occurring at every level of development of a social action program; repetition of the depiction emphasizes the critical nature of the intermediate feedback-review-monitoring steps. Application of this principle to the conceptual programming model is illustrated schematically in Figure 6-1.

The Relation of Evaluation
to Other Program Activities

A schematic view of the relation of evaluation to other activities encompassed within programming appears in Figure 6-2. The intent of this diagram is to demonstrate the feedback function of evaluation at multiple levels of programming.

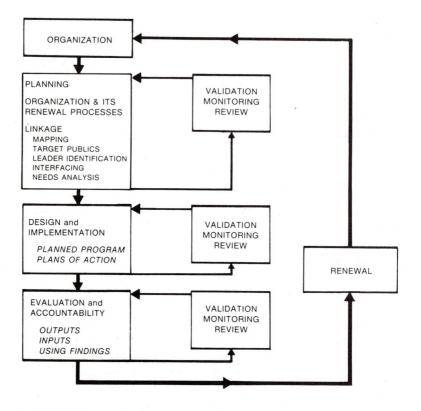

FIGURE 6-1   Schematic view of macro and micro feedback relationships in the programming process

Four categories of evaluation are suggested in Figure 6-2: intended and unintended, and manifest and latent outcomes. The first category of evaluation is *intended outcomes*, essentially the achievement of specified objectives. This loop is the one suggested in the foregoing brief description. But, as Tyler (1971) points out, learning activities generally have multiple outcomes, some of which will be incidental, *unintended outcomes*. Figure 6-2 suggests this category of outcomes or behavioral change is an equally important focus for evaluation.

In rural eastern North Carolina, structural and technological innovations have brought many changes to small farm operators. Faced with spiraling costs and a depressed economy, small farm operators, with limited resources and usually obsolete, shopworn equipment, experience tremendous odds in competing with large-scale operations. To assist these small farm operators, a vocational education program was designed to instruct them in developing new equipment and repairing, refurbishing, and enhancing existing equipment. Activities of the program included teaching 30 small farm operators basic and intermediate welding skills. Six months after the workshops, a simple evaluative

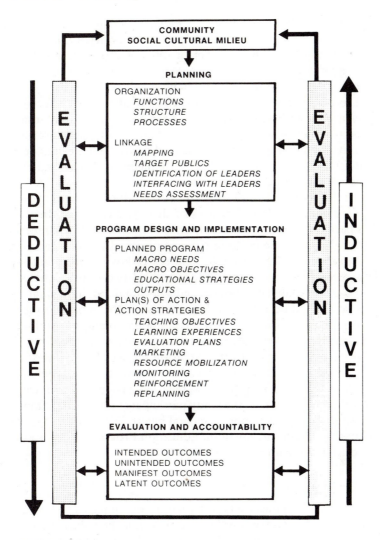

FIGURE 6-2   Relationships of evaluation and accountability to the programming process

follow-up effort was made to ascertain the number of farm operators who had used their welding skills on their own farms. To the dismay of the evaluators, only 8 of the 30 farm operators reported having used the skills developed in the workshop. While the outcome fell far short of that intended, the follow-up also revealed that 21 of the 30 farm operators were now employed full time in a naval shipyard, certainly an unintended outcome. To be sure, their families and their community profited from the unintended outcome of employment in the shipyard for these 21 small farm operators.

The third category of evaluations, *manifest outcomes*, are those that are evident, obvious, observable immediately. A fourth category, *latent outcomes*, also is suggested in Figure 6-2. Earlier, it was noted that learning experiences involve a temporal dimension: some experiences take longer than others to work through and, while some behavioral changes will be immediately observable (manifest), other experiences may be expected to show their effects at a point in time well after the learning activity has been completed. Now, some of these latent outcomes may be intended; others, perhaps the majority, are unintended. In both cases, the implication is that delayed or follow-up evaluations have a specific utility in assessing latency and permanency of behavioral change due to educational experiences.

The major asset of a 4-H program is the adult volunteer who provides leadership for building life experiences of these young people. Increasing emphasis has been directed toward recruiting low-income adult volunteers to work particularly with the often neglected, economically disadvantaged youth. In a recent programming effort to recruit and retain low-income adult volunteers as leaders, researchers investigated the impact of two instructional strategies: a traditional group-centered approach and a personalized, individual approach. A quasi-experimental design was utilized to assess the impact of these stimuli on behavioral changes among the low-income adult volunteers. Major emphasis was on changes in knowledge about extension programs, changes in self-esteem, and changes in attitudes toward the extension service. The manifest outcomes revealed at posttesting reflected the intended behavioral changes among the participants. However, the posttesting also revealed a latent, unintended outcome of the educational experience: the study participants experienced improvement in their self-reported perceptions of mental health. No such change was noted among Expanded Food and Nutrition Education Program (EFNEP) volunteers who served as a control group for this project.

The Intent of Evaluation

We hesitate to summarize in a few words as complex a task as an evaluation might become. Yet a few guiding questions may help the reader as we progress through the discussion that follows. Briefly, the intent of evaluation in the conceptual programming model is to develop information aimed at answering the following questions:

1. To what extent did the planned program and plans of action result in individual behavioral change, intended or unintended, manifest or latent, among learners?
2. To what extent did the planned program and plans of action result in aggregate behavioral change in the target public?
3. To what extent were planned program and plans of action inputs and program activities associated with such change?
4. To what extent were organizational mission, philosophy, structure, functions, and processes effective and efficient in producing outcomes intended in the planned program and plans of action?

Questions 1 and 2 imply achievement of objectives at the various levels of the objectives hierarchy; parallel concerns with satisfaction of needs associated with objectives also are implied. Question 3 hints at something that is virtually impossible to demonstrate in educational situations: cause-and-effect relationships between program input/activities and the resulting behavioral change or outputs. Question 4 refers to the program's organizational environment and points toward the analysis of organizational settings as they relate to the achievement of program objectives.

The notion of parallel hierarchies was illustrated in Chapter 5. There it was suggested that micro needs are nested under macro needs, and that micro objectives are nested under macro objectives. To complete the picture, we suggest that "micro" evaluations are nested within "macro" evaluation steps. That is to say, macro evaluations or judgments depend on cumulated micro evaluations of collated individual behavioral change data. Thus, there is a bottom-to-top flow of evaluation information through the evaluation hierarchy. The analogy to a river system is graphic and apt: individual droplets collect into small streams, feeding into creeks, then into rivers. Individual educational achievements are aggregated as, for example, class performance, grade-level performance, school-wide indications, and city, county, state, and national norms.

Note again the importance of pursuing the individual learner, target public, and organizational implications of both intended and unintended outcomes. Both occur and, even if one were to conclude that all intended outcomes incorporated in micro objectives were achieved, it is nonetheless essential to follow the ripples through individual life structures and the life of publics, as well as ties to organizational mission, philosophy, functions, structure, and processes. Even when planned change is completely attained, evaluation has a broader application and mandate.

OPERATIONAL DEFINITION OF EVALUATION AND RELATED PROCESSUAL TASKS

The following operational definition of *evaluation* is offered to provide a working model for the evaluation dimension of the evaluation/assessment subprocess and to account for the major issues involved:

> *Evaluation* is a coordinated process carried on by the total system and its individual subsystems. It consists of making *judgments* about planned programs based on established *criteria* and known, observable *evidence*.

Following this definition, execution of evaluation involves five basic processual tasks:

1. Describe program outputs, intended and unintended, manifest and latent, with appropriate documentary evidence.

2. Examine relations between activities/inputs and outcomes/outputs with the intent of inferring nominally causal associations.
3. Review implementation of objectives in relation to the input/output associations.
4. Scrutinize the translation of analyzed needs into objectives statements.
5. Probe the adequacy of needs identification, assessment, and analysis steps.

At this point we can see how the evaluation dimension and its processual tasks relate back to the prior planning and design/implementation subprocesses of programming. Goals of evaluation are to relate program outputs to program objectives and to program inputs and activities. Thus, the planning and design/implementation subprocesses provide guidelines by which evaluation is carried out. In turn, a primary utilization of evaluation findings is to modify the planning and design/implementation subprocesses of a planned program, within its organizational framework and environment.

Parallel with and complementary to the previously stated processual tasks is a taxonomy of evaluation tasks, developed by Stufflebeam (1971), that outlines the mechanics of program evaluation:

Developing a climate among educators that is supportive of evaluation.
Planning and focusing the evaluation.
Selecting or constructing appropriate measuring instruments.
Collecting and processing data.
Analyzing, interpreting, and reporting information.
Assisting decision makers in utilizing evaluation information.

These tasks will be interwoven with a discussion of the major processual tasks involved in the program evaluation dimension.

Having provided an introductory framework for the consideration of program evaluation, we will now examine each of the major processual tasks. In that examination, specific mechanics of evaluation actions will be interpolated among the more general processual tasks.

Task 1. The adult educator must describe the outcomes of the planned program, intended or objective-based, unintended, manifest, and latent. Evidence must be collected in line with professional standards to document outcomes.

This briefly stated processual task conceals a variety of thorny issues. One subset of issues derives from the notion that outcomes are specified in objectives. A further series is related to the analysis, summary, and documentation of evidence of feedback. A final area is that of comparisons with or interpretation relative to objectives.

Outcomes/outputs of a planned educational program can take any or all of four forms: intended and unintended, manifest and latent. *Intended outcomes* are those behavioral changes stated as objectives of the planned program.

Unintended outcomes are any other behavioral changes that occur subsequent to program activities. We commented earlier that both forms may include manifest and latent outcomes. *Manifest outcomes* are those that are evident, obvious, observable immediately. *Latent outcomes* are those that appear displaced in time from the educational activities, that is, in the future. Latent outcomes are those that perhaps require some "incubation," or the occurrence of some special circumstances or stimuli, or the acquisition of additional information before they become overt and observable. Tyler (1971) emphasizes that educational activities have multiple outcomes; we can add that some are predictable and some are not.

Given the point of view that social change is an end toward which programming is aimed, it would be appropriate to keep in mind that such changes may well be latent, that is, observable only at some time in the future. Note also that social change has incremental effects, affecting individuals and other linked systems beyond those to which the planned program may have been directed. For example, a man who, on the advice of his physician, takes up an exercise program, perhaps walking a regular route through his neighborhood, may influence others to begin exercising. Educating that one individual to exercise has a latent effect on his local system, one which was not intended in the doctor's objective. The broader community effect is also delayed in time.

Hierarchies of Objectives

In Chapter 5, we pointed out that programming entails hierarchies of micro objectives, derived in deductive fashion from macro objectives and including expressed and translated needs of the target public. Macro objectives are defined as broader in scope and as typically requiring longer periods of time to attain. In describing outcomes of a program, one must keep in mind that outcomes/outputs also must be examined hierarchically. That is, the program statement of objectives, at both the planned program and plans of action levels, suggests that outcomes at all hierarchical levels must be examined. Granted the macro objectives, and hence outcomes, often are essentially cumulative from micro objectives. Nonetheless, for each objective stated, some description of outcomes, that is, evaluation, is required.

One may argue that a strong possibility exists for observed macro outcomes to be more than the sum of the micro outcomes. In other words, emergent *aggregate* behaviors may occur that are not easily, if at all, predictable from a consideration of anticipated individual behavioral change outcomes. For instance, suppose we operate a program on automobile tire care for a community school group. Individual behavioral change could be documented through class performance, or at a later date in terms of improved tire wear on individual automobiles. A predictable, cumulative effect might be reduced aggregate expense for automobile maintenance, a macro objective. An emergent, nonpredictable, aggregate outcome, however, might be some social action with the goal of repairing neighborhood streets through a petition drive aimed at the local city council.

The point here is that, while the description of outcomes must begin with descriptions of individual behavioral change, it cannot end there. Outcomes (again, intended and unintended, manifest and latent) must be described at *all* levels of preexisting objectives hierarchies. We want to know if what we intended to have happen actually happened and, in addition, *what else* happened.

Yet another system of objectives should be kept in mind. To this point, we have discussed educational objectives aimed at individual behavioral change. In a major sense, that behavioral change is the product of the programming organization. We gave the analogy earlier of a manufacturing plant; at this point, it might be useful to refer again to that analogy. To manufacture a product, the plant personnel, functioning in their various departments, must execute certain duties to given levels of performance or output. These levels of performance or output are often referred to as objectives, and management-by-objectives (MBO) is widely recognized as an effective means for efficient control of production of goods and services. Adult education organizations also have management objectives, referring to allocation of time and effort in the performance of organizational functions and processes.

It is sometimes difficult for the beginning programmer to keep educational objectives distinct from management objectives, but it is essential that this distinction be made and maintained. *Educational objectives* are those intended changes in behavior of learners/learner systems. *Management objectives* are those performance standards intended to guide the efforts of organizational personnel. Both sets of objectives are usually hierarchical and both may be keyed to hierarchical levels of responsibility in the organization.

Again by analogy, consider the manufacture of pieces of fine jewelry. The jewelry company has to set its needs in terms of space, tools, personnel, and so forth, within its organizational structure. The overall objective of producing jewelry means that a whole system of intermediate objectives has to be worked out, department by department, all feeding into the overall production objective. Thus, the design department will have objectives centered on producing various patterns, in given materials, by certain deadlines. The personnel department will be required to recruit, process, orient, train, and assign individuals who can craft the pieces. The purchasing and procurement departments similarly will have objectives related to their functions, and so on. Finally, as a result of meeting these management objectives in the various departments, craftspersons will be supplied materials and tools to work with. Now there is a second set of production objectives to be met, which will result in transforming raw stock into finished pieces of jewelry. The stock must be shaped into component parts; the jewels to be set in the piece are selected, cut, and polished; the parts are carefully assembled, step by step; and, finally, the completed piece is polished and inspected by the quality control department.

The analogy to an educational program is fairly direct. The adult education organization has management objectives inherent in its operation, all of which converge on teaching-learning activities in which a teacher (craftsperson) employs a predefined set of procedures (teaching strategies and learning experiences) to transform raw material (the entering learner) into a "finished jewel." The product then is "inspected" through evaluation efforts.

A necessary area of inquiry in evaluating the outcomes of a planned program is the degree to which management objectives are attained. This inquiry may be viewed as paralleling the assessment of achievement of educational objectives, in one perspective. However, a more useful approach might be to consider management objectives as one subset of inputs that support the achievement of educational aims. Other forms of input include human (instructional and support), material, and financial resources, as well as the particular activities involved in the teaching-learning environment.

To summarize outcomes with relation to objectives, the description of what happened as a result of programmatic efforts begins with a consideration of outcomes or learner behavioral change, which can be classified as intended and unintended, each in turn considered as manifest or latent. Objectives in the programming process are hierarchical; thus a hierarchy of description is implied. Higher-level outcomes may involve nonpredictable emergent aggregate effects. Therefore, all levels of the hierarchies of both macro and micro objectives need to be examined. Management objectives, stated in terms of performance by or functions of components of the organization and its personnel, must be distinguished from educational objectives, stated in terms of behavioral change in learners/learner systems served by the organization. Degree of attainment of management objectives is indirectly an assessment of the availability of inputs (resources and processes) for implementing behavioral change in learners/learner systems.

Describing Program Outcomes and Inputs

The prescribed description of outcomes implies that some observable indicators of those outcomes can be *collected, documented,* and *communicated.* The three functions are related, at least in the sense that the form of communication depends on the nature of evidence collected.

Program outcomes/outputs. Descriptive evidence for or documentation of outcomes/outputs can take a variety of forms; indeed, much literature is devoted to this task. For present purposes, a concept offered by Webb et al. (1966) seems appropriate. These authors discuss measures in the social sciences, including education, as falling into two broad categories, which we will term *intrusive/reactive* and *unobtrusive/nonreactive.* Intrusive/reactive measures are those in which the learners/learner systems are actively involved and which require two-way communication between the learners/learner systems and the evaluator. Examples include interviews, questionnaires, ratings, tests, and any other technique in which the learners/learner systems are aware of and involved by the evaluator. Unobtrusive/nonreactive measures are those in which the evaluator does not actively involve the learners/learner systems and in which they typically are unaware that the evaluation is being conducted. Examples include some forms of direct observation; some instrumental measures, such as door-opening counts; archival measures, such as proportion of students passing the Tests of General Educational Development; and others.

Another form of categorization of evaluative evidence is clinical or qualitative versus psychometric assessment. The principle involved in *clinical assessment* is that the trained human observer is a highly sophisticated data-collection device, with processing capability. Allied to the clinical approach is the ethological, in which detailed observation is made with the intent of seeing regularities and patterning in behavior. The *psychometric approach* emphasizes controlled measures treated statistically.

No clear prescription can be given for the best means for collecting evidence on program outcomes, particularly where both intended and unintended outcomes must be taken into account. Some reasonable but very general guidelines, however, may be helpful.

Intended outcomes/outputs are those stated in objectives. The most appropriate time to consider measuring outcomes of objectives would seem to be when the objectives are being written. Mager (1962) emphasizes the importance of stating what data will be acceptable for defined objectives. His point is that the intended outcomes must be translated into an observable and thus quantifiable form. Given that the objectives of the planned program are stated in observable terms, the obstacle for evaluation is less a psychometric than a sociopolitical one.

To elucidate, we must remember that the usefulness of any educational program in which participation is voluntary depends ultimately on the learners and their leaders understanding and accepting the relevance of objectives, methods, activities, and program evaluation to their needs and sociocultural environment. Acceptance of evaluation by learners/learner systems is critical to the acceptance of social change through participation in the program in question, regardless of the statistical or psychometric qualities of the measure. Helmstadter (1964) refers to this as *face validity*; the measure, "on its face," has to appear relevant to the measurement context.

Credibility on this level is a function of the strength and breadth of the linkages developed early on and maintained through constant interaction with and involvement of target public leaders. The type, extent, and quantity of evidence to be used in evaluation that is acceptable to the target public must be an issue for exploration in the design dimension of the design/implementation subprocess such that evidence of objectives achievement is equally clear to learners, their leaders, and the programmer.

The type, amount, and scope of evidence of intended outcomes nonetheless is open. Given that observable learner behavior is to be measured within a restricted range, various psychometric decisions, from standardized tests to more locally normed performance tests, probably would be appropriate. Appropriate provisions to ensure statistical reliability and validity can be built in during the planning subprocess.

Unintended outcomes appear to lend themselves more to observational, clinical, ethological, or case-report approaches. This may be particularly true where outcomes of interest are restricted (limited perhaps to a single individual). The heuristic value of such evidence, in directing future analyses, planning, or larger-scale inquiries, should be noted. Major difficulties in assessing unintended outcomes obviously include the fact that more formal measures may not be possible. Further, in this context, psychometric qualities of measure may be less than desirable (but see also Webb et al., 1966).

Latent outcomes present a special problem. The ideal solution is follow-up testing and observation on several levels. First, one would like to know that knowledge acquired by learners during program activities will be retained. For instance, if young homemakers have learned what foods make up the basic four food groups, it would be useful to know if they will be able to recall that information a year later. Second, one would like to know whether or not the learning derived from the program has been incorporated into routine behavior. Do the young homemakers actually plan family meals around the basic four food groups? Truly latent effects may require additional questions; for example, what other time-delayed outcomes have occurred? To extend the example, our young homemakers may have begun growing gardens to ensure access to the food groups they learned about, or may have formed a food-buying cooperative, or may have begun using the information only after the birth of a child.

Latent effects are not easily predictable. Therefore, devices such as in-depth interviews, direct observations, or secondary indicators (e.g., in the case of the homemakers, relative increases in vegetable sales at the neighborhood grocery store) are indicated as most useful.

Program inputs.   Evidence on inputs used—resources expended, institutional processes employed, and so forth—also must be documented. And again, the programmer must understand *why* this documentation is needed. At some point in the evaluation process, if at all possible, we want to be able to make justifiable claims that the outcomes/outputs of the planned program are a causal result of the inputs applied. There is no way such statements can be offered unless inputs actually used are documented.

A causal argument is extremely difficult to make, particularly in operational situations where the control of potentially confounding elements is almost impossible, as is the case in most educational settings. A number of authors have recognized this point and have offered alternatives that might be helpful in arguing for causality (cause and effect). Weiss (1972) is an accessible entry into that literature.

At the least, the program evaluator would like to see covariation between input expenditures and outcome production; that is, outputs will vary in terms of inputs provided. This bare correlational approach requires some level of quantification of both inputs and outputs.

On another level, documentation of inputs provided is a basis for assessing achievement of management objectives, answering questions such as, How much money was spent in what area (s)? Were resources available where and when they were supposed to be? Were assigned tasks carried out as scheduled? These issues relate to the control of work flow in the organization and, in addition to potentially explaining the degree of success in achieving educational objectives, point up areas of greater or lesser effectiveness in organizational functions, structure, and processes.

Analysis and Summary of Program Descriptions

Basically, two forms of analysis and summary of program descriptions are used in evaluation. The first form of analysis is statistical and includes the well-known quantitative devices of mean, median, and mode descriptors of average response or activity and associated measures of variability such as range, interquartile deviation, and standard deviation. At the simplest level, tallies of observations, by category, can summarize sets of observations, for example, a count of the number of learners finishing a program.

A second level is a nonsummarized collection of observations, such as case reports, transmitted without analysis. There may be situations where this approach is appropriate, for instance, when only a very few individuals have participated in a program. More typically, some order or pattern in observations is sought and reported.

The limited scope of this discussion precludes detailed explanations of analysis techniques used, particularly statistics, a technical area requiring a depth of treatment we cannot readily supply here. Note, however, that professional preparation for the programmer role requires some proficiency with analytical tools, including evaluation and statistics. From the point of view of planning toward evaluation, the outcomes expected and the measures to be collected should be chosen with consideration of statistical, analytic, and descriptive limitations and potentialities in mind.

Our operational definition states that evaluation consists of judgments about planned programs against established criteria, using observable *evidence*. Some basic conclusions about worth of the planned program in its various aspects is expected, which implies a value judgment in the evaluation process. The difficult issues here are value-related: What are the values involved? Whose values are they? How do we come to know them or incorporate them into the evaluation process?

The programming process, as an organic whole, provides answers to these value questions and, indeed, incorporates the idea of value throughout. We noted in Chapter 4 (Planning) that values are a major element in both social systems and target publics. In mapping a target public, as a preliminary step toward needs identification, assessment, and analysis in the program planning sub-process, the adult educator must learn that public's values; otherwise, any program aimed at that public is doomed to failure.

Needs are identified and assessed through dialogue with the target public's leaders and their followers, based on linkage established between the adult education organization and these leaders. Consensus on needs statements is achieved through this dialogue. Leaders and their followers state the needs in their terms and the change agent restates or translates these expressed needs to check understanding with the leaders. Similar dialogue is required as macro and micro needs and their associated objectives are explicated. If agreement between the change agent and the learners and their leaders is checked and rechecked throughout the programming process, it is reasonably certain that the values important to these learners will be incorporated in needs statements, in objectives statements, and in specifying intended outcomes, as well as acceptable evidence of intended outcomes to be used in evaluation.

In a sense, linkage, as established and maintained over the entire programming process, is the means by which the target public's values are woven into the planned program as it takes form. Similarly, criteria for the worth, the "success," of the program are negotiated through collaborative linkage dialogue and are validated as acceptable to the target public. Knowles (1976), for example, calls for including criteria for acceptable performance in the statement of educational objectives. If these performances are not specified in the statements of objectives, the prudent change agent will confirm an understanding of criteria, in some written form, before committing resources to program implementation. The potential for "shifting" criteria over the course of a planned program, particularly in the minds of the public, means that there may be no agreeable basis for concluding "success" of the program.

To sum up, values are always the basic pivot for evaluation. Programming acknowledges values in assessing needs, setting objectives, deriving criteria for judgments, and specifying acceptable evidence for intended outcomes. The means for validating the incorporation of values is constant dialogue between the adult education organization, through the individual adult educator, acting as change agent, and the target public, through its identified leaders.

Evaluation of unintended outcomes is a problem that can be addressed only in context, because unintended outcomes, by definition, are unpredictable. Presumably, unintended outcomes will be relatively small-scale and will involve relatively few people. Their primary importance will be heuristic and thought-provoking. Nonetheless, the programmer, as evaluator, must at least come to grips with possible unintended outcomes.

For example, suppose a program is offered to youth in a small town, with the intent of making them more employable. Further, suppose that leaders in the area support the expressed aim of the program and that, at the level of intended outcomes, the program is successful; that is, increased numbers of youth get jobs. One unintended, latent effect of the program might be increased mobility of these youth. They buy cars and begin to expand their social sphere to include other towns or cities, with the ripple effect that some marry and move away or bring newcomers to the home area. The unintended outcome of greater geographic and social mobility, with its impact on traditional family structure and interaction, may be more or less acceptable, under the value system of the target public, than was the original employability training program.

The credibility of the programmer and the future success of programming efforts may hinge on the programmer's shrewdness in handling unintended outcomes relative to the value system of the target public. Again, the programmer's professional preparation in systems analysis and interpersonal communication and negotiation skills are underscored.

> *Task 2.* The adult educator must examine associations between input and output variables with the intent of inferring causal relations.

The types of output to be described in program evaluation are listed in processual task 1. Processual task 2 focuses on the need to establish that the observed outputs were caused by the program activities themselves, rather than some other factor or set of factors outside the scope of the planned program effort. For example, all programs take time, and human behavior changes across time. Can we conclude that a given program, and not simply human development across time, produced the observed behavioral change?

Causality is difficult to demonstrate under almost any circumstance and is almost impossible to show clearly in any form of behavior. Rather, by convention, we accept probabilistic statements relating antecedent activities, stimuli, or treatments to subsequent observable change. Social interventions, including education, are extremely challenging environments within which to attempt to infer causality, because the range of potential influences on behavior is so great and because control, in the form of isolating one suspected causal influence from all others, is so difficult.

Nonetheless, judgments about effectiveness and efficiency depend on examining, in an inferential causal context, relationships between the human and material resources employed, the methods and techniques applied, and other inputs, on the one hand, and outputs, on the other. These relationships are to be scrutinized in terms of quantified antecedents (inputs) and quantified consequences (outcomes/outputs). The means by which inputs are applied also are worthy of study.

We want to look particularly, however, for covariation in outcomes and inputs. Even when nominally the same methods, materials, and procedures are used, we need to assume a range of measurable variation in actual methods, materials, and procedures. As simple examples, the amount of time spent using a family account book may vary from homemaker to homemaker, or the number of questions asked in guided discussion sessions may vary from adult educator to adult educator, or the frequency of supervised practice using a piece of equipment may vary. Any of these measures could correlate statistically with outcome measures.

Now the astute reader will quickly argue, and correctly so, that correlation does not imply causation. However, a *lack* of correlation does imply a *lack* of causation. And, in cases where individual, assumed, causal factors cannot be isolated, as in a controlled experiment, correlation may be the only possible suggestion of causation. According to Labovitz and Hagadorn (1976), "the greater the magnitude of the association . . . , the more confidence that one has that the relation is truly causal" (p. 5).

In addition, there is a pragmatic principle here: correlations do not have to be proximally causal connections to be useful. As long as the correlation exists at some significant level, input can be said to "explain" some portion of the variance in output. Consequently, changes in input can be used to *predict* changes in output. For instance, suppose in our evaluation we discovered that the larger the number of addition and subtraction practice problems completed in an adult math class, the lower the probability that the adults would have a check returned for insufficient funds within the six months following the program. (Of course, there is a reasonable causal connection here, but not a perfect one). Further, suppose that the correlation between the input variable (number of practice problems) and the output variable (bounced checks) is $-.30$. Several factors may enter into keeping sufficient funds in a checking account. But, if we view that as an important goal, it would seem reasonable to increase the number of practice problems, regardless of the actual causal links to not bouncing checks that might exist.

Again, the issue of causal inference is complex. Often, firm conclusions of causality cannot be made for educational programs. But the program evaluator, in the present context, should always seek causal information as a means to provide a basis for *recommending* change in programs.

Task 3. The adult educator should review the implementation of objectives in their hierarchies with regard to intended output specifications as compared to input/output associations.

Processual task 2 feeds into processual task 3. In examining the association between inputs and outputs, one necessarily reviews the logical steps that were taken in specifying the intended outputs or objectives. A feedback loop is implied here. One derives objectives in terms of observable, measurable, intended outputs and then selects or constructs teaching methods and learning experiences that will lead to those outputs.

Input/output associations test this logic. A relatively weak association may suggest several possible alternative hypotheses. The first is that the wrong inputs (materials, methods, procedures, experiences, and so forth) were chosen to promote the specific objective, or were used inexpertly. If so, a recommendation to use other inputs, or perhaps other instructors, could be made. A second possibility is that the theoretical framework was in error, that the hypotheses about input/output associations were incorrect and led to unworkable selections of inputs for intended outputs. In essence, the evaluation becomes a test of the hypothesis and, on a broader scale, our "theory" of instruction. Third, while we may have a clear idea on an abstract level of what kinds of learning experiences lead to what kinds of outputs, we may have inappropriately or inadvertently implemented one or the other, or both.

Let us see if we can be quite clear on this important point. Frequently, we enter a program design phase with a clear, verbal description of the personal characteristics, skills, attitudes, knowledge, or whatever we see as objectives related to needs. The problem, then, is to translate that description into observable actions.

Here is a simple example. Suppose we have an objective of producing "good table manners" among the members of a family. What are the behaviors that we can observe (count, measure) that reveal good table manners? Many possibilities come to mind, including picking up a napkin at the right time and using it correctly; using the silverware in proper sequence and with appropriate foods; employing correct ways of eating particular food items, from soup to fried chicken; making conversation at the table; and so on. Because good table manners encompass a variety of activities, we cannot choose just one of these. But, even if we choose a range, we *make choices* and the choices we make form our *operational definition* of good table manners. How can we know we have done a good job with our operational definition of good table manners?

Given an operational definition of good table manners, we next face the problem of choosing inputs (materials, teaching methods, learning experiences) that will lead to behaviors we have chosen to call good table manners. Here, again, we turn to an operational definition. We may say that "good table manners are learned from good examples," and proceed to display good examples. Or, "good table manners are learned by trial and error." Or, "good table manners depend on fear of embarrassment." Again, there are many possibilities. We may lecture or show films; we may invite individual learners to dinner parties and let them learn through embarrassment. At the end of the time allotted for the learning experience, observations reveal little or no behavioral change in our learners. Choice of inputs reflects our theory may be wrong. Even if it is not wrong, we or whoever we chose as instructor may be inexpert in applying an appropriate teaching method.

What becomes apparent from examining the association between inputs and outputs is the degree to which our operational definitions of inputs and outputs and our theory of learning, both of which guide our conceptualizations, are basically correct. Generalizations such as those given in Chapter 5 are excellent means by which to avoid gross errors in implementation. But no set of generalizations ensures totally against error. Therefore, all action or operational steps must be reexamined, given the observable outcomes. The benefit of such reexamination is that steps may be taken to revise and refine operational steps in the continual evolution of the planned program.

Task 4. The adult educator must carefully check the translation of objectives, within their hierarchies, from needs, within their hierarchies.

This task, as stated, collapses two interrelated steps. In the development of programming, we stress the macro nature of the long-range planned program and the micro nature of the short-term plans of action. It should be clear by now that a deductive relationship has to exist between the two levels of program statement, the micro needs and objectives hierarchies derived from the planned program statements of needs and objectives. In both instances, a translation step must be taken, such that needs are rephrased as objectives. While, overall, this step is relatively uncomplicated, it is worth remembering that the intended outcomes/outputs must be observable in the statement of objectives and that the leaders and learners in the target public must concur on the validity of the needs statement.

The translation of analyzed/expressed/felt needs into needs statements also is the point in evaluation at which the logic of the deduction entailed in elaborating the needs and objectives hierarchies should be reexamined. The first point to be confirmed is whether or not the expressed needs of the target public are adequately reflected in the hierarchies. Again, this should have been negotiated with the target public's leaders and learners. Since programs, in practice, often stray from intent because of the availability or nonavailability of resources, the particular mix of personalities, and so forth, a review of needs with leaders of the target public can be a useful step.

We suggested that needs and objectives hierarchies, with the macro needs and macro objectives of the planned program as the pinnacles of each, are the products of both inductive and deductive processes (as illustrated in Figure 6-2). Macro objectives are inferred that subsume analyzed expressed needs. Needs analysis also reveals associated unexpressed needs at the same hierarchical level as the expressed macro and micro needs. These unexpressed needs have to be sequentially and cumulatively met to serve the analyzed expressed needs, while leading toward the even broader macro needs fulfillment. The intellectual steps involved in elaborating the parallel needs and objectives hierarchies are complex. They require a high degree of judgment and decision-making skill, both founded on well-developed knowledge and experience bases. Because these are complex undertakings, the possibility of overlooking important component needs and their objectives is ever present. Any "missing" needs/objectives will result in the program being stated, and consequently carried out, in an incomplete form. The obvious result is that overall macro needs and objectives will not be completely met.

Most instructors are aware of the truism that the best "evaluators" of planned methods or materials are the learners themselves. The best way to check the soundness of one's planning and preparation is to try them on one's learners, while monitoring what happens through critical observation. In a sense, the same modus operandi is suggested here for needs and objectives. Critical observation of the plans of action may suggest "gaps" in the needs and objectives hierarchies, perhaps in the form of lack of abilities assumed to be present in learners or in the form of required behavior components that were either overlooked or simply not thought of.

There are no foolproof means to ensure completeness of needs and objectives hierarchies, but two approaches would appear to be helpful. Typically, more than one person will be involved in developing a planned program, so these developers can both check and reinforce each other as they "brainstorm" needs and objectives hierarchies. And the programmers should, of course, continually check and recheck their emerging ideas with the learners and their leaders. However, when a "final" set of needs and objectives is developed, it may be worthwhile to seek an outside expert or consultant to review the product. Such a person is often better able to detect omissions or flaws in the program than those who were closely involved in its construction. In much the same sense, several observers of the planned program in action are more likely to perceive missing pieces than is a single observer. Here, too, an outside perspective may be useful.

In summary, evaluation of the adequacy of needs and objectives hierarchies has both vertical and horizontal dimensions. The development from analyzed expressed needs to both macro and micro needs represents the vertical dimension and requires collaborative monitoring by programmers—among themselves, with target public leaders and learners, and possibly with outside experts, as the construction of the needs hierarchy proceeds. The horizontal dimension represents translation of the needs hierarchy into the "observable" language of the objectives hierarchy, again under monitoring by programmers, leaders and learners, and perhaps consultants. During implementation of the planned program, ongoing monitoring of learner behavior may suggest oversights in the needs/objectives development process. Several observers help ensure reliability of observation and provide a broader aggregate observational and experiential base.

We cite here an example of how multiple-level evaluations can be built into a planned program for middle managers in an industrial complex. The target public consisted of the first-line supervisors in a large utility company. A major responsibility of these supervisors was to teach their subordinates how to perform those tasks defined in their job descriptions. Poor job performance by trainees led the company to look for possible weaknesses in the training procedures used by their supervisors.

The company's training staff, in collaboration with several of the informal leaders among the supervisory personnel, identified as the major need of the supervisors that they know how to design, implement, and evaluate effective on-the-job training programs for their trainees. Further study and analysis of this macro need led to identification of several other specific macro needs of supervisors: the need to know how to (1) identify and assess job-related training needs of their workers; (2) understand the worker as a learner; (3) translate trainee needs into teaching-learning objectives; (4) understand and be able to draw upon basic adult learning concepts in selecting and organizing learning experiences; (5) recognize and acquire skills in the use of various teaching and instructional strategies, methods, and techniques; and (6) evaluate the effectiveness of on-the-job training programs, with particular emphasis on assessing/measuring behavioral changes related to job performance. These macro needs provided the training staff with the basic information for designing a training program.

Further analysis of the macro needs led to six micro objectives, which became the focus of the planned supervisory training program. These micro objectives, in ascending levels, were to have the supervisors acquire the abilities to (1) recognize and assess job-related training needs; (2) understand the unique characteristics of the worker as a learner; (3) translate needs into objectives; (4) draw upon and use learning concepts in designing learning experiences; (5) use various teaching strategies, methods, and techniques; and (6) design and conduct evaluations in assessing and measuring changes in cognitive skills, affective behaviors, and in the performance of job skills expected to result from the educational intervention.

Program activities included three intensive workshops, assigned readings, teaching demonstrations, video tapes, and various other simulated learning activities. A unique feature of the program was the levels of evaluation designed and conducted to determine its impact.

The first level of evaluation, labeled "reactions," was designed ··· provide the supervisors an opportunity to react to various aspects of the training program. These reactions ranged from simple responses, such as "this is super" or "this is terrific," to no reaction. Included in this level of evaluation were participant reactions to the trainer, the subject matter, the teaching methods, the setting for the training, and feelings about fellow participants. Feedback obtained at the reaction level of evaluation was used by the trainers (change agents) to make adjustments or modifications in several aspects of the program.

The second level of evaluation was entitled "learning." The focus here was to determine the actual cognitive changes that occurred among the supervisors, with particular emphasis on changes in behaviors specified in the objectives. Tests were constructed and administered during and at the end of the program to measure the participants' actual behavioral changes between the time the program started and those times at which the tests were administered. Data obtained from the tests enabled the trainers to modify, where necessary, both the program content and the teaching methods.

The third level of evaluation was entitled "job behavior." Because experience has shown that, in many instances, trainees learn the content of the training, but experience difficulty in applying it, this level of evaluation was designed to determine whether or not the supervisors could transfer their "newly acquired behaviors" to their performance of the job of training workers. The participant-observer technique was used to assess actual changes in the supervisors' job behavior that could be attributed to the training program. Data obtained indicated that about 80 percent of the supervisors applied the new knowledge and skills acquired in the training program.

The fourth level of evaluation, "organization," was designed to assess the impact of the planned program on the functioning of the utility company. To determine impact on the company, data were obtained on the performance of trainees supervised by the newly trained supervisors. The question asked was, "Does the application of the new knowledge and skills acquired in the program positively affect the functioning of the organization?" Systematic observation and analysis of data compiled by the utility confirmed that the functioning of the organization improved as a result of both the improved training performance of the supervisors and improved performance of the workers they trained.

This example illustrates how several levels of evaluation can be built into a planned program. The first two levels provide data that enable training staff to adjust or modify the ongoing program. The third and fourth levels of evaluation speak, respectively, to the application of newly acquired knowledge and skills to the job and the subsequent impact of these new behaviors and skills on the functioning of the organization itself.

During implementation of the planned program, ongoing monitoring of learner behavior may suggest oversights in the needs/objectives development process. Several observers help ensure reliability of observation and provide a broader aggregate observational and experiential base.

Task 5. The adequacy of needs identification, assessment, and analysis must be examined as associated with the degree of learner participation and observed outcomes/outputs at individual and aggregate learner levels.

Three of the more difficult concepts for beginning or aspiring change agents to come to grips with are mapping publics and, perhaps to a lesser degree, the associated ideas of identifying and interfacing with the leaders of target publics. The entire programming process, as described in the conceptual programming model, depends on the tasks of mapping and identifying and interfacing with leaders of target publics being done well and thoroughly, because they are the foundation on which needs are identified, assessed, and analyzed. The programming process likewise is totally disrupted if needs are improperly identified or inadequately assessed and analyzed. Further, it is crucial to the overall evaluation process and to organizational renewal that the needs identification, assessment, and analysis steps themselves be assessed for adequacy, especially as related to observed outcomes of the planned program.

Part of task 5 was alluded to in task 4. If elaboration of a needs hierarchy begins with needs expressed by target public leaders only, one must constantly be aware that individual learner needs are being passed, at second hand, through leaders. An obvious efficiency principle operates here; we avoid the difficulty and expense entailed in directly assessing the needs of individuals, so we assume that the perspective of the leader(s) of target publics adequately reflects individual needs. Some benefits accrue from working through leaders: the analysis of individual responses means that interpretive error (our own biases) can creep into the expression of needs; the leaders are "leverage points" for acceptance of programs, as well as information sources; and leaders have a broader perspective (closer to the macro view) of their public's needs.

But here the issues blur. As pointed out in Chapter 4 (Planning), identification of leaders is far from an exact science. Thus, identification of publics' expressed needs and, through logical processes, individual needs, would depend on the selection of leaders with whom to interface and collaborate. The change agent may err in selecting such leaders to the degree that identification of needs resulting from collaboration may be off target. How much off target will be difficult to say until we examine two factors: first, the degree to which individuals are willing to participate in the planned program, which is surely an indicator of adequacy of needs analysis and of the influence exercised by the identified leader(s) and, second, the observed outcomes/outputs of planned program activities.

Identification of leaders depends, in turn, on how adequately the change agent mapped the publics in the area of interest. Again, this is a difficult task for which there are no rigid rules or recipes. Certainly, some guidelines are available, as discussed in Chapter 4. But, once more, the expertise, experience, observational ability, and creativity of the adult educator in the role of change agent are key factors. There can be no guarantee that conclusions drawn are entirely correct. Hence, at an even earlier stage in the programming process, serious errors can be made that affect the remainder of the programming steps.

The task of evaluating needs analysis has two "ends." The first is to look at program outcomes/outputs and then back at needs analysis as a potential causal factor in the degree of success of planned program activities. The second is to monitor, review, and validate conclusions drawn from mapping of publics and identification of target publics and their leaders. Campbell and Fiske (1959) address a technique of "multitrait-multimethod" assessment in which any psychological attribute can be applied in several ways. According to these authors, this assessment leads to more adequate indications of psychological "status" by employing multiple measures, each of which can be applied to multiple attributes or traits. While the "multitrait-multimethod" notion may not apply directly to evaluation of the adequacy of linkage—that is, system mapping and identification of target publics and their leaders—it might serve as a metaphor or a heuristic.

Communities have multiple attributes, as was brought out in the discussion of factors to be considered in mapping; adequacy of mapping can be improved by requiring multiple measures of a given attribute. There are at least two ways to do this. First, for a given social system variable of interest, one can predict what measures would be consistent with that variable and, in mapping, use more than one variable and test their consistency with a correlation statistic.

Suppose, for a given geographical region, we are interested in family income level as an indicator of socioeconomic status. What measures consistent with actual family income might we choose? Value of real estate owned would be one; makes, models, and numbers of automobiles owned would be another; proportion of children in public versus private schools would be another; and so on. A similar procedure could be carried out for other indicators. Taken as a set, consistency among measures would help the change agent avoid erroneous conclusions in mapping.

In much the same way, leader identification was discussed in Chapter 4 (Planning) on a "multitrait-multimethod" basis, if not in those specific terms. For instance, if we see an individual who has served or is serving as a formal leader (e.g., as a city council member), has been active in nonformal community activities (e.g., has served in United Way campaigns), and is publicly identified as an opinion leader (e.g., is frequently quoted by the local newspaper), we can safely assume that person is indeed a leader. What we would have taken, in effect, are multiple measures of that person's leadership position/status/function in the community. In this instance, a single change agent takes multiple measures. Generally, a number of individuals in the adult education organization will be in a position to make relatively independent judgments about social system maps and leaders. Agreement among these individuals may further indicate correctness of judgment.

In a similar way, as individuals from the community become involved as participants in a program, a further opportunity for validation becomes available. Observation, inquiry, and monitoring of individual behavior and interactions will help "flesh out" assessments of social system dynamics and, through these assessments, point toward centers of influence, power, and leadership in the social system or public of interest.

We turn now to accountability, the second dimension of the evaluation/accountability subprocess in the conceptual programming model.

ACCOUNTABILITY

Accountability refers to the process of reporting efficiency of planned program operation, primarily to the learners and leaders of the target public, the organization, funding sources, the profession, and, where appropriate, the governance body. We hold that reporting of what does and does not work to professional colleagues is a responsibility incumbent on every professional. Overall, resources are finite; therefore, any information that can be used to promote efficiency in any program ought to be reported to others who might be able to use such findings elsewhere.

Accountability is a relatively new concept to the professional practice of adult education. However, its usage can be traced as far back as Plutarch (ca.

A.D. 46–120), who put the matter forcefully into education. Barrow (1967) tells us how Plutarch admonished those fathers who entrusted the tutelage of their sons to paid strangers to call those instructors to account, periodically, for their teaching. In more modern times, accountability is well defined in business and industry. For example, a supermarket is accountable for the produce it sells; if the produce is spoiled, the consumer may return it for a refund. A corporation is accountable for its earnings record; if the net returns are low, the shareholders may replace the management. Further, accountability has long been a concern of political officeholders. Politicians study public problems, consult with their constituents, weigh their alternatives, and anticipate consequences. These elected officeholders have learned the intricacies of accountability. They know the pressures and consequences of being held accountable to a variety of groups and individuals for decisions made and supported. Experience has taught political officeholders to be sensitive to the needs, goals, and expectations of their constituencies, their colleagues, indeed, of their society. Elected officeholders search for answers, guided primarily by their experience, beliefs, and insight, all of which are influenced by those to whom they are accountable. Accountability also applies to numerous other persons, professions, and groups. The doctor, the office manager, the educator, the plumber, the newsboy, as well as a host of other individuals who provide a service, are held accountable by their clientele. The degree to which each is held accountable is a function of the quality of service provided and of the users who receive it.

A number of contemporary writers in education and adult education have defined the concept of accountability. Browder, Alkins, and Kaya (1973) speak of *accountability* as the requirement of the occupants of a role, by those who authorize that role, to answer for the results of work expected from them in that role. Gephardt (1975) refers to accountability as an essential part of the process of education. He suggests that accountability involves a relationship between the funding sources, the educator, and the learners. He declares that the educator, in being accountable to funding sources and learners, must perform three functions, namely, (1) provide information on which determinations can be made regarding the nature of work carried out; (2) provide evidence of the quality of accomplishments on work undertaken; and (3) report on relationships between nature of work and quality of its accomplishment. Steele (1970) defines accountability as an investment concept involving those who provide resources and those who use these resources to carry out programs.

OPERATIONAL DEFINITION OF ACCOUNTABILITY AND RELATED PROCESSUAL TASKS

Accountability, as used in the conceptual programming model, refers to the process whereby the adult education organization and its practicing adult educators are held accountable for planned program outcomes/outputs and the effectiveness and efficiency of their efforts or inputs in producing the intended outputs. Accountability always involves external imposition of demands for evaluative evidence. External groups to which the adult education organization and its adult educators are accountable include the learners and leaders of target publics, the organization, funding sources, the profession, and, where appropriate, the governance body. Last, but not least, is the notion that adult educators must account to themselves for evidence regarding the quality of their professional efforts. Further, they must be prepared to take the actions dictated by the evidence.

Three processual tasks related to the accountability dimension of the evaluation and accountability subprocess speak to the adult educators' responsibility to (1) report evaluation results, (2) analyze the organization in tems of evaluation results, and (3) make recommendations, based on evaluation results, to their organization.

> ***Task 1.*** The adult educator has the responsibility and the obligation to report the results of evaluating the planned program to the learners and leaders of the target public, the organization, funding sources, the profession, and any others who have a stake in the program and its outcome.

The evaluation/accountability subprocess described thus far culminates in a report to the learners and their leaders, the organization, the sources of funds for the program, the larger professional community, and, where appropriate, the governance body. Let us look at each of these separately.

One would have to say that the learners and their leaders are of paramount importance, for without their participation the planned program cannot exist. It becomes necessary then to keep the learners informed about the aims and achievements of the planned program, both directly and indirectly through their leaders. Several types of benefits accrue from such reporting. First of all, success breeds credibility. At minimum, a report to the learners says, "We claimed we would do such-and-such (our objectives) and we did thus-and-so (the degree of achievement of our objectives)." All marketing authorities agree that word of mouth is the most effective means of promotion; therefore, the most effective "salespersons" for a planned program will be participants who see quality and value in their experiences with the program. "Contagion" or "snowball" effects of successful programs help recruit future participants. In that sense, reporting to the learners is a tool for public relations. Reporting to and through leaders to the learners is an additional means to strengthen linkage for future needs identification and community cooperation.

Documentation

Accountability, in the form of evaluation reports, is essential to the organization for carrying out management control functions. Thus such reports, planned programs (including any revisions of needs, objectives, and strategies of implementation), allocation of resources, and plans for contingencies are adapted to the program context as defined legally, economically, socially, politically, technologically, or otherwise. The challenge for the organization is adaptation to social, cultural, and economic change, based on experience in the environment. Accountability reports provide a data base on which rational organizational adaptation or renewal is founded.

From the perspective of educational objectives, accountability reports contain critical information about the adequacy of management objectives and, therefore, have a central function in the development of adapting and adaptable sets of management objectives. From an educational perspective, accountability also may impinge on organizational functions, structure, and processes. A more detailed account of those consequences is offered later in this discussion.

American society and American institutions value efficiency. Funding sources for educational programs are far from exceptions in this regard. In fact, these sources usually require parallel reporting of financial and performance statuses. The general thrust is that the funded organization accepts responsibility for providing, at the most reasonable cost, services it purports to be able to provide. On that basis, it is important to maintain, summarize, and report records of expenditures versus objectives achieved at various hierarchical levels, along with other outcomes. Observed benefits to a community or target public are of particular interest to government funders.

To illustrate the concept of accountability in programming, attention is directed to the results obtained through a program planned, implemented, evaluated, and reported by the Sampson County (North Carolina) Agricultural Extension Service. The program originated from the identified, assessed, and analyzed educational needs of farmers engaged in the commercial production of peppers. The county agent and leaders of the pepper industry and agribusiness, in a collaborative analysis of the producers' needs, identified as their macro need the need to increase net income per acre of peppers produced. After thorough study and analysis by the agent and these leaders, several specific needs were identified as parts of the macro need. These included the needs to (1) determine and adopt a means of growing pepper transplants that would produce more peppers at an earlier harvest date, (2) determine and adopt methods for reducing the field costs of transplanting, (3) reduce labor costs, (4) control insects, and (5) develop and adopt a higher germinating pepper seed.

The most basic need was to find a more effective method for growing pepper transplants. Fortunately, this need had been recognized earlier by the county agent, and much information about plant production and transplanting had been obtained. Borrowing from the success of containerized plant production in Florida, field tests of types of containers, growing media, and size of transplants had been conducted under the aegis of the Sampson County Agricultural Extension Service two years prior to involvement of Sampson County farm and agribusiness leaders. The results of these field tests provided proof that container-grown pepper transplants outproduced the bare-roots transplants being used and could be harvested more than two weeks earlier. Market information gathered by the county agent indicated that a higher price per bushel could be obtained from peppers at this earlier harvesting date.

Armed with this information, the county agent, in collaboration with leaders of the local pepper industry, designed and implemented a program aimed at meeting the educational needs of pepper producers and thus helping them to increase their net income per acre of peppers grown. The first-level micro objective was to introduce local farmers to the container-grown transplant method and have them adopt this new technology. The learning experiences, scheduled to extend over an 18-month period, included on-the-farm tests strategically located throughout the pepper-growing region of the county, special educational meetings for both farmers and agribusiness leaders, circular letters, tours, newsletters, and other media forms. The county agent estimated that more than 90 percent of the local pepper producers were reached during the first 12 months of the planned program.

Evaluation of the adoption of this new transplant practice and its subsequent economic impact on the pepper producers was conducted by the county agent at the end of 18 months. Data obtained revealed that (1) three-fourths of the producers adopted the container-grown transplant practice during the first 12 months of the program and (2) income netted by those producers who had adopted the new practice amounted to $690 per acre more than the net income per acre obtained by producers who used the conventional method of growing and transplanting peppers. It is now observed that almost 100 percent of the pepper producers in Sampson County have adopted the container-grown transplant practice. In terms of the time and effort of the county agent, coupled with the public funds that were invested in his salary and support services, and the increased net income per acre realized by the pepper producers, the cost-benefit ratio of this planned program was computed as 1:49.

This experience illustrates how sound programming practices can effectively produce change. Further, it provides substantive evidence that can be used to convince the public, county commissioners, and other relevant groups of the positive economic returns that can be realized from public funds invested in an effective adult education planned program.

In becoming a member of the professional community of adult education, the adult educator accepts a responsibility to contribute to the knowledge base of the profession and its advancement. A major activity in support of that responsibility is reporting to other members of the profession the results of programming efforts. Particularly important are any cause-and-effect relationships that can be demonstrated, as these may serve as foundations for decisions other programmers may face in the same or other localities and environments.

Types of Documentation

Several types of reports may be useful to other programmers. Some examples, in addition to causal relations, are statistical summaries of participation and outcomes; observations of novel, surprising, or unexpected outcomes; innovative marketing techniques; creative approaches to instruction such as methods, materials, and experiences; elaborated needs hierarchies and associated objectives hierarchies in which applicability may be generalizable beyond local contexts; diagnostic and evaluation instruments that proved especially useful; program documents or descriptive plans that may serve as examples or guides to others; case studies showing the development of needs, programs, plans, strategies, and outcomes, again, as examples; and other characteristics of local programs. If a guiding principle exists, it most likely goes something like this: if there is any aspect of your program that could help other programmers in similar situations, you have a duty and an obligation to attempt to disseminate that information.

Means by which the profession can be informed include publication of reports in professional journals; publication of organizational reports and newsletters; oral reports at professional meetings, workshops, seminars, and the like; and deposit with the Education Research Institute Clearinghouse (ERIC). The principal responsibility is to make the information available to those who can use it.

Governance bodies such as boards of trustees and boards of directors generally require that the adult education organization report on its accomplishments and failures. Such information is deemed essential by governance bodies in making decisions about policies and allocations of resources to the organization.

> *Task 2.* The adult educator should analyze the mission, philosophy, functions, structure, and processes of the adult education organization as associated with input to the planned program, achievement of planned program objectives, observed outcomes/outputs, and the need for organizational renewal, that is, continual adaptation to a changing service environment.

Lippitt, Watson, and Westley (1958) point out that a critical requirement of modern life is to acquire a facility for change. This is as true for the adult education organization as it is for the adult educator. The function of the organization is to foster such change in a rationally directed manner. Thus, to the degree that the organization is successful in its aims, it operates in a continually changing context.

The thrust of processual task 2, then, is to emphasize the necessity for the programmer, in an evaluative mode, to analyze the organization's mission, philosophy, functions, structure, and processes in relation to the social, political, economic, legal, and technological climate or environment in which the organization exists and must operate. This analysis begins with an understanding of and commitment to the organizational mission and philosophy; continues through the mapping of the publics in which the organization functions, with the stipulation that the relations between organizational and community values be clarified and examined; takes into account the documentation of program outcomes in relation to organizational structure, functions, and processes; and ultimately points toward the course(s) of action needed to refine and renew the organization to attain a better fit between its mission and philosophy (its culture) and the culture of its target publics. To effect this analysis, the programmer must bring to bear expertise in organizational development, sociology, anthropology, psychology, education, and evaluation and measurement, not to mention some small skill as a juggler of tasks!

In a way, the analytic steps proposed here mirror those indicated earlier in documenting input-output associations. It is from such analysis that organizational functions, structure, and processes should be studied: the learner is, in a sense, the product of the organization; the organization and its functions are intended to support efficient design and manufacture of that product in a market. As the product flows back to the market (the target social system), the market is changed and requirements for its product are altered. If we were, indeed, in the business of manufacturing some good, obviously our continuation in business would depend on our ability to adapt our organization, its functions, structure, and processes, and its product to a changing market. The same is true with programming in adult education organizations.

Conclusions from analyses of adult education organizations derive from answers to a general question applied, in particular or specific terms, to a given unit or component of the organization: To what extent were the efforts of this unit effective and efficient in helping to achieve planned program objectives? The ramifications of this question are many and varied. Issues of work flow and organizational communication may arise, for example, or spatial arrangements of individuals or units in the organization, or access to resources inside or outside the organization, or delegation/reporting channels, or interpersonal relations (team or group cooperation, conflict), or inadequate practical skills or cognitive skills such as decision making or problem solving, or any of a thousand others. The important point is that the question must be asked and the examination must be made, under an organizational commitment to renewal for adaptation to its service environment.

> *Task 3.* Drawing on expertise in programming as a whole, knowledge of the unique relationships between the organization and its target public(s), and the outcomes from continuing evaluation throughout the programming process, the adult educator, in accounting for the outcomes of the planned program, recommends any means by which the organization, through renewal, might become more adaptive in serving the needs of those publics.

At the beginning of the discussion of accountability, we pointed out that this dimension raises and attempts to address questions about organizational effectiveness, impact on target publics, and quality of learning experiences offered. Answers to such questions may have some utility in supporting the credibility and public image of an adult education organization. Perhaps more importantly, such answers provide the input for the critical process of organizational renewal. This notion has been brought out before; it is reiterated in processual task 3 to emphasize that the evaluation responsibilities have not been completed until the programmer, in reporting findings to representatives of all those involved, proposes recommendations through which the organization, and the planned program, might be improved in their capacity to serve the target publics.

Recommendations for organizational renewal are derived by juxtaposing knowledge of the environment or operating climate as it exists with an "ideal" of how it ought to exist. The intellectual task is reminiscent of Tyler's (1971) notion of a need as a gap between existing and ideal behavioral competencies. Analogous organizational competencies, present versus ideal, can be imagined.

The descriptive and analytical steps outlined in the accountability processual tasks define, in a diagnostic sense, the current capabilities or competencies of the organization, as revealed from measuring inputs, processes, and outputs of the planned program. The divergence of performance from objectives is one measure of a gap that points toward revision of either the planned program or the organization's functions, structure, or processes, or all four.

The measurement and interpretation flow we suggest calls for examining each step of the programming process, along with the utility of organizational capabilities in supporting each step. It is totally predictable that some component or aspect of the planned program or the relevant institutional mechanism will be inadequate, to a greater or lesser degree. The first step toward recommending change is to recognize where such inadequacies lie. A list of areas for improvement can be made in the course of evaluating the program.

The second step is to rank order the organizational or program problems identified on the basis of their relative importance to the success of the planned program. These, in a sense, are "needs" assessed in terms of "needed" organizational or program change.

The problem then becomes to develop recommendations that can be incorporated into the organizational framework or into a revised program that will close the gaps identified. Obviously, there is no recipe for recommendations; they depend on peculiarities or individual situations. In all cases, however, the programmer's observational, integrative, and interpretive powers will feed the creative abilities that each programmer either must have or must develop.

One can imagine four broad scenarios. In the first, all objectives of the planned program are met in a timely and cost-efficient manner. In the second, objectives are generally well met. In the third, objectives are not met. In the fourth, the degree to which objectives are met is problemmatical.

For this last case, recommendations probably would fall into two groups, aiming at two different overarching questions: What should be changed in the program itself to promote achievement of objectives? What alterations in organizational functions, structure, and processes would better support achievement of objectives? Clearly, the two questions are interdependent but, in our view, the programmatic issues ought to have priority, because the adult education organization exists to serve programmatic ends rather than vice versa. Hence, one would begin by looking for problem areas in the statement of the planned program, as described in this chapter. Once those areas have been identified, one would critically review, in their context, the organization's functions, structure, and processes, looking for obstructions and areas of inefficiency that may have contributed to inadequacies in carrying out the program. Recommendations for change would follow from such identification. Two cases are cited as examples.

In the first case, objectives are inadequately met. Here one would strongly suspect that the program is fundamentally misdirected. A thorough review of the planned program, particularly of needs/objectives statements and the linkage steps, clearly would be required. Recommendations focused on needs identification, assessment, and analysis, and the translation steps that lead to a viable planned program presumably would follow.

In the second case, objectives are fairly well achieved. In this case, organizational mechanisms would be a preferred focus. Recommendations for streamlined procedures, more efficient reporting/delegating channels, perhaps decentralization of some decision making, and a host of other changes could be put forth.

A program in which *all* objectives are met will be the greatest challenge for organizational renewal. If all the objectives initially set are achieved, then the identified needs will, in principle, have been met. Why should such astounding success be a problem? There are several reasons. By achieving its planned program objectives and thus fulfilling the learners' needs, the organization, from one perspective, eliminates its initial reason for being. To the extent that a planned program has been successful, the organization has *changed* the character of the target public it set out to serve, at least in the sense of reducing or eliminating a set of needs. The public for the planned program, therefore, becomes a *different* public with *different* needs, some of which may have surfaced only after the original set of needs was satisfied.

It is from the perspective of the successful program that the notion of renewal gains its force. The successful organization can continue to be successful in meeting the needs of its target publics *only through change* in its planned programs, functions, structure, and processes, as those organizational changes adapt to the changing needs of its publics. The programming process, therefore, is a cyclically continuous, evolving, and adapting mechanism, reacting to its own success through evaluation and accountability.

To complete this last scenario, the programmer-as-evaluator, in the face of success, must recommend the *programming process in its entirety* as the appropriate route to organizational renewal. The cycle completes itself.

The world, alas, rarely offers simple solutions to clear-cut outcomes. More typically, some things work well, while others do not; most things we see, a few we overlook. Many of our departments function smoothly and efficiently, most of the time; others are disappointing in both smoothness and efficiency. The adult educator's task is to discuss as clearly as possible, through accountability reports, where these problem areas exist and to give reasonable approaches to their elimination. Can we be right all of the time? Hardly! But we can work at it, build experience and expertise and, from those foundations, grow toward professionalism in program content and toward efficiency and effectiveness in operation.

The literature on program evaluation, in its many forms and spheres, is immense and constantly growing. Novel approaches are continually being proposed and tested, many with strikingly innovative features and apparent utility (e.g., Smith, 1981).

With the plethora of evaluation models available, it is not surprising that some rational disagreement or lack of consensus exists as to the acceptability of one approach versus another. There is even lack of agreement on what criteria should be used to judge the worth of evaluation approaches. This latter concern is referred to as *meta-evaluation,* and has a degree of relevance to the conceptual programming model in at least an intuitive sense. Evaluation is one dimension in the total programming process. One can argue that evaluation, itself, as a dimension of the evaluation/accountability subprocess, needs to be evaluated. While a separate evaluation processual task could have been added here to include meta-evaluation, it would not have fit readily into the flow of ideas being discussed. Rather, the notion of meta-evaluation calls for a degree of skepticism about any formulaic approach to evaluation, and certainly requires open-mindedness when selecting evaluation approaches.

EVALUATION AND ACCOUNTABILITY IN RETROSPECT

The evaluation/accountability processual tasks listed are pragmatic questions we regard as justifiable for the programming process as it is envisioned in the conceptual programming model. There is no magic in the evaluation/accountability scheme, and throughout this explication we have emphasized the importance of adapting the evaluation/accountability methodology to the particular programming environment.

The invocation of the evaluation/accountability subprocess is straightforward. We review the evaluation frameworks (values, data, criteria, judgments) with the same aims of observational clarity, logical consistency, and methodological completeness that guide every other phase of evaluation and, indeed, programming, in general.

The same notion applies to accountability. As stated earlier, adult educators have the ethical responsibility for keeping their target publics, organizations, funding sources, the profession, and, where applicable, the governance body informed about the successes and failures of their planned program and why they occurred. Sharing such information may be helpful to other professionals who are attempting planned programs in adult education or in other areas.

REFERENCES

BARROW, R. H., *Plutarch and His Times*. Bloomington: Indiana University Press, 1967.

BEAL, G. M., R. C. BLOUNT, R. C. POWERS, and W. J. JOHNSON, *Social Action and Interaction In Program Planning*. Ames: Iowa State University Press, 1966.

BOYLE, P. G., and I. JAHNS, "Program Development and Evaluation," in *Handbook of Adult Education*, ed. R. M. Smith, G. F. Aker, and J. E. Kidd. New York: The Macmillan Company, 1970.

BROWDER, L. H., JR., W. A. ATKINS, JR., and E. KAYA, *Developing an Educationally Accountable Program*. Berkeley, Calif.: McCutchan Publishing Corporation, 1973.

CAMPBELL, D. T., and D. W. FISKE, "Convergent and Discriminant Validation by the Multitrait-Multimethod Matrix." *Psychological Bulletin,* 56 (1959), 81–105.

FOREST, L., "Program Evaluation for Reality," *Adult Education,* 26 (Spring 1976), 167–175.

GEPHARDT, W. J., ed., *Accountability: A State, a Process, or a Product?* Bloomington, Ind.: Phi Delta Kappan, Inc., 1975.

GROTELUESCHEN, A. D., "Program Evaluation," in *Developing, Administering, and Evaluating Adult Education,* ed. A. B. Knox and Associates. San Francisco: Jossey-Bass, Publishers, 1980.

HELMSTADTER, G., *Principles of Psychological Measurement*. New York: Appleton-Century-Crofts, 1964.

KNOWLES, M. S., *The Adult Learner: A Neglected Species*. Houston, Texas: Gulf Publishing Company, 1976.

LABOVITZ, S., and R. HAGADORN, *Introduction to Social Renewal*. New York: McGraw-Hill Book Company, 1976.

LIPPITT, G. L., *Organization Renewal*. New York: Meredith Corporation, 1976.

LIPPITT, R. L., J. WATSON, and B. WESTLEY, *The Dynamics of Planned Change*. New York: Harcourt, Brace & World, Inc., 1958.

MAGER, R. F., *Preparing Instructional Objectives*. Palo Alto, Calif.: Fearn Publishers, 1962.

————, *Measuring Instructional Intent*. Belmont, Calif.: Fearn, Pitman, Publishers, 1973.

PFIFFNER, J. M., and F. R. SHERWOOD, *Administrative Organization*. Englewood Cliffs, N.J.: Prentice-Hall, Inc., 1960.

SMITH, N., ed., *Metaphors for Evaluation*. Beverley Hills, Calif.: Sage Publications, Inc., 1981.

STEELE, S., "Program Evaluation—A Broader Definition," *Journal of Extension,* 8 (Summer 1970), 5–18.

STUFFLEBEAM, D. I., chairman, *Education Evaluation: Decision-Making*. The PDK National Study Committee on Education. Itasca, Ill.: F. E. Peacock, Publishers, Inc., 1971.

THIEDE, W., "Evaluation and Adult Education," in *Adult Education: Designing an Emerging Field,* ed. G. Jensen. Washington, D.C.: Adult Education Association of the USA, 1971.

TYLER, R. W., *Basic Principles of Curriculum and Instruction*. Chicago: University of Chicago Press, 1971.

WEBB, E. J., D. T. CAMPBELL, R. W. SCHWARTZ, and L. B. SECHREST, *Unobtrusive Measures: Nonreactive Research in the Social Sciences*. Chicago: Rand McNally & Company, 1966.

WEISS, C., *Evaluation Research*. Englewood Cliffs, N.J.: Prentice-Hall, Inc., 1972.

Chapter Seven

Programming: A Challenge to Adult Education

Now is the time to review briefly where we have come from and the route by which we came. This brief review constitutes what we will refer to as the three concluding phases of this presentation. Secure in the knowledge that we have "closed the loop" in the programming process, we are ready for the second phase: an examination of applications and implications of the conceptual model for programming in adult education. The third and final phase consists of an examination of some means by which the conceptual programming model might be subjected to further research.

The model proposed herein is described as a conceptual approach to programming in both formal and nonformal contexts. The intent is to develop a way of thinking about programming and how it might be applied to many situations of practice. The conceptual programming model suggests a number of more specialized areas on which inquiry might be focused. Such inquiry may have two aspects: (1) critical personal inquiry, a means by which individual adult educators develop and enhance their professional competence in the roles of change agent and programmer, and (2) professional practice. Thus the task at hand is to summarize the content and consequences of the conceptual model for programming in adult education.

THE CONCEPTUAL PROGRAMMING MODEL IN RETROSPECT

Beginning with a review of the key elements of the programming model, we will recount its conceptual flow. A principal belief upon which the conceptual programming model is predicated is that programming in adult education takes place in specifiable contexts. Two contexts, in particular, are viewed as central to the model: (1) the social/functional context of the adult education organization, and (2) the sociocultural context within which change is proposed. While one may visualize adult education programming as occurring outside a formal organization, for the most part, this simply is not the case. Adult educators generally are employed by formal organizations, such as universities and colleges, public schools, industry, social service groups, allied health systems, churches, and other systems. Almost always, some type of formal organizational setting is the context for their programming efforts.

The importance of the adult education organization is obvious. The organizational context facilitates or constrains (or both) the adult educator's efforts through (1) its mission, philosophy, functions, structures, and processes; (2) its available resources and the means by which those resources are allocated; and (3) its historical relationships to other organizations. Consequently, adult educators need to be thoroughly knowledgeable about the context of their organization.

Equally imperative is consideration of the sociocultural context of the publics toward which the adult education program will be directed. The reasons are obvious: the sociocultural context of the target public influences (1) the context of the program to be offered, which is based on the expressed needs of the publics; (2) the ways and means through which the program will be offered; (3) the objectives that may be reasonably set; and (4) the strategies through which objectives may be approached. If the adult educator ignores the sociocultural context of programming, the probable outcome will be little or no participation by those for whom the program is intended.

These two central contexts of the conceptual programming model interact. That is, the adult education organization is typically part of its sociocultural environment, and the culture of the target public may be expected to influence and, to a degree, filter into the culture of the adult education organization. Conceptually, one might separate the two contexts; however, they often overlap, interact, and fuse.

Belief in the importance of the sociocultural context of the organization and its target public is a basic assumption underlying all of the subprocesses and concepts in the conceptual programming model. Other assumptions are noted throughout the text, as required in the development of the model. Collectively, these assumptions represent an implicit philosophy of adult education and programming. Other assumptions are entirely possible. Yet another programming model, based on different assumptions, will differ from the conceptual model developed herein. To illustrate, Kohlberg and Mayer (1972) describe three different philosophies about human development and show how the types of values, objectives, and methods will differ for each philosophy.

Genesis of the Conceptual Programming Model

The evolution and development of the conceptual programming model are explicated in Chapter 3, in which the overall philosophical tenets guiding the thinking that went into the model are cited. A review of the chapter may be useful in emphasizing to the reader that the conceptual programming model rests on a base of assumptions and concepts, integrated through the application of a set of philosophical tenets. While a listing of all those components of the model would be repetitious, it is important to recall that each of the three major subprocesses of the conceptual programming model contains a system of assumptions and concepts. Critical assumptions are emphasized and addressed in detail throughout this presentation. In Chapter 5 (Design and Implementation), for example, the assumptions are presented upon which the design/ implementation subprocess is predicated. In other chapters, even more basic assumptions are emphasized, especially in Chapters 3, 4, and 6.

The reader should keep in mind that some assumptions about the nature of programming, the nature of planned programs, and the functions of adult educators as change agents and programmers are critical to understanding the rationale for the conceptual programming model. A view of the philosophical tenets as they affect programming is elaborated in Chapter 3. Any philosophy is selective, in that a few of many possible points of view are taken as primary and basic, guided by underlying values of congruency and consistency. As noted earlier, different ideas often lead to different conclusions and systems of concepts, constructs, and, ultimately, theory. Therefore, a critical examination of one's own systems of assumptions and concepts and their interrelatedness is both valuable and essential to understanding the programming process and the roles of the adult educator as change agent and programmer. From the author's point of view, the system of concepts about programming, as presented here, is consistent, logical, and verified to a satisfactory degree by the experience of practicing adult educators.

The presentation of the conceptual programming model differs from that of the other models reviewed in Chapter 2 in that an overt effort is made to explicate the basic assumptions, concepts, and processes of concern. Thus, the reader has the option of questioning the assumptions, concepts, and processes as a means for accepting, rejecting, modifying, extending, or developing a new conceptual model. Testing the conceptual programming model is facilitated by an understanding of the model itself. Such understanding is facilitated when its basic assumptions, concepts, and processes are clearly stated.

That the conceptual model encompasses three major and highly interrelated subprocesses is repeated throughout this text. The adult educator must never forget that the three subprocesses—planning, design/implementation, and evaluation/accountability—are essential to the practice of adult education. The three subprocesses (depicted in Table 3–1) form the foundation that supports the programming process on more refined levels. One cannot overemphasize that these subprocesses, their dimensions, assumptions, and concepts, are interrelated *as components of a system,* with all the implications within the concept of a system.

Programming is an organic whole in quite the same sense that the human body is an organic whole. While, for the sake of analysis and study, one might dissect from the human body some part or subsystem, one cannot expect that isolated part or subsystem to function effectively. In point of fact, the structure of a book into discrete chapters does some violence to its integration. Likewise, presenting each of the three programming subprocesses as a separate chapter suggests they might be viewed discretely, when the only appropriate and realistic way to understand the entire conceptual programming model is in terms of its units and the interrelatedness of program planning, design and implementation, and evaluation and accountability.

A unique component of the conceptual programming model is the introduction and elaboration of processual tasks for each of its three subprocesses. Processual tasks identify and define an orderly progression of actions that need to be engaged in when applying concepts to particular situations in planning, design and implementation, and evaluation and accountability. These orderly actions provide a sense of organization, continuity, and logic to the programming efforts of the adult educator.

Practical Aspects of the Model Often Overlooked

On a practical level, several aspects of the conceptual programming model deserve special comment, because they may be overlooked. These are (1) the linkage process of mapping, (2) identifying target publics and their leaders and interfacing with those leaders, (3) marketing the planned program, and (4) evaluating and accounting for the programming effort. The reason these aspects may be overlooked is that their usage and relative importance are somewhat unfamiliar in the experience of many adult educators.

The first of these aspects, the concept of mapping, derives not so much from the field of education as from the social sciences. Consequently, the importance and means of executing mapping may be unfamiliar to many adult educators. Insightful, in-depth study, analysis, and mapping of the publics to be served are essential to the adult education organization's success in identifying and ordering its target publics. Embedded in this axiom is an implicit assumption, which applies throughout the conceptual programming model: successful programming depends on the need for, access to, and generation and availability of adequate information about publics to be served. As time passes, more and more adult education organizations are coming to realize the pivotal import of knowing in detail the social and cultural context of the publics they are to serve. The range of publics extends from religious groups to educational, political, and social action groups. Failure to gather needed information through mapping has resulted in a long list of ineffective programs over the past several decades of adult education programming.

A second aspect to be emphasized is identifying target publics and their leaders and interfacing with those leaders. The conceptual programming model underscores the necessity of identifying target publics as well as both formal and informal leaders of those publics. Likewise, the importance of interfacing with individuals, through their leaders and as learners, cannot be overstated. Collaboration between change agents, leaders, and learners is essential in needs identification, assessment, and analysis. A number of sources point out that a feeling of "ownership" among the learners and their leaders is vital to the success of an adult education program. The conceptual programming model restates that requirement. No substitute exists for the effort that goes into building such linkages. Because linkage is an important part of the entire programming process, the degree of success in this endeavor influences the ultimate work and impact of the planned program.

Three categories of learner-leader involvement might be mentioned. *Leaders* of the target public obviously are to be included. *Members* of the target public clearly are necessary as participants in and consumers of the educational program(s) offered. Both groups can be advocates of the planned program to the target and other publics. A third group, whose importance should not be overlooked, are *volunteer leaders* from among the publics. Such volunteers will both extend the organizational resources available to the planned program and will be the most easily accessible representatives of the public for the purposes of acquiring and disseminating information about the planned program. Volunteers historically have given considerable support to the adult education movement.

A third aspect to be emphasized is that the planned program has to be marketed to its target public(s) and other groups. Many adult educators have had little if any exposure to the marketing concept. As pressure increases for accountability, in the face of declining resources and the projected expansion of demand for services, adult educators will be forced to an in-depth consideration of the ramifications of marketing their programs. One suspects, and experience confirms, that most adult educators do not market and perhaps are not adept at marketing their products and services. The success of any adult education planned program requires both consideration and implementation of marketing strategies.

The fourth and final aspect of the conceptual programming model that is often overlooked is the importance of evaluating and accounting for programming efforts. Too frequently, adult educators defer consideration of evaluation strategies and techniques until the program is either well under way or completed. Because accountability is dependent upon the development and utilization of an evaluation system, adult educators who are knowledgeable about good programming practices plan for evaluation in the early stages of the programming process and use evaluation philosophies and methodologies as guides in selecting and utilizing various program strategies. The conceptual programming model points out that allowances of time, effort, and resources must be made for monitoring and evaluating the planned program, the subprocesses of programming, and the processual tasks subsumed under each subprocess.

Evaluation and accountability are central to adaptation of the organization and its programs to the sociocultural environment. The history of the adult education movement should be consulted for examples to support this contention. Philosopher George Santayana is widely quoted as saying, "Those who cannot remember the past are condemned to repeat it." We infer from this that we learn from experience—our own and others. The relationship between organizational demise and failure to evaluate and account for program outcomes adequately, as a base for organizational and program renewal, is recorded in the history of adult education.

Generality of the Conceptual Programming Model

The conceptual programming model is intended to provide a framework that might be applied in a wide range of settings. Certain assumptions set boundaries on situations in which the model can be applied, and the model is couched in general concepts. A few of the assumptions of the model will be reviewed. For example, it is assumed that adult educators, as change agents and programmers, do not and cannot act alone; rather, they act only as part of an adult education organization. A pervasive assumption is that the offerings of the planned program will be to individual learners in a target public or social system.

This assumption does not limit the applicability of the conceptual programming model. The model emphasizes the role of the adult educator, as change agent, in the linkage processes of mapping, identifying target publics and their leaders, and interfacing with leaders and learners in those publics in collaborative needs identification, assessment, and analysis.

The contexts within which the model may be applied are quite broad. This is a strength of the conceptual programming model. It allows a common basis for preparation, for practice, and for communication among adult educators. Sufficient flexibility is allowed to make it possible for a given organization, within its environment, to tailor its efforts to particular educational needs. It is hoped that application of the conceptual programming model in different situations will contribute to further refinement of the model and to its support through successful marketing and application. The challenge is to subject the assumptions and concepts of the model to further tests in various programmatic situations.

The organization of the conceptual programming model, based on relatively abstract and detached concepts, suggests another mode of applicability and utility. The model draws from several disciplines, among them sociology, anthropology, psychology, economics, organizational science, all in addition to education. Thus, the interdisciplinary nature of programming in adult education is affirmed. The history of scholarly inquiry demonstrates how interdisciplinary examination of a given problem area can lead to new insights and productive advances in knowledge. Advances in each of these disciplines may contribute to revisions in the adult education programming process.

Similarly, the interdisciplinary nature of the conceptual programming model suggests that the special expertise of individuals from contributing disciplines can be drawn upon in analyzing programming and its subprocesses. For example, the professional skills of an organizational theorist might be applied in analyzing the mission, philosophy, functions, structure, and processes of an adult education organization. The services of a marketing specialist would be helpful in developing a plan for marketing adult education programs. A media specialist might provide insights into how one uses mass media to acquire information about a public. A sociologist may note overlooked means of analyzing a public's structure. The general point is that the interdisciplinary nature of the conceptual programming model suggests the inherent potentialities of input from and interaction with specialists from other disciplines.

Within broad and relatively nonrestrictive boundaries, then, the model, as a conceptual framework, is broadly applicable and useful. Given that some boundaries are defined, obvious questions are, What lies outside those boundaries? What types of problems are not covered or addressed under the present model? Although this issue will be discussed later, some points need to be mentioned here.

In general, any model that has the "internal validity" discussed in Chapter 3 can be applicable when the assumptions underlying its derivation are sound.

One might say that any time the basic assumptions of the conceptual programming model are not violated, the model ought to hold. Conversely, one might ask to what degree can successful programming be carried out when its underlying assumptions are violated? This question cannot be answered a priori; it requires testing in practice. The question, however, is aimed directly at the issue of generality of the model, which needs to be subjected to further inquiry.

Along the same lines and consistent with the previously suggested notion of interdisciplinary analysis, the assumptions of the programming process and its subprocesses can and should be subjected to further study. A subsidiary question of generality lies here, too, in that the content of each subprocess and its accompanying generic and specific concepts depend on the surrounding and supporting assumptions and processes. For instance, can some or any of the processual tasks of the subprocesses be circumvented or eliminated? The model suggests that the answer to that question is "probably not," but only practice can test the assertion.

The argument is not so much that the model's conceptual framework is complete and rigid; rather, that the model is consistently constructed from a set of assumptions, philosophical tenets, and experience. The need is for its further application and testing in practice. In this sense, all aspects of the model are hypothetically correct, and these hypotheses remain such until subjected to further tests. This conceptual programming model calls for such tests.

SUBJECTING THE CONCEPTUAL PROGRAMMING MODEL TO FURTHER INQUIRY

The conceptual programming model is based on assumptions, concepts, and the actual experience of adult educators as change agents and programmers. To test its validity and applicability, the model must be subjected to further inquiry. Thus, we focus on that task and raise questions derived from the model that may form the basis for further research. The objective will be to consider the means of "testing" this conceptual programming model, beginning with applications and moving on to research problems, questions, themes, and hypotheses suggested by the model.

Testing the Validity of the Model

How might one confirm a conceptual programming model in adult education? Two approaches come to mind. One obvious means is through statistically testing hypotheses drawn from the model. This is an important avenue of inquiry to which a later discussion will turn. A second approach is to look for applications, the general rationale being that the usefulness of any model is judged by the breadth of its applicability. Therefore, one might look at historical examples, at more or less current endeavors, and at anticipated situations to which the model might be applied. Allied to such a review, one might also search for situations to which the model applies less well. In a related way, one might list the range of problems, with some notation of the relative importance of these problems, that the model might address or help solve. The converse also should be examined: the range and importance of the problems for which the model obviously is not helpful.

Application of the Model to Scholarly Inquiry

As noted, applications have a time factor associated with them. The applicability of the conceptual programming model can be assessed in terms of (1) analysis of historical examples, (2) present situations and practices, and (3) future or anticipated situations.

Historical programs as examples.   In his scholarly and insightful history of adult education, Grattan (1955) comments that the history of adult education enterprises is replete with failed efforts, efforts begun with high hopes and the promise of success. Why were such efforts not successful in the time allotted to the programs? One approach to the question would be to examine each one from the perspective of the conceptual programming model in much the same fashion as proposed in the evaluation and accountability subprocess. Such analysis may help to bring into focus various inadequacies in these historical programming efforts that may have contributed to their failure.

As an example, consider the discussion of the rise and fall of the Mechanics' Institute to Britain (ca. 1820, but with threads back as early as 1796). Grattan describes the interest of major patrons of these institutes and early successes in involving workers in classes of vocationally oriented training in basic science. But, he continues, "promoters were unable permanently to engage the support of the class of people they set out to serve." Those who lasted for some time he described as "oddly persistent vestigial remains" of the original efforts, lacking a "vital spark" (p. 84).

Why did such an interesting and apparently useful program, from the perspective of over a century and a half, fail to maintain its viability? Grattan (1955) suggests a main cause: inability or unwillingness to continue to meet the changing needs of the target public. He remarks that the Institutes "seem to have been related to a need of the time," but that "many workers were interested in politics" (pp. 84–85), a topic the Institutes were unwilling to teach or have discussed. Politics, economics, history, and even fiction were viewed in some circles as dangerous studies.

Grattan's (1955) quotation from J. W. Hudson's *The History of Adult Education,* published in 1851, bears repeating, for it clearly demonstrates the violation of a basic principle of programming; namely, the social context for the programming effort must be taken into account.

Ten years after the formation of the Mechanics' Institutions in the principal towns of England [i.e., by around 1833], it was proved, upon undoubtable testimony, that these societies had failed to attract the class for whom they were intended, by their founders, to benefit. . . . The universal complaint is that the Mechanics' Institutions [sic] are attended by persons of a higher rank than those for whom they were designed. (P. 86)

According to Grattan, "the cry against the workers was that they were apathetic. . . . They were not apathetic to what they themselves knew they wanted, but they were to what 'do-gooders' thought they ought to want" (p. 87). Grattan listed additional factors in the decline of the Institutes: lack of "ownership" (no direct voice in management, outside rather than inside support), inferior teaching methods, inadequate or totally lacking library resources, failure to consider the learners' starting level of educational attainment, and, underlying all this, misperception of the learners' actual needs.

What lessons for the contemporary adult educator are inherent in this example from the past, particularly from the point of view of the conceptual programing model? The answers by now should be obvious. The model stresses that linkage between the adult education organization and its target public must be firmly established early in the development of the planned program. The needs of the target public, once identified, must be delineated in rational form and negotiated in collaboration with appropriate representatives of the target public, that is, with its learners and their leaders. The design of a realistic planned program and plans of action must take into account diagnostic steps such as determining where the learner is at the beginning of the program activity, the appropriateness of the teaching methods, and whether or not adequate supporting resources, both physical and material, have been developed. Simply stated, all these principles were violated by the founders and directors of the Mechanics' Institutes. With the hindsight of over a century and a half, it is easy to say, "No wonder the effort failed." (We should all assume a more charitable stance; the programmers of a century and a half hence may cast a similarly disdainful eye on us.)

As an oversimplified and too brief illustration, the Mechanics' Institutes show how the conceptual programming model may be used to evaluate the success or failure of an adult education enterprise. Through such evaluation, we see more clearly the importance of the concepts described in the conceptual programming model and have the opportunity to learn from others' experiences.

On a more positive historical note, one might cite the adult education success story of the Cooperative Extension Service (Boone, 1970). The story of Seaman Knapp, the Smith-Lever Act of 1914, development of the demonstration farm concept, and all other details of this movement are too well known to warrant repeating here. But note some of the principles of programming that undergird that success story. Linkages were established with the target public to be served; members of that social system were actively involved in needs identification, assessment, and analysis; linkages were and continue to be maintained through a system of agents from the adult education organization; great effort went into devising effective methods of teaching that addressed real problems of the target public, not problems imagined by some "expert" at a distance; materials to support the educational effort were prepared and made widely available. The result? A viable and successful system of adult education that has operated in the United States for nearly a century and has spread its influence throughout the world.

Again, the principle illustrated is that the programming model can be used as a conceptual framework for evaluating historical adult education efforts, either to document potential causes for failure or to establish cause-and-effect relationships in successes. This historical case study approach to adult education apparently has not been seriously and thoroughly attempted; it might result in a highly productive area for scholarly inquiry, the product of which might be most useful to the field of adult education.

Present situations and practices as examples. If the concepts espoused in the conceptual programming model are useful in analyzing historical adult education enterprises, they are even more useful in present-day situations, at least for the reason the information (personal, documentary, observational) is more readily available. Although a number of potential motivations exist for such an analysis, two will be cited for discussion here. The first focuses on the needs of the individual adult educator who is considering employment with a given organization. The second, mentioned only briefly, has to do with the usefulness of evaluation in responding to the mandates of funding agencies, governments, citizens groups, and the like, who may have a stake in the operation of the adult education organization somewhat different from that of persons within the organization, for example, those who may be primarily interested in the renewal process.

Adult educators almost always operate as members of an adult education organization. At some point the individual educator who is considering employment with a given organization has to become acquainted with that organization in order to decide whether or not to accept a position, if one is offered. The conceptual programming model can be very useful for such an individual. First, the model provides a highly useful conceptual framework for inquiring about the adult education organization, on the assumption that the most rational decisions about that organization can be made when the most complete information is available. Often, such information must be obtained within a limited period of time. Using the programming model as a source of questions about an organization, the information can be obtained more efficiently and, consequently, better decisions can be made by the job seeker about the advisability of working with that organization.

In this case, questions might focus on the organization's mission, philosophy, functions, structure, and processes. These are some of the forces that impact directly on the day-to-day work of the adult educator. What are the mission and philosophy of the organization? Is the mission tied to the actual practices in the organization's programming process? What is the organizational chart for the organization in question? Who reports to whom? Who delegates responsibilities to whom? What are the levels of responsibility and authority at the various levels of the organization? What are the sources of funding for the organization? These are a few of the questions our jobseeker probably would raise.

The main point of such an inquiry is to examine the match between, on the one hand, one's own philosophy of adult education, one's own skills and abilities, and one's own personal and professional goals and, on the other hand, the implicit or explicit philosophy of adult education as expressed in practice by the organization, the functional needs of the organization, and the educational and social aims of the organization. It is unrealistic to expect to be effective as an adult educator in a situation in which one's goals are incompatible with those of the employing organization. Further, it is unethical to accept a position with an organization in which one's skills and abilities cannot be effectively utilized.

Evaluating an organization and its program(s) from this individual perspective may be useful. The conceptual programming model provides a set of ideas for making such an evaluation. Evaluation by an external group is another perspective that might be encouraged. Adult education professionals often are called upon to make external evaluations of particular programming efforts; in fact, some federal aid programs require that an external evaluation be made as a condition of funding. A question that can be raised is how to go about such an evaluation. We propose, again, that a thorough grasp of the concepts outlined in this text provide a fairly comprehensive framework for asking the appropriate questions.

The foregoing examples suggest two applications of the conceptual programming model, in something of an ongoing model. One also may find it useful to consider the range of adult education arenas in which the conceptual model might be applied. The obvious cases include (1) community college programs, (2) cooperative extension programs, (3) continuing education in public and private institutions, (4) professional development activities in an array of occupational areas, (5) leisure and recreational programming for adults under the aegis of social service agencies, (5) extension programming in colleges and universities, and (6) community education programs through the public schools, including adult basic education, literacy, and high school equivalency programs.

Are there other situations in which the model might be applied? Yes! *The conceptual programming model can be applied anywhere there is a need for adults to engage in educational activities in fulfilling personal or group needs.*

Other adult education arenas in which the conceptual programming model may be applied are (1) social action programs to remedy neighborhood, city, county, or other civic problems, such as housing, street repair, sanitation, health care, and public transportation, in which groups of people need educating about the problems and possible solutions; (2) campaigns for needed legislative reforms or remedies, such as tax relief, crime control, gun control, and toxic waste disposal, which are issues of current concern; (3) civil rights efforts such as the current educational activities on both sides of the Equal Rights Amendment to the U.S. Constitution; and (4) religious education. The whole arena of transfer of technology from one country to another, especially from developed to less well-developed countries, presents a gigantic educational challenge with unlimited potential for benefit. Programming, as described in the preceding chapters, can be used to facilitate the transfer process.

In the realm of educational technology, a well-developed understanding of the conceptual programming model can form a useful foundation for guiding the development of innovative teaching methods and materials. In programming, one begins by understanding the nature and needs of the target public to be served. The same order of understanding is needed in designing educational materials and methods. The clear necessity to take into account the sociocultural characteristics of the group to be taught, when designing learning experiences for them, was cited in Chapter 5.

Many technological and educational experts stress that emerging technologies hold the potential to revolutionize adult education. The microcomputer is one example. The availability of the microcomputer requires one to understand the broader context for applying it to adult education. The educator with access to such technology, but without a clear grasp of programming, is much like a carpenter with fine tools, but no blueprint for a house to build.

Touching on these emerging educational technologies points up that we face a mushrooming adult population that is maturing into an age characterized by change so rapid that one can barely keep track of it, much less respond and adapt to it. Cross (1981) provides a cogent and thoughtful review of some of the forces that will shape adult education in the foreseeable future: (1) a changing population age structure; (2) radically altered attitudes about marriage, families, and childbearing; (3) career patterns that feature multiple occupations across the working life span and, under some projections, longer working lives; and (4) increased leisure time. Expectations have changed in recent years. Everyone expects to have a "good life," free from some of the hardships their parents or grandparents experienced. Cross (1981) points out that education is part of both the reason for and the solution to problems entailed by such changes. Increasing educational attainment expands the horizons of the population, extending expectations and suggesting more far-reaching goals. Education, too, is the means by which educators and the general public suggest that those ends may be attained. The adult educator and the adult education organization must take these expectations into account in programming. Clearly, a comprehensive conceptual programming model can provide considerable support in making relevant programs available to the adult population of the future.

Examples of questionable areas of model application.   Given the foregoing, one might reasonably ask, Are there any areas of adult education to which the conceptual programming model does not apply, or does not apply so well? In fact, there are some areas in which the model can be applied only with some difficulty. Broadly speaking, the areas of difficulty for this model are those in which some of the basic assumptions of the model are violated (see Chapters 1 and 3, particularly). For example, the model is founded on a basic assumption of democracy; implicit in that assumption is the notion of freedom to accept or reject ideas and to participate or not in any given activity. If a society does not embrace these ideas, the conceptual programming model, which is built on such an assumption, is unlikely to work very well.

The conceptual programming model also assumes that social change is possible through education; that is, that social mobility is a realistic outcome of education. In those societies with very strict class stratification, where social mobility and social change are proscribed, success of the model will be unlikely.

The underlying assumptions of the conceptual programming model are described in detail all through the discussion of the various programming subprocesses. It might be instructive for each adult educator to review from time to time just what those assumptions are and the degree to which they may be violated in a given situation. The assumptions set some conditions on the contexts for success of the model and their validity is crucial to the application of the model.

On another level, it is assumed that (1) adult education programming, in most cases, is aimed at group processes; (2) that social change emerges as a result of individual behavioral change; and (3) that such behavioral change will occur in a client–change agent interaction. Tough (1971) reminds us that a great deal of adult learning and change takes place in self-directed learning projects. It is not clear how the conceptual programming model applies to self-directed learning projects nor that it reasonably should, given the incredible variety of individual interests such projects address.

On the whole, it would appear that the conceptual programming model has wide applicability. Exceptions would be cases in which basic assumptions are violated or in which operational conditions differ from those assumed by the model, for example, self-directed learning versus client–change agent interactive learning.

Testing Research Questions in the Model

We mentioned earlier that the conceptual programming model needs to be subjected to further study under a range of practical situations. Besides the rather broad situation of model generality is another level of testing; that is, the model suggests a range of research questions that can be addressed in more limited fashion, restricted to specific hypotheses derived from the assumptions, concepts, and processes of the model.

In one sense, the model includes a set of implicit "if, then" propositions. For instance, one may infer the proposition, "If publics or systems are mapped, educational needs can be derived" (noting the several intermediate steps between mapping and needs identification). As stated, this proposition is clearly open to test: one could compare needs derived by approaches that begin with mapping versus approaches that do not, for example, by analyzing the local newspaper and related publications, then checking the resulting list(s) of needs with a sample of potential clients.

On another level are a series of technological or methodological questions that are open to empirical research. In the discussion of the mapping aspect of linkage (Chapter 4), means are suggested through which such mapping might be executed and expedited. But, perhaps other methods could be used. How do the various methods compare? For instance, do the methods developed by direct mail merchandisers have any utility as a means to identify subpopulations within a given larger population or public?

The foregoing two areas for research seem to be particularly important: (1) to test the "if, then" proposition that can be derived from the model and (2) to explore the methodological aspects of the model and its processes. Given these two overarching concerns, let us now turn to each of the three major subprocesses of programming—planning, design/implementation, and evaluation/accountability—for a brief look at some of the research questions suggested by them.

The planning subprocess begins with an analysis of the organizational context for adult education programming. It then moves to linkage, which involves study, analysis, and mapping of the public, identifying the target public, and identifying and interfacing with its leaders and learners. It concludes with identification, assessment, and analysis of expressed needs in collaboration with the learners and their leaders. Each of these activities suggests research themes and issues. Within this brief discussion, we can only sketch, rather than detail, research questions. For practical testing, each of the ideas alluded to would require substantial elaboration.

The organizational context suggests comparative studies: What types of organizational structures are better contexts for the delivery of adult education programs? One may cite hierarchical, network, task force, and other forms of organizations, for instance. Is one better than the other in supporting the programming process? Similarly, are there organizational policies and practices that can either facilitate or impede the programming process? As one instance, we might examine staff development, from recruiting to orientation, through continuing staff training.

Analysis of the organization clearly requires the acquisition of accurate and valid information about the organization. What are the most effective or least effective ways of acquiring such information? For example, how do in-depth interviews compare with checklists or with open-ended questions? This type of question frequently is raised by organizational development practitioners (French and Bell, 1978). At this point, the interdisciplinary nature of inquiry into adult education programming and its practice comes into force.

Conceptual tools and techniques for mapping are an area of inquiry in which a great deal of research effort could be expended profitably. As mentioned in Chapters 3 and 4, mapping a social system is no easy task. Accessible techniques would be an important contribution to the entire field of adult education. This is a topic to which sociologists, community development specialists, and market research experts could all add unique perspectives. The advent of computer technology to the analysis of U.S. census data and the development of extensive data banks by governmental and private agencies suggests that innovative approaches to mapping may be possible.

The principle addressed by mapping is specificity of needs assessment. How effective and efficient is full-scale mapping of the organization's public in identifying educational needs? Are other approaches as effective and more efficient? The conceptual programming model indicates that a major function of mapping is to identify and describe the target public within which the adult educator will identify and interface with leaders who, in turn, will be the principal sources of information about needs of the target public. Are there other uses for social system structural information in the programming process?

How can the leaders of a target public be identified? Chapter 4 contains a number of approaches to such identification. For programming purposes, which approaches will be most effective in identifying and interfacing with target public leaders for purposes of educational needs identification, assessment, and analysis? To what extent is it necessary to identify leaders of target publics? The conceptual programming model suggests (and the literature supports) that such identification is very necessary. But is that necessity specific to some situations and not to others? If so, how can we know when identification of target public leaders is or is not necessary?

Collaborative needs identification, assessment, and analysis are consistently thorny problems for change agents. Do the values that accrue from such collaborative effort outweigh those from other approaches? What means for identifying and assessing needs, even given the interfacing-with-leaders approach of the model, are better or worse: interviews with leaders, field trips with leaders, panel discussions among leaders, checklists, open-ended questions, or some other means? Again, the model seems to imply an efficiency principle. What are the most efficient techniques? Do these techniques differ in validity; that is, do they differ in their capacity to evoke the "real" educational needs of the target public? How can validity of techniques be tested in such situations?

In each aspect of the planning subprocess, questions arise as to possible connections with other disciplines. Are there, for instance, specific theories in other disciplines that might suggest explanations of means of action in any of the aspects mentioned? At the same time, how does information obtained from studies within the programming process relate to those other disciplines? For example, how does information about organizational development in adult education organizations relate to other organizational development situations? One would hope for the development, maintenance, and enhancement of this type of interdisciplinary flow of information and support.

The design/implementation subprocess in programming is the most complex of the three, at least in the sense that it includes so many disparate activities and a broad range of research opportunities. Basically, the flow of the design/implementation subprocess includes (1) developing a long-range planned program that encompasses hierarchical sets of macro needs and macro objectives derived from analyzing identified and assessed needs, (2) developing appropriate educational strategies, and (3) including plans for evaluating the outcomes of the planned program. Further implementation of the planned program requires the development of plans of action that include sequential teaching objectives, learning experiences, and plans for evaluating outcomes. Plans of action are implemented through marketing, recruiting and training volunteers, and continuous monitoring and evaluation of progress toward attaining the objectives. Each of these components of the design/implementation subprocess provides opportunities for research.

While some of the components and their connections seem nothing more than common sense, others might be examined empirically. For instance, a crucial concept in the design of the long-range planned program is the translation of analyzed expressed/felt needs into a more comprehensive set of needs statements, on higher (more macro) and lower (more micro) levels. The concept of a hierarchy is central to this perspective of needs assessment: Are there other ways of conceptualizing the relationships of needs to each other? An analogy might be to compare the hierarchical structure of an organization versus a network of organizations. Is something similar possible in thinking about needs relationships? How might one validate a needs hierarchy, once it has been elaborated? Are ways available to the programmer to check the thinking that goes into elaborating needs/objectives hierarchies? Are statistical methods available (for example, cluster analysis) that might be helpful? Because hierarchies of needs and objectives are basic to the design of both the long-range planned program and plans of action, it might be highly useful to examine the cognitive processes and skills of the programmer in generating such hierarchies. What information, for instance, is available in the literature on decision making and logical thought that might be relevant to the program design dimension?

Considerable effort and focused thinking are being devoted to learning strategies. As a research issue, the adult educator needs to know what sociocultural characteristics of the adult learner are important to the effectiveness of proposed teaching-learning activities. An obvious social dimension is contained in this statement and should be explored. Technological advances suggest that application of emerging computer hardware and software may be particularly effective in adult learning; the theme needs to be scrutinized for its importance. Similarly, for evaluation methodologies, assessment of individual learning experiences is far from a static field of inquiry. New information needs to be acquired and developed, with special focus on adult learners, and incorporated into strategies for ongoing evaluation in program design.

Mention of the sociocultural characteristics of adult learners points toward an additional theme, one that was referred to in earlier discussion of mapping. Learning has a developmental dimension at all age levels. Consequently, the adult educator must be familiar with information on adult development, in whatever form such development takes. Research on adult development is in its infancy. Adult educators looking for an area of inquiry might do well to consider the field of adult developmental psychology and the learning consequences of that development.

Some normative information about adult learners that has become available over the years is, in a sense, a form of "market research" for educators (see Cross, 1981). Even broad-scale findings about factors that either lead to or hinder participation in adult education activities are useful in planning marketing approaches for a given program, if for no other reason than they provide starting points for questions one might ask in a particular sociocultural environment. Expanding on the theme of marketing, a surprisingly small body of knowledge exists about the techniques of marketing that can be, have been, or might be applied in the field of adult education. A whole range of research questions could be generated and followed up in this area.

To summarize, the design/implementation subprocess offers a plethora of questions that a research-oriented adult educator might wrestle with. The questions range from the abstract (e.g., cognitive processes in decision making) to the most practical (e.g., the effectiveness of a particular piece of newspaper advertising). The adult educator might be challenged on any of these levels and, in meeting the challenge, has the prospect of contributing something of value to the entire field of adult education. We should stress that many of these issues and themes are fruitful, interdisciplinary research areas in which collaboration among adult educators, sociologists, psychologists, anthropologists, economists, media specialists, statisticians, and others is desirable, if not essential. New theory, new research techniques, and new perspectives on problems are all predictable consequences of such efforts.

The evaluation/accountability subprocess of programming focuses on the central theme that programmers must have "good" information about the outcomes of their programming effort as it is ultimately implemented. In the conceptual programming model, this information is intended as feedback for future program planning and organizational renewal or adaptation to a changing operational environment.

Several contrasting points of view on evaluation might be taken. Evaluation at one level, as described in Chapter 6, is a straightforward extension of the assumptions and values that motivate the preceding subprocesses of programming. At other levels, the scope of the evaluation might be broader or narrower than that suggested in Chapter 6. For instance, the evaluation dimension of the conceptual programming model indicates that both unintended and latent outcomes should be anticipated and studied; some might argue that the focus of the evaluation should be only those outcomes that were originally intended. Even with that issue in abeyance, the methodologies that could be elected vary tremendously. Recent publications speak directly to this methodological issue (see, for example, Smith, 1981).

Analysis and interpretations of evaluation information depend on the types of questions that motivate evaluation, as well as the types of evidence or data collected. The research issues that emerge from the evaluation/accountability subprocess of programming thus occur at a number of levels. What should be the motivating philosophy of evaluation in programming? How does that philosophy affect the strategies and techniques incorporated in the evaluation? To what extent does the strategy chosen affect the types of measures or sorts of data or evidence collected? What then will be the more or less appropriate methods of analysis?

It may be useful to reiterate that program evaluation/accountability is an area of great activity, divergent opinions, and innovative thought. It clearly has an important impact on the activities of the adult educator, as both change agent and programmer and must not be ignored. At the same time, the evaluation/accountability subprocess appears to be an area in which significant and far-reaching contributions might be made to the field of adult education.

The implication drawn here is that so many questions about program evaluation/accountability need to be answered that even suggesting a few seems presumptuous. The literature in that area is extensive, and in some sense entertaining because of the variety of approaches described. Nonetheless, the technical sophistication of program evaluation/accountability and the concomitant well-developed quantitative, logical, and qualitative skills needed in that area make it perhaps the most challenging of any of the principal areas of investigation suggested in this brief review of research questions.

Four primary issues should be kept in mind in considering research questions evolving from the conceptual programming model. First, questions may arise out of the principles and generalizations described in the model. The interrelationships of the concepts and subprocesses of programming advanced in the conceptual programming model should be viewed, skeptically or critically, as hypothetical. The conceptual model becomes more refined through testing, as do all such theoretical constructs. Therefore, tests of principles and generalizations of the model are essential first stages in research directed to the model as a whole.

Second, the range of technological and methodological issues incorporated in each of the subprocesses and their accompanying assumptions and concepts are open to research in the form of either comparative evaluation of those suggested or development of new approaches. Many of the advances in any area of knowledge have depended on the thinking engendered by and avenues of activity made possible through new methodological approaches.

Third, the interdisciplinary nature of the conceptual programming model, drawing as it does from the disciplines of education, psychology, sociology, anthropology, and economics, among others, suggests an advantage in applying to adult education programming some of the prevailing advances in those other disciplines. This pursuit will require individuals who are willing to become knowledgeable in at least a second discipline and to commit themselves to attempts to keep track of both education and the second or other disciplines. The implication here is that a special breed of professional, one with the flexibility and capacity to deal effectively with disparate areas of knowledge, might be recruited to the field of adult education.

Fourth and finally, basic processes support and sustain the conceptual programming model. As founded on the Bloomian hierarchy of cognitive skills, the most basic processes are those involved in decision making, judgment, and choice, that is, knowledge, comprehension, application, analysis, synthesis, and evaluation. On other levels, interpersonal skills (what they are, how they are acquired, how they may be improved) support programming activities. Research questions might be derived from an interpersonal skills task analysis. Aspects of learning, as applied to adult learning situations, offer clear avenues for research: (1) what theories work and why; (2) are new theories needed and, if so, what are they; and so forth. The fact that adult learning so often takes place in group situations points toward further areas of inquiry into group processes and group dynamics: (1) what they are; (2) how they develop; (3) how they help or hinder the achievement of learning objectives; and (4) how they can be manipulated or controlled for maximum benefit in the learning situation. Some answers to this order of inquiry are available; others remain to be discussed. An important starting point is to perceive what the important questions are, to organize them, and to order our efforts in pursuing them.

Research demands an element of creativity. The adult educator who feels that spark and perceives the kinds of questions that require "good" answers can make a substantial contribution to the entire field of adult education.

IMPLICATIONS OF THE CONCEPTUAL PROGRAMMING MODEL

A thoughtful consideration of the conceptual model for programming in adult education will reveal the possibility of a number of implications beyond the direct application of the model to adult education program services delivery. Some of these implications will be reviewed in this section; others will be apparent to individual readers, depending on local or individual situations. One important implication, that of the guidance of professional preparation, will be emphasized in the discussion.

We noted in the preceding discussion of research issues, themes, and questions that a fairly general principle of research involves comparing methods of organizations or other components/elements (perhaps as suggested in the model) versus some competing method or components/elements. The notion of comparison is elaborated somewhat, particularly when discussing the analysis of historical attempts at comparisons in adult education. Implicit in such comparisons is the concept that a well-thought-out conceptual framework guides the analysis. So, one implication of the conceptual programming model is that contemporary approaches such as organizations, programs per se, and programming frameworks can be compared in terms of the principles and generalities laid out in the model. In fact, that is the basis for much of the content of Chapter 2, in which several prominent programming theories or models are presented and described and for which similarities and differences are identified. The general idea that a common conceptual framework helps in such comparisons is the principal point. Whether or not the conceptual programming model is the best guide for such comparisons is a matter for scholarly debate, but it does provide at least a reasonable starting point and a useful initial framework for such debate. The value of the interchange made possible by such comparisons cannot be underestimated, for it is through such interchange that progress is made and consensus emerges.

At least two levels of organizational implications emerge from the conceptual programming model. The first concerns the adult education organization and the second refers to professional organizations of adult educators.

While the conceptual programming model can be used to suggest a range of questions about the functions, structure, and processes of the adult education organization, the model also provides some guidance as to specific functions that are to be executed by the organization. Consequently, in designing or redesigning the organization, a catalog of functions is easily derived. In this way, the functional "architecture" of the organization can be planned such that all programming functions are accounted for within the organization. The interrelationships of the subprocesses of the conceptual programming model also suggest where attention should be focused on organizational communication channels for the most efficient and effective flow of information. The hierarchical structure of the needs and objectives components of the conceptual programming model suggests that a parallel organizational structure may be effective. Other structures may be considered, of course, but even there the model provides a set of criteria that can be used in evaluating alternative forms of organization.

On quite another level, that of the functions, structure, and processes of professional organizations, the conceptual programming model may be useful as a guide to structure, for instance, how subgroups or special-interest groups might be chosen or set up. More important, the model suggests an organizational agenda, a set of problem areas to which the organization might profitably turn its collective attention. For example, in the concepts and processual tasks of its subprocesses, the conceptual programming model details a number of areas in which governmental regulations and support may be important. Lobbying efforts could, in principle, be ordered on the basis of their relationship to the processes encompassed in the model. While it may be both premature and presumptuous to intimate that the conceptual programming model be incorporated into legislation, certainly some aspects of the model might be useful in guiding legislation affecting the delivery of adult education programs.

As a prominent example, one could point to the linkage of the adult education organization to its target publics as an area that appears to be frequently neglected. Similarly, the government has resources, in the form of data banks that may not now be available to adult education organizations, that could be of significant benefit to activities such as mapping. A valuable contribution to the entire field could be made through professional adult education organizations helping to make such resources available.

And, of course, there is always the problem of adequate funding for adult education programs. A generally accessible and agreed-upon conceptual framework for programming, among adult educators, would tend to enhance credibility of the entire field and could be used as a reasonable set of criteria in evaluating proposals for adult education program activities submitted for funding. Common understanding among adult educators has clear and significant value in the adoption of any programming model, and certainly one that has the intent of generality asserted for the conceptual programming model.

It goes without saying that adult education is both a national and an international priority. Extensive efforts have been made over the years to export adult education concepts, expertise, and materials, particularly to the developing nations of the Third World in Africa, the Mideast, Southeast Asia, and South and Central America. The United States has been a leader in this effort, with substantial assistance from Western European nations. Indeed, adult education is the basis for a vigorous community of international scholars and practitioners. One can argue rather strongly that the effectiveness of continuing international cooperation and international extension of adult education activities can be sustained under a degree of consensus as to the overall aims, approaches, and methods of the professional field of practice. It is suggested here, then, that a commonly held model for programming in adult education might have additional utility in promoting international consensus in the field of adult education.

The conceptual programming model might be a reasonable provisional form for such consensus. It has the virtue of implicit generality and implicit, broad applicability. Certainly, as the principles included in the conceptual programming model developed over the years, a variety of international students contributed their experiences, reflections, and reactions to the model. Thus, as presently stated, the model already contains many ideas that are acceptable to and compatible with an international community.

Lippitt, Watson, and Westley (1958) conclude their classic work on planned change with some suggestions for the professional preparation of adult educators for the role of change agent. Their prescriptions are couched in abstract language appropriate to their theory of planned change. The general notion is that a model of professional activity can be used as a basis for designing preparatory educational experiences for professionals. A more circumscribed model of change, aimed at more restricted areas (as with the conceptual programming model) might be used as a more specific foundation for planning professional preparation. Lippitt and his co-workers refer to some issues that are general to the development of professional capability; those suggestions apply as well in the present model. They also refer to the distinction between the generalist's preparation and that of the specialist. In some sense, the conceptual programming model is one "speciality" in planned change; in another sense, it encompasses a number of specialties. Consequently, a useful approach to choosing an area of specialization appears to be, as the Lippitt group suggests, to look at overarching general areas of preparation and subsequently list some more specialized areas.

We can only echo the Lippitt group on some issues. First, they point out, and quite correctly, that all professional change agents must develop expertise in several areas. First among these is the derivation or adoption of a conceptual framework for the work they intend to do. That principle is patent throughout the development and discussion of the programming model, which itself is intended to be such a conceptual framework. Second, they indicate that every student must come to grips with a theoretical orientation to his or her professional activities. A number of theoretical slants in adult education have potential for adoption by students of the field. In fact, a number of theoretical orientations should be considered: theories of organization and management, theories of social structure, theories of evaluation, and so forth.

Each of the programming subprocesses and their accompanying concepts contain elements of theory that the student should draw out, reflect upon, and incorporate into a personal philosophy of adult education. No single book can present all sides of that sort of critical intellectual analysis; in fact, the student is better served by both investigating in depth and thinking through the relevant concepts. However, a consistent theoretical orientation is maintained throughout the design and development of the conceptual programming model. The thinking that went into its construction is adequately reflected in Chapter 3. The existence of a coherent model in no sense relieves the student of the responsibility for the critical and reflective thinking required to develop a personal philosophy of adult education. Rather, the model should be used as a guide for thinking, as a means to help sort out the important issues and questions, and not as a source of ready-made answers.

A philosophy of adult education necessarily implies a social philosophy as well, again mirroring an aspect of professional preparation suggested by Lippitt, Watson, and Westley (1958). A view of humankind, based on observation, reading, discussion with teachers and other students, and experience gained as an adult, is requisite to effective practice as an adult educator. The historical antecedents of present-day practices and organizations are indispensable sources of experience gained, through considerable effort and difficulty, over the years; such documented experience should be used to buttress contemporary experience in developing maturity and sophistication in the science and art of programming. Philosophical works, specifically, can give insights on problems and responses to problems as they have been reported by scholars of the past and present, based on their particular personal preparation and expertise. The conceptual programming model clearly requires and implies a high degree of both social awareness and the social perfectibility of humankind. Other orientations may suggest differing views of programming. The student must develop a view of humankind or a social philosophy that can be worn comfortably.

Values and ethics structures accrue to most adults over years of social participation, reflection, and study. Adult educators are challenged to clarify for themselves the dimensions of those values and ethical principles. Such values and principles have important and obvious consequences for individual professional participation in programming in adult education.

Going beyond these first principles of professional preparation are two main areas of professional education. One is preparation for research inquiry; the other is preparation for practice. (This distinction is arbitrary, for the sake of discussion; practitioners need research skills and researchers must be familiar with practice.) Research skills likewise have at least two notable aspects. First, research skills that contribute to practice are essential. Two practical applications (of research skills) are mapping and evaluation. Mapping, discussed in detail in Chapter 4, is a research problem that requires the adult educator to discover the dimensions of importance on which subgroups of a public differ. And mapping is certainly a nontrivial task, because the sources of information are not always obvious and the dimensions of importance are not always clear. Evaluation, discussed in Chapter 6, is a research problem in that some of the outcomes of a given program, such as unintended outcomes and all latent outcomes, are not clear and require observational and measurement skills of a relatively high degree. Also in evaluation, the documentation of causal relationships, to the extent that they can be documented, further reflects as important, practical application of research skills.

Research on programming, in the sense of enlarging and enhancing the knowledge base of the professional field of practice, was discussed in detail earlier in this chapter. None of that type of research is executed by accident, and the skills that undergird the research have to be gained through study, observation, example, and application. Any field advances only as fast as its research professionals can derive supporting and new data that, in turn, can be translated into practice in the field. Adult educaion is no exception; the importance of the adult education professional who devotes a career to advancing the state of knowledge in the field must not be underestimated.

Turning to the specific types of skill needed by the adult education professional practitioner, as opposed to a researcher, a number of important areas of preparation can be cited. First among these is, as mentioned, a conceptual framework within which to operate. Such a framework is gained through study of existing models, integration of their principles, and reflection on their similarities and differences. Allied to this framework is the development of a consistent and coherent personal philosophy of adult education and a social philosophy.

More specifically, the adult educator must develop a range of interpersonal skills necessary for successful interaction with clients, both as individuals and as groups. Among these interpersonal skills are empathy, observation, effective listening habits, interviewing, asking productive questions, negotiating, salesmanship, and a sense of humor. Information-seeking skills are essential: using public archival sources of data, library skills, knowledge of public and private sources of aid, and the like. All these information skills support the particular skills and abilities that are embedded in the subprocesses and their accompanying concepts of the conceptual programming model, without necessarily being specifically part of the model. It goes without saying that a thorough grasp of the programming subprocesses is imperative.

Where and how are such skills to be developed? Clearly, the curriculum of the professional school is the first source. That curriculum should reflect the processes and attendant skills of some adequate programming model, if not the one advanced here. Opportunities to develop operational skills through laboratory experiences, internships, or practicums aid materially in promoting superior professional practice.

The conceptual programming model might be used as a basis for analyzing the curriculum of an institution being considered by a potential adult education student. Does the department or institution offer the courses and opportunities necessary for preparation for a professional role in the field of adult education? What courses offer the needed specific training in adult education programming? What theoretical and philosophical orientations are represented among the course offerings and the faculty's expertise? These types of questions help to ensure better, more utilitarian learning experiences for students of adult education.

Coupled with the notion that adult education programming is a viable area for scholarly inquiry and research, and the necessary inference that the area will not become static, is the notion that, to sustain currency in the field as either practitioners or researchers/scholars, adult educators must maintain a posture of continuing professional development throughout their careers and, more particularly, *beyond* their formal education. Avenues toward this end include attendance at professional meetings; reading professional journals; enrollment in additional formal courses, workshops, or seminars; and continuing contact and discussion with professional colleagues.

At several points in this discussion of professional preparation we have called for a questioning, a searching and inquiring attitude toward programming. It is totally predictable that such an attitude will, over time, result in altered views of the field of adult education, its content, its philosophies, its theories, its methods, and its practice. No one who claims the status of "professional" can ignore the changes that surely will occur. For the true professional, "school is never out." The difference is that the learning becomes self-directed and is consistently developed.

MAJOR AREAS SUGGESTED FOR FURTHER INQUIRY

No book on a topic as broad as programming in adult education can expect to do justice to the many content areas that are touched on. This book is by no means an exception to that generality. So many important and extensive areas of inquiry are intimately involved in adult education that this work can serve only as the barest introduction to what they are. For example, allusions have been made to sociology, anthropology, psychology, economics, management science, and other disciplines throughout the discussion of the conceptual programming model. Consequently, it seems necessary to point out a number of areas into which the serious student of adult education might look to gain a fuller grasp of programming and the disciplines that buttress programming.

Examining each of the major components of programming may give some excellent leads to further literature or topical areas. Among the more important of these components, treated here, are the three subprocesses of programming and the cognitive map of programming.

Planning

Since the planning subprocess begins with a consideration of the organizational context for programming, organizational *theory,* organizational *design,* and organziational *development* form a connected set of topics useful in understanding organizational processes. Aspects of management and administration, as they apply to educational services delivery organizations, also are indicated, particularly with regard to the development of organizational policies and practices. The areas of organizational sociology and psychology have components that impinge on educational services delivery organizations and might be examined with profit.

Systems thinking, based on the interrelationships among elements of groups (including organizations, communities, cultures), is a generic area of study that might contribute to an overall understanding of organizations and publics. Loomis's (1965) work is an outstanding example of the application of systems thinking to sociology. Loomis suggests that *sociology* and its ally *anthropology* contain ideas useful to understanding and utilizing the conceptual programming model. Particularly important are topics such as group or public structure; leadership patterns and dynamics; the acquisition, development, and maintenance of power structures in groups; and others (see Loomis, 1965, for further topical areas). Inquiry into systems thinking should be supportive of linkage efforts in the field, that is, in mapping publics, identifying social systems and subsystems, and identifying and interfacing with both formal and informal leaders of such systems. An understanding of interpersonal relationship dynamics, gained perhaps through study of in the field of *social psychology*, might be helpful in promoting cooperation with systems leaders and, through them, with their followers.

Design and Implementation

While some of the following skill areas could be invoked with regard to any of several components of the conceptual programming model, mention of the complex and varied nature of the activities incorporated in the design/implementation subprocess seems particularly appropriate at this point. Reference is to the personal administrative and managerial skills that sustain all the activities, the most important of which is the *ability to make decisions.* A growing literature exists on decision making, choice, and the components of judgment that go into them. Because so much of the programming process involves making and influencing decisions, choices, and judgments, the student of programming in adult education would be well advised to explore at least some of that literature.

Goal setting and *stating objectives* have both personal and programming dimensions. Adult educators, as change agents and programmers, should develop the ability to set personal goals and exercise that ability continually in their professional career and personal life. One expects that such personal ability, well formed and well used, will transfer to the parallel activity in programming. Goals and objectives are pivotal aspects of educational programs to be planned; they are central to the organizational activity that supports the planned program in the form of administrative or managerial objectives (see Chapters 5 and 6).

We tend to assume that a professional has developed effective *communication skills*; too often, experience demonstrates the fallacy of that assumption. So it will be said here: as in any other profession, the adult educator must develop and use effective oral and written communication skills. Very frequently, representatives of the adult education organization are called upon to speak to public and other groups on the goals and activities of the organization. Face-to-face communication is essential in developing linkages with publics and social system representatives. A precise, written statement of the need to be addressed by the planned program, program objectives, and anticipated program outcomes is critical to the success of any programming effort. Note, too, that effective communication also requires effective *listening* and *comprehension* skills.

Turning more to the specific tasks incorporated in the design/implementation subprocess, an important and challenging task is entailed in translating the need expressed by and communicated from the target public or social system into a macro need and its corresponding macro objective. Translation of the stated macro need into a hierarchy of needs and the macro objective, derived from the hierarchy of needs, into a hierarchy of objectives depends on effective use of the cognitive skills of *critical thinking* and *logical analysis*.

The construction and content of educational objectives are areas for fruitful additional study by the adult educator in the role of programmer. The taxonomies of Bloom et al. (1956) and Krathwohl, Bloom, and Masia (1964) provide useful models of both the process of objectives development and of the hierarchical nature of objectives.

The discussion in Chapter 5 stresses the affinities between program design and curriculum development. While a variety of pertinent sources are cited, the reader should be aware that only a selection of those available could be included. Thus, the literature on *curriculum development* is yet another area for additional professional study.

Implementation of a planned program depends on selecting or inventing appropriate learning experiences, materials, and methods. Again, here is a rich area for further inquiry. *Learning theory*, as it may apply to adult learners, is basic to the choice of learning materials and methods. *Learning technologies* such as group discussion, demonstrations, computer-aided instruction, and audiovisual aids must be mastered to the extent that they can be used effectively and matched appropriately to the sociocultural characteristics and needs of the target public.

Selecting learning experiences, and indeed to some extent the statement of objectives, requires *diagnostic* skills; this reflects the point of view expressed by Lippitt, Watson, and Westley (1958). Diagnostic skills provide means to discover "where the learner is" before designing learning experiences. Such diagnosis often involves *testing* and *test interpretation*, coequal in importance for the adult educator. In much the same sense, *evaluation* of the degree of attainment of objectives also may involve testing for achievement.

Effective implementation at the teacher-learner interface requires expertise in assessing and promoting *group dynamics* and *group processes*—again, an area in which there is a relatively rich and interesting literature. Related to this implementation, the necessity to monitor and reinforce learners and teachers demands an awareness of such processes, based on developed *observational skills*.

Evaluation and Accountability

Perhaps the most technical of the three programming subprocesses, evaluation/accountability is itself a topical area, the literature on which the professional adult educator as programmer would do well to explore in detail. Much of the evaluation design methodology is based on *statistical techniques*, which are totally critical to anything approaching a complete understanding of evaluation. Consequently, the professional programmer should exert the effort required to gain competence in statistical applications in evaluation.

The requirement that evaluation be reported to the various constituencies of the planned program again places a premium on good communication skills.

This requirement is complicated somewhat by the typical inclusion of quantitative information and the use of relatively technical language and ideas. But those aspects of evaluation/accountability should be taken as added emphasis on the need for refined and practiced communication skills.

The evaluation/accountability area is one of relatively intense activity, with new procedures, perspectives, and interpretations continually evolving. Programmers involved in evaluating and accounting for planned programs, as well as those who use the resultant information, should monitor the related literature on a continuing basis so that an adequate understanding of evaluation procedures and accountability reports can be gained.

Evaluating and accounting for a given planned program is a major means by which the organization adapts to changes in its environment and that of its publics. Evaluation is used, in one form, to pinpoint those aspects of the organization on which indicated change or renewal efforts should be focused. This is the field of *organizational development*, mentioned earlier.

The Cognitive Map of Programming

Early in this presentation, the need for a connected set of concepts or a *cognitive map* of programming was introduced and developed. Further study in programming should be guided by that cognitive map, with the overall aim of making it more complete and more comprehensive. Segregated into broad aspects, the programmer's continuing study should focus on substantive topical areas; on continuing development and refinement of personal skills related to programming; and on programming itself, its history, its application, and its many forms. The cognitive map for programming should never be taken as static. Rather, it should be viewed as dynamic and open, subject to revision based on a never-ending flow of additional information from reading, from study, from observation, from interaction with peers and colleagues, and from experience in applying the programming process.

THE CHALLENGE OF COMMITMENT

Statements from a number of authorities in the field of adult education strongly indicate that the future of education generally will see growing emphasis on the adult learner (see Cross, 1981). That being the case, one may only conclude that leaders in the march into the future will be those who can most effectively plan, design and implement, evaluate and account for adult education planned programs. That leadership role is an exciting opportunity, a challenge, and an awesome responsibility.

The model presented and analyzed is intended to be a theoretical yet practical conceptual framework for programming in adult education. As such, it is a coherent, consistent, and logical system of ideas and activities for adult education. It also is complex, as it draws significant concepts from a broad variety of ancillary fields of knowledge.

Those adult educators who strive to refine their roles as change agents and programmers, from the point of view of this conceptual programming model, will be an elite corps of scholars who bring to the challenge significant intellectual capabilities and a singular commitment to what must become an increasingly technical and sophisticated enterprise. The real challenge of programming in adult education is in this commitment. Adult educators have the capacity to grasp the intricacies of the complex programming model. And only a complex model offers the generality required.

Roles for specialists in the field of adult education are clearly indicated by this model. The development of these specialist roles is certainly to be encouraged. For example, we may see individuals who have become particularly skilled in mapping publics, or in marketing planned programs, or in evaluating and accounting for planned programs. Those individuals, however, will not be change agents and programmers.

Change agents and programmers will be generalists, those remarkable individuals who can see the forest while still noting the trees, who can see the landscape without having to focus on individual landmarks. These individuals will have both foresight and broad perspectives on the place of the adult education enterprise in the flow of time and in the fabric of society.

The challenge in the field of adult education is to identify such individuals within its ranks, and to recruit others who can fill these critical leadership roles. The conceptual programming model provides some initial criteria that may be used to select those future leaders.

As adult educators in the roles of change agents and programmers, and as educators of adult educators, we must accept the challenges of programming. To meet these challenges will entail a continuing commitment to the leadership roles in adult education programming that inevitably will fall to us.

We raise a final question with our readers: Is the conceptual programming model in adult education, as presented here, a theory or a model or neither? We recall Inkeles's (1964) contribution: "It is not always possible to distinguish between a scientific model and a scientific theory. . . . A theory ordinarily can be proved wrong. In the case of a model, it can only be judged incomplete, misleading, or unproductive" (p. 28). As with the lady and the tiger, we leave the answer to the good judgment of our peers, our colleagues, and our students, as they scrutinize, probe, implement, analyze, test, and retest the conceptual programming model.

REFERENCES

BLOOM, B. S., M. D. ENGLEHART, E. J. FURST, W. H. HILL, and D. R. KRATHWOHL, *Taxonomy of Educational Objectives. Handbook I: Cognitive Domain.* New York: David McKay Company, 1956.

BOONE, E. J. "The Cooperative Extension Service," in *Handbook of Adult Education,* ed. R.M. Smith, G. F. Aker, and J. R. Kodd. New York: The Macmillan Company, 1970.

CROSS, K. P., *Adults as Learners.* San Francisco: Jossey-Bass, Publishers, 1981.

FRENCH, W. L., and C. H. BELL, JR., *Organization Development.* Englewood Cliffs, N.J.: Prentice-Hall, Inc., 1978.

GRATTAN, C. H., *In Quest of Knowledge.* New York: Association Press, 1955.

INKELES, A., *What Is Sociology? An Introduction to a Discipline and Profession.* Englewood Cliffs, N.J.: Prentice-Hall, Inc., 1964.

KOHLBERG, L., and R. MAYER, "Development as the Aim of Education," *Harvard Educational Review,* 42 (1972), 449–496.

KRATHWOHL, D. E., B. S. BLOOM, and B. B. MASIA, *Taxonomy of Educational Objectives: Handbook II: Affective Domain.* New York: David McKay Company, 1964.

LIPPITT, R., J. WATSON, and B. WESTLEY, *The Dynamics of Planned Change.* New York: Harcourt, Brace & World, Inc., 1958.

LOOMIS, C. P., *Social Systems.* Princeton, N. J.: D. Van Nostrand Company, 1965.

SMITH, N., ed., *Metaphors for Evaluation.* Beverly Hills, Calif.: Sage Publications, Inc., 1981.

TOUGH, A., *The Adult's Learning Projects: A Fresh Approach to Theory and Practice in Adult Learning.* Research in Education Series, No. 1. Toronto, Canada: Ontario Institute for Studies in Education, 1971.

Index